COMMUNITY POWER IN
A POSTREFORM CITY

COMMUNITY POWER IN A POSTREFORM CITY

Politics in New York City

ROBERT F. PECORELLA

M.E. Sharpe
Armonk, New York
London, England

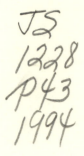

Library of Congress Cataloging-in-Publication Data

Pecorella, Robert F., 1948–
Community power in a postreform city:
politics in New York City
p. cm.   Includes bibliographical references and index.
ISBN 1-56324-136-6
1. New York (N.Y.)—Politics and government—1951–
2. Neighborhood government—New York (N.Y.)
I. Title.
JS1228.P43   1993
320.8´5´097471—dc20
93-22409
CIP

Printed in the United States of America
The paper used in this publication meets the minimum
requirements of American National Standard for
Information Sciences—Permanence of Paper for
Printed Library Materials, ANSI Z 39.48-1984.

⊗

BM   10   9   8   7   6   5   4   3   2   1

For Melody, who smiles knowingly.

CONTENTS

LIST OF TABLES

ACKNOWLEDGMENTS

This book represents the culmination of several years of research on community politics in New York City. It could not have been completed without the assistance of several groups of people. First, colleagues with whom I discussed the research helped me immeasurably. Their comments, suggestions, and arguments made the finished product more interesting and ultimately more satisfying. In this regard, I am particularly grateful to Bob Bailey from Columbia University, Doug Muzzio from Baruch College, Joe Viteritti from the Wagner Graduate School at New York University, and Ed Rogowsky from Brooklyn College. I also wish to acknowledge Clarence Stone from the University of Maryland, whose positive reactions to an earlier version of chapter one gave me confidence in the overall model.

I am also grateful to all the community board members from around the city who took the time to fill out and return the questionnaires, to the representatives of the borough community relations offices who spoke with me about the board system, to the officials at the Department of City Planning who helped clarify land-use issues, particularly ULURP, and to the officials at the Office of Community Board Relations at the New York City Office of Management and the Budget, whose courtesy and assistance made the somewhat tedious task of coding some two thousand community board budget proposals more tolerable. I also wish to acknowledge the American Political Science Association, whose small-grant program helped defray some of the costs involved in preparing and sending out the board members' questionnaires. I also extend special words of thanks to Kelly Ronayne, whose patience and care in reviewing and proofreading the manuscript was of great assistance, and to Eileen M. Gaffney, whose careful copyediting was greatly appreciated.

Needless to say, all errors of fact, misinterpretations of information, or lack of clarity in the presentation are my own and I take full responsibility for them.

Finally, I want to acknowledge my spouse and other household friends without whom the book would have been finished sooner but with much less joy.

COMMUNITY POWER IN A POSTREFORM CITY

CHAPTER ONE

Introduction: Fiscal Crisis, Regime Change, and Political Legitimacy

Although the assertion that New York City politics is crisis-driven is an exaggerated description of day-to-day life in the nation's largest city, it nevertheless serves as a precise, analytical observation. This chapter presents a contextual approach to urban politics that suggests that periodic fiscal crises have resulted in regime changes in New York's governance. The approach provides a historical perspective to city politics from the machine era through the reform era as well as a method for analyzing New York's current postreform regime within its larger context. That postreform regime is characterized by a large welfare state under extragovernmental fiscal control coupled with the nation's most ambitious attempt at urban decentralization, New York's community board system.

The contextual approach considers periods of both crisis and normal politics in New York. Crisis politics occurs when credit markets close to city debt; normal politics occurs the remainder of the time. Normal politics is characterized by the sometimes structured, sometimes informal, political interactions between government officials and private-sector members of the current governing coalition. It is these interactions that define regime politics. "A regime thus involves not just any informal group that comes together to make a decision but an informal yet relatively stable group with access to institutional resources that enable it to have a sustained role in making governing decisions" (Stone 1989, 239). Historically, political interactions with government officials have been more direct for some members of the coalition than for others. For some, interactions take place on a one-to-one basis; for others, they are channeled through mediating mechanisms such as elections and group activity.

Although periods of normal politics are, by definition, more frequent and long-lasting than periods of crisis, their relevant political interactions are defined by periods of crisis. Fiscal crises and retrenchment politics redefine normal politics by replacing one governing coalition with another and by changing the rules governing political behavior. As a result, both the process of supporting economic growth, necessary for fiscal health, and the process of democratic governance, necessary for political stability, change dramatically in the wake of fiscal crisis. Each new regime is characterized by a new coalition of "political winners," some with direct access and others with indirect access to officials.

The contextual approach does not presuppose that economic factors determine politics. The view here is that politics unfolds within a socioeconomic environment that constrains, more or less rigidly, the breadth of options open to public officials. During periods of normal politics in cities, the constraints are relatively loose and the policy options open to city officials rather broad. However, during periods of crisis, socioeconomic constraints narrow dramatically and local politics becomes more a function of local economics than an independent enterprise.

In developing a theory of urban politics that addresses both proximate and long-range issues, I begin with a review of several familiar approaches to the study of urban politics, including pluralist, statist, and stratificationist models. Following this review, I present the contextual approach to urban politics, which clarifies the analysis guiding the remainder of the book.

Approaches to Urban Politics

To present the contextual approach, it is useful to review the ways urbanists have viewed power in American cities and the conclusions they have drawn based on these views. Stated simply, political relationships in American cities have generally been portrayed through either pluralist or stratificationist models, with each general model including multiple subapproaches. The literature in the area is large, the substantive and methodological issues are fundamental, and the debate is unending. This section makes a brief pass at the general issue with a specific focus on studies of New York.

Group Accommodation: The Pluralist Approach

Pluralism, with its roots in the group theories of Arthur Bentley (1908) and David Truman (1951), suggests that local politics evolves incrementally through a process of accommodation among a diverse and wide-ranging collection of interest groups. From this perspective, the fluidity of group competition within an open political system is protected by a number of factors, including the large number of groups vying to influence local policy, the noncumulative nature of the resources useful to these groups, the extent of crosscutting pressures within and overlapping memberships among the various groups, the potential for new groups to emerge, and the overall social consensus on democratic norms.

From the pluralist perspective, even those interests achieving preeminence in a particular policy area at a particular time are constrained by the potential mobilization of countervailing forces. Pluralist theory suggests that the continual competition among diverse groups, with none able to accumulate sufficient resources to monopolize the political game, is conducive to the development of polyarchy where democratic norms govern.[1] This pluralist system, where policy is the result more of political negotiation and compromise than of coherent planning, moves incrementally in balancing the pressures for stability and change. Stability is the empirical and normative standard; change, which must be possible to avoid stagnation and is possible given system fluidity, occurs within the constraints of existing policy.

David Ricci (1971) argues that pluralism is a form of neoliberalism in that it substitutes the notion of group actions, under the rational leadership of the politically active, for the liberal concept of the rational individual acting alone. Indeed, pluralists, borrowing from the theory of the free-market economy and substituting interest groups for Adam Smith's rational individual, envision a local political arena that is essentially self-regulating. Norton Long (1958), in his aptly titled piece, "The Local Community as an Ecology of Games," argues explicitly for this position: "A great deal of the communities' activities consist of undirected co-operation of particular social structures, each seeking particular goals, and in doing so, meshing with others" (1958, 252).

Robert Dahl's (1961) study of New Haven is the most notable example of pluralist research on urban politics. Employing a decision-based approach to examine three areas of local public policy—education, urban renewal, and political nominations—Dahl concluded that political power in New Haven was widely dispersed, with different groups involved with and influential in different policy arenas. The only political actors influential across all three policy areas were public officials, notably the mayor, a situation theoretically consistent with the pluralist notion of polyarchy.

Pluralist research on politics in New York has emphasized group competition when analyzing both periods of normal politics and periods of fiscal crisis and retrenchment. The city has been viewed as a diverse political arena where competing interest groups interact with city officials to secure some share of the prizes of local politics. The interactions and the political competition are portrayed as open, fluid, and nonideological. Moreover, the competition for public resources occurs solely in the political sphere, where it is adjudicated by public officials.

Wallace Sayre and Herbert Kaufman's (1960) remarkably in-depth analysis, *Governing New York City*, is a pluralist classic. Having introduced their study with reviews of the "stakes and prizes of city politics," the "contestants for the prizes of city politics," and the "rules of the contest," the authors come to conclusions that are quintessentially pluralist.

> The most lasting impression created by a systematic analysis of New York City's political and governmental system as a whole are its democratic virtues: its qualities of openness, its commitments to bargaining and accommodation among participants, its receptivity to new participants, its opportunities for the exercise of leadership by the unmatched variety and number of the city's residents new and old. (1960, 738)

In analyzing periods of fiscal crisis and retrenchment politics in New York, pluralists remain analytically true to their worldview. Charles Levine, Irene Rubin, and George Wolohojian (1981) argue that the 1975 fiscal crisis resulted from economic decline following a temporary imbalance in the city's interest group configuration. This imbalance, caused by the windfall growth of urban social programs in the 1960s, reformulated the relationship between interest groups and city officials and permitted a coalition of social spenders to increase the city's fiscal obligations. The combination of slower economic growth and federal retrenchment in the 1970s put pressures on the city's budget, with which the existing governing coalition, committed as it was to extending social services, could not cope. Consequently, a countervailing conservative coalition of business interests, state government, and fiscally conservative local officials assumed power in order to manage retrenchment. The pluralist concepts of social equilibrium and policy incrementalism are very much in evidence in the authors' conclusions concerning retrenchment politics in New York: "Power has shifted somewhat from the city's municipal unions to business groups. These shifts have been gradual and do not represent a total reversal of prior political relationships on city politics" (1981, 34).

From the pluralist perspective, the 1975 fiscal crisis was simply the result of group imbalance, and the solution involved the ascendance of countervailing power. The causes of the crisis were temporary, aberrant, and nonsystemic; the solutions were paradigmatically consistent, equally temporary, and definitely systemic.

Interest Group Liberalism: The Statist Critique

In recent years, a number of internal critics have emerged to question mainstream pluralist ideas.[2] For example, several pluralist scholars have challenged the notion of balanced group competition. "Businessmen play a distinctive role in polyarchical politics that is qualitatively different from that of any interest group" (Dahl and Lindblom 1976, xxxii). Indeed, John Manley (1983) suggests that the internal criticisms concerning business influence are substantial enough to give rise to a neopluralist paradigm, although the precise shape of the new model remains unclear. What is quite clear, however, is the growing disquiet among some pluralist scholars about the effects of the "privileged position of business" on the ideas of self-regulating group competition.

Another mainstream assault on the pluralist paradigm arises from those who point to the increasing tendency to disregard formal public authority in American politics. These critics contend that the devaluation of statism in pluralist societies produces a disaggregated political order where accommodation overwhelms governance. Indeed, when the lack of formal public authority is coupled with economic growth, the continued accommodation of group demands appears almost costless (Peters 1980, 39). However, statists contend that this "unconstrained policy entrepreneurship" eventually produces political crisis at the local level (Beam and Colella 1980, 58).

Theodore Lowi (1979a) argues forcefully for this position in his book *The End of Liberalism*. Lowi defines "interest group liberalism" as a philosophy that accepts an expansive government role in American life, sees interest groups as the primary vehicle for citizen–government interaction, and makes no judgment about various group claims on government (1969, 51). He goes on to argue that this "vulgarized version of pluralism" fragments public policy and parcels out the various pieces to the very groups that benefit directly from the policy, effectively neutralizing all central authority over these programs. "It provided a theoretical basis for giving to each according to his claim, the price of which is a reduction of concern for what others are claiming. . . . [I]t transformed access and logrolling from necessary evil to greater good" (1979a, 55). The absence of public authority at the policy formulation stage and the often decisive influence of organized interests at the policy implementation stage mean that pluralism's virtues of group competition, open access to officials, and policy incrementalism become interest group liberalism's problems of group entrenchment, subgovernments allocating resources, and policy stagnation.[3]

This fragmented political order resulted from the adaptation of pluralist principles to the exigencies of social modernization. Lowi argues that the merger of pluralism and modernization negatively impacted government authority in three ways (1979b, 46–47). First, by decentralizing policy-making in a host of quasi-independent bureaucratic agencies, modernization led to a situation where public policy was largely determined within subgovernments, which made overall management very difficult. Second, by encouraging home rule, the forces of modernization increased the responsibilities but weakened the formal authority of city governments by making them accountable for policy areas over which they had little effective control. Third, by delegating responsibility to cities and thereby decreasing the size of the political arena, modernization empowered a host of local interest groups, which might have been less influential in the larger political arenas, to establish domains of influence in American cities. "Within this power imbalance most cities found themselves literally too small to handle their policy problems but politically too weak to resist trying" (Lowi 1979b, 47).

From the statist perspective, in the absence of a central authority with the legitimacy to evaluate and coordinate group demands, pluralism has degenerated into a pattern of group entrenchment within specific policy areas. The problem here is not of the privileged position of business interests but of the privileged position of all interests. Statists argue that, although resources are noncumulative from a systemwide perspective, the agency–client relationships that characterize group entrenchment represent cumulative power within a particular policy area. The ability of entrenched interests to exclude countervailing groups from their policy domains negates the pluralist concepts of political competition.

Reflecting the statist view, Frederick Wirt's (1974) research on San Francisco characterizes that city's decentralized interest group and governmental sector as "hyperpluralism." Douglas Yates (1977), in a book notably titled *The Ungovernable City,* coins the phrase "street-fighting pluralism" to describe the process of political breakdown in American cities.

Lowi (1967) himself viewed New York City as a classic example of the breakdown of public authority. He notes that in New York, the mayor stands "denuded of authority" in the face of huge and largely autonomous city bureaucracies; the political parties have been replaced by organized interest groups; and city government is best characterized as "organized decentralization" (1967, 100). Lowi concludes that "cities like New York became well-run but ungoverned" (1967, 99).

In an analysis of post–Sayre-and-Kaufman New York, Donald Haider (1979) emphasizes a statist perspective. He argues that in the period 1965–70, a rapid increase in city resources, fueled by national economic growth and national social spending programs, resulted in large increases in city government's commitments to groups throughout New York. These commitments, however, were hostage to intergovernmental and group pressures, which "contributed to the parceling out of public authority from the center" (1979, 138). City government lost the capacity to govern as control over the allocation of resources "flowed away from City Hall and the primary overhead agencies of the local government—up, down, and laterally" (1979, 140).

From the statist perspective, then, urban fiscal crises are the predictable consequence of government's inability to exercise authority and choose among different claims on public resources. Such crises are not necessarily the result of general economic decline or of temporary imbalances in group accommodations: they are the consequence of "weak governance and lack of public control." Martin Shefter (1977, 1985) presents a picture of fiscal irresponsibility resulting from the inability of New York City officials to assert the role of public authority in the 1960s and 1970s. By acceding to the demands of municipal unions for higher wages and of minority groups for increased social services, city officials incorporated new and expensive claims on the public treasury. By refusing to risk alienating middle-class homeowners with further tax burdens, officials maintained artificially low revenue bases. By combining the two processes, governmental weakness produced fiscal crisis. "Faced with growing expenditure demands as well as demands for tax reductions or controls, many public sector officials have chosen to borrow rather than seek the necessary tax increases to cover the expenditures" (Peters 1980, 26). At the federal level, such borrowing can act to "prime the pump" and generate economic growth; at the local level, such borrowing can lead to fiscal crises.

Economic Primacy: Stratification Approaches

Whereas statists question pluralist assumptions about group competition and social equilibrium, stratification theorists challenge the basic principles of group theory. From this perspective, local politics is essentially the domain of economic elites whose policy influence overrides that of any other group or coalition in the city. To the stratification theorists, urbanization itself is a consequence of elite action, and urban policy continues to reflect the primacy of these elites.

Stratification theorists argue that by concentrating their attention on public decision-making processes group theorists miss the determinant role that economic elites play in local politics.

Stratification theory incorporates two distinct perspectives. One view, evolving from the elite-power school of urban sociology, sees city government as hostage to the economic power of local upper-income interests and their political allies. This *elitist* branch of stratification theory contends that wealth is a cumulative resource that provides the fortunate few with the means to control local policy. The other branch of stratification theory sees local politics as a manifestation of the larger socioeconomic forces that define capitalism. This *structuralist* perspective looks beyond the interests of local economic elites and sees urban politics as simply another arena where the continuing class struggle and the evolving crises of capitalist societies are played out.

Elite theory has a long history in the sociological study of urban politics. The studies of "Middletown" by Robert and Helen Lynd (1929) concluded that local businessmen and wealthy families, through their domination of material resources and social prestige, controlled political decisions in the community. Floyd Hunter's (1953) seminal reputational analysis of "Regional City" (Atlanta) found that only four of forty "influentials" in that city were public officials; the remaining "influentials" were businessmen and professionals. Moreover, Hunter found that the elites had developed a network of interlocking directorships that allowed them to coordinate both business and politics in the city (1953, 75). And G. William Domhoff's (1978) replication of Dahl's study of New Haven found that, Dahl's original findings notwithstanding, the city's major development programs, including urban renewal (one of Dahl's three important issues), were controlled by local economic elites with ties to national elites.

Based on work stretching over seven decades, therefore, elitist researchers have concluded that city politics is characterized by several common elements. First, there is an economic elite that controls most major public policy decisions, has extensive professional and social interactions, and operates under conditions of low public visibility. Second, city politics includes a visible political class whose members contest for office but who are, in the final analysis, subservient to the local economic elites. Third, urban politics is followed only peripherally by an apathetic and largely politically irrelevant public.

From the perspective of elite theorists, urban fiscal crises are the consequence of the self-interested policies pursued by the economic elites who control cities. Jack Newfield and Paul DuBrul (1981), for example, locate the roots of New York's 1975 crisis in the capital construction projects and tax expenditure programs designed to socialize corporate production costs and to secure higher rates of return for investors. These ever-increasing costs, together with the self-serving decision by large banks to dump city bonds in favor of more profitable investments in 1974, precipitated the city's fiscal crisis.

The structuralist branch of stratification theory is founded on several basic assumptions. First, the city is a reflection of the larger socioeconomic realities encompassed by the term *mode of production*.[4] The class struggle inherent in the capitalist mode of production causes periodic crises, which, in turn, produce political coping strategies to deal with crisis. These strategies, while mitigating the crises of one period, generate new social contradictions that result in the reappearance of crises in later periods. From an urban perpective, changes in the mode of production produce changes in urban form, that is, the physical layout of cities. David Gordon (1984), for example, connects three historical changes in urban forms—the commercial, the industrial, and the corporate city—to changes in the mode of production. Ann Markusen (1978) relates the idea of urban form specifically to class conflict when she writes, "An inquiry into the origins of this form reveals that it has evolved from the resolution of past class conflicts, each of which in turn was shaped by existing political form" (1984, 91).

Structuralist analysis sees government as an active partner in sustaining a particular mode of production and in maintaining class control. This point is emphasized by James O'Connor (1973) in his analysis of how structural mandates force local governments to socialize private-sector costs and implement expensive social legitimation programs. Eventually these costs generate a fiscal crisis for the state. To the structuralist, then, "fiscal crisis—the gap between expenditure demands and available resources—becomes the state budgetary expression of class conflict in a monopoly capitalist society" (Hill 1984, 301).

Structuralists reject the pluralist view of cities as independent social and political entities. "Urbanism, as a general phenomenon, should not be viewed as the history of particular cities, but as the history of the system of cities within, between, and around which the surplus circulates" (Harvey 1973, 250). Urban fiscal crises have both long-term historical roots and regional geographic implications. Historically, "the fiscal problems of municipal governments tend to be cumulative as a result of the institutionalization of past concessions" (Friedland, Piven, and Alford 1984, 276); geographically, regional disinvestment highlights the tendency toward uneven development in capitalist societies (Bluestone and Harrison 1980).

From the structuralist perspective, New York City's 1975 fiscal crisis was the consequence of the need to remake the city into a worldwide corporate service center. Because this is only possible through a coordinative effort and because the process of dealing with the previous crises enlarged the role and fragmented the institutions of city government, the fiscal crisis, by initiating a period of restructuring built around the idea of "blaming the victim," permits the required consolidation of government. In his analysis of the 1975 fiscal crisis, William Tabb (1984) focuses on the need to coordinate policy in New York in order to restructure the city into the world corporate capital: "Overextension of borrowing by shortsighted and opportunistic politicians was the immediate trigger to the crisis, but the extent of city borrowing cannot be explained without full consideration of this restructuring process" (1984, 323).

The Approaches Assessed

The various approaches have been criticized on both methodological and substantive grounds. Pluralists are attacked for a variety of paradigmatic problems, including basing their conclusions on relatively few public issues (Anton 1963); employing the term *salient issue* to characterize policy areas that generate little interest among local notables (Danziger 1964); overemphasizing the overt manifestations of local political power and ignoring the influence of nondecisions on public policy (Bachrach and Baratz 1962); and undervaluing the extent of the upper-class bias on their interest group system (Schattschneider 1960).

The elite branch of stratification theory has also been questioned on methodological grounds. Critics suggest that elite methodologies, like Hunter's reputational approach, presuppose the very issue under examination (Polsby 1963). Elitist theorists are also charged with equating potential and actual power; subscribing to economic determinism by ignoring the independent pressures of a democratic political system; assuming the existence of a cohesive elite; and generalizing from specific instances of influence to the notion of a wider scope of influence (Polsby 1963; Wolfinger 1962; Dahl 1958). The structuralist wing of stratification theory is sometimes critiqued as too abstract to address the day-to-day realities of urban politics. "No one lives or experiences capitalism in general" (Katznelson, Gille, and Weir 1982, 222).

Regardless of the methodolgical and substantive battles over the various approaches, each of them has a reasonable empirical claim on validity. Pluralism appeared to have modeled the dynamics of American politics during the 1950s quite astutely. At the national level, political conflicts were moderated by the distributive capacities of economic growth as the welfare state, created by Democratic administrations, was institutionalized during the Republican administration of Dwight Eisenhower. In American cities, the concept of the social crisis was as yet undiscovered, and the cleavages between haves and have-nots and between Protestant and immigrant cultures were considered treatable through continued economic growth and eventual ethnic assimilation.

In New York City, there appeared to be a reasonable balance among competing groups as an open political system accommodated their concerns. Characterizing political participation in the New York of the 1950s, Sayre and Kaufman wrote, "The channels of access to the points of decision are numerous, and most of them are open to any group alert to the opportunities offered and persistent in pursuit of its objectives. All the diverse elements in the city, in competition with each other, can and do partake of the stakes of politics; if none gets all it wants, neither is any excluded" (1960, 720–21). However, despite Sayre and Kaufman's conclusion that there was a "reasonable balance" between stability and adaptability in the city, they do include an interesting caveat in light of the statist interpretation of events: "The fact is clear that only a few institutions in the city produce decisions made on the bases of premises relevant to the entire community" (1960, 719).

As political conflicts during the 1960s and early 1970s intensified, the statist critics emerged to confront anomalies in the pluralist model. As group competition degenerated into open, frequently violent, group conflict, urban politics took on a distinctly nonpluralist tone. Increases in federal aid fueled the growth of local government responsibilities to lower-income groups. Federal War on Poverty efforts were intended to increase the responsiveness of urban bureaucracies in part by organizing and empowering local service recipients. Donald Haider observed that in New York City the result of such programs "provides considerable credence to Lowi's contention that new structures of power tended to build upon rather than replace or diminish older structures" (1979, 139).

In the social upheavals of the period and the fiscal instability of a later period, statists saw clear evidence of the predictable breakdown of pluralist society. The statist model seemed to capture the dynamics of this period perfectly. The non-zero-sum politics of growth and accommodation had become the zero-sum politics of stagnation and conflict. As the political conflicts intensified, as the group demands became more adamant, and as the social fabric of the city came under increasing strain, no central authority emerged to coordinate policy. The statists argued that no coordinative authority emerged because such authority had been neutralized by decades of interest group liberalism.

If pluralist theory seemed to be a reasonable guide to politics in the 1950s and if the statist critics seemed to offer plausible explanations for the intense conflicts and fiscal crises of the 1960s, neither had a particularly compelling explanation for retrenchment politics in the 1970s. The emergence of centralized authority in the form of quasi-public agencies, such as the Municipal Assistance Corporation and the Emergency Financial Control Board in New York City, the Financial and Policy Service Board in Cleveland, and Economic Development Agencies in Detroit, fit a pattern of directive business control of local governments. To argue that this extragovernmental centralization was necessary to cope with fiscal crisis is reasonable though not incontestable; to argue that it reflected self-regulating group equilibrium, temporary imbalances in group competition, or the absence of coherent authority is unconvincing.

The mid-1970s belonged analytically to the stratification theorists. In the financiers who sat on the boards managing retrenchment in New York, the elite wing saw examples of the public ascendance of a formerly less visible but always dominant local economic elite. Elite analysts argued that retrenchment managers, in many cases the same individuals who profited by dealing in city debt for the prior decades, were careful to ensure that the crisis was solved at the expense of others and not themselves. "New York City's sovereignty, home rule, was lost, not to a pluralist coalition government, which might have been acceptable under the emergency circumstances of possible default and unremitting federal hostility, but to a group dominated by one economic interest, one economic class, with scarce comprehension of common life in the city beyond Manhattan" (Newfield and DuBrul 1981, 163).

Structuralists saw the retrenchment politics that followed the 1975 crisis as part of the necessary restructuring of the local economy in light of changes in the mode of production. For example, in analyzing the structural imperatives of the period, David Gordon distinguished the socioeconomic constraints around the "old cities" of the Northeast and Midwest from those around the new cities of the South and the Southwest. According to Gordon, fiscal crisis is primarily a regional manifestation of larger socioeconomic changes. "It is a crisis of Old Cities in the corporate stage of capital accumulation. Capitalism has decreed that those cities are archaic as sites for capital production" (Gordon 1984, 49).

It is clear that pluralists and stratificationists differ as to the causes and effects of fiscal crises. It is also clear that within each model there are distinct views of urban politics in general and fiscal crises and retrenchment in particular. To pluralists, fiscal crises are anomalous events that reflect equally anomalous periods of windfall growth; to statists, they are the predictable results of the destruction of formal public authority in pluralist societies; and to stratificationists, these crises are a function of local elites or of the larger structural constraints on local governments.

In dealing with retrenchment, group theorists are faced with paradigmatic dilemmas. If urban politics is either self-regulating group competition or an example of the absence of coherent authority, from where did the authority to manage retrenchment arise? If it arose from emergency powers—that is, from outside of paradigmatic relationships—why were the agencies managing retrenchment dominated by representatives of large financial institutions? If emergency circumstances required that financiers intervene, what does this say about the influence of these interests in general? In other words, how far does the influence of financial forces stretch during periods of normal politics? Is it not conceivable that these financial interests represent a centralizing component of urban politics that, although not vested with the authority of the formal governmental sector, does help coordinate urban fiscal policy? Finally, are those pluralist scholars who express concern about a "privileged position" for business in the American polyarchy actually understating the extent of business influence at the local level? These questions seem particularly salient given the recurring patterns of crisis and financier intervention in American urban history.

Stratificationists were understandably anxious to address these questions. Because of the determinant power wielded by economic elites within their models of urban politics, the directive role that financiers play during retrenchment is not unexpected from the stratificationist perspective. However, although stratification theorists offer paradigmatically consistent explanations for the form that retrenchment politics takes, their analyses have weaknesses overall. Elitists often equate resources with power; the potential for influence with influence; and the capacity to control with the desire to control. The structuralist wing of stratification theory is often too abstract to explain the day-to-day dynamics of normal urban realities.

A Contextual Approach to Urban Politics

The approaches reviewed above provide useful snapshots of urban politics at particular points in time. The contextual approach overcomes this temporal limitation by focusing on how changes in the socioeconomic conditions around cities interact with local political developments to shape urban policy over time. In so doing, the contextual approach employs the other models as more or less accurate reflections of urban politics at specific and recurring historical phases in the evolution of urban regimes rather than as general characterizations of urban politics across time.[5]

The contextual approach is not an effort to split the intellectual difference (indeed, there are basic disagreements between the structuralist wing of the stratification approach and the other models); rather, it is designed to employ aspects of the existing approaches to analyze two recurring historical processes in American cities. First, it provides a framework to examine the regime changes that follow periodic fiscal crises and that result in the fundamental restructuring of political interactions in cities. Second, the approach includes guidelines for monitoring the incremental transformations that occur during periods of normal urban politics.

This section of chapter one, which introduces the contextual approach, is divided into three parts. The first part clarifies the terminology employed in the approach and offers a number of general propositions about urban politics. The second part develops the relationship among fiscal crisis, retrenchment politics, and regime change in American cities. The third part explores the process of internal regime evolution.

Terminology and Propositions

Urban politics in the United States involves three broadly defined sets of interests. In a democratic society, local officials are accountable to the electoral coalitions that put them into office and to the governing coalitions that support their policies. In a market economy, within a federal political system, such accountability means that local officials must cope, on the one hand, with the demands of the *economic elites,* who produce local wealth, and, on the other, with the aspirations of *attentive nonelites,* who are the politically organized elements of the urban citizenry. In a general sense, economic elites embody socioeconomic constraints on government activity, and attentive nonelites represent political constraints on government.[6]

Economic Elites and Local Officials

Because wealth production in the United States occurs largely in the private sector and because government at all levels depends on the producers of wealth for the resources it is charged with allocating, interests involved in large-scale wealth production are critically important to public officials. Such interests are particularly crucial to officials at the subnational levels of government, where corporate mobility is often an option and operating budgets have to be balanced.

There are two types of large-scale economic interests in American cities: major industrial concerns and financial institutions. Representatives of industrial concerns interact with local officials from either a monopoly or a competitive position. In the former case, industry may have substantial, perhaps directive, influence over local government policy; in a more competitive situation, however, industry's interests are generally more diversified and its influence consequently less dramatic. Financial institutions, on the other hand, have more predictable relationships with city governments. As the source of capital for entrepreneurs, financiers promote local economic growth; as the source of financing for housing, they help maintain residential neighborhood stability; and as the primary purchasers and underwriters of city debt, they provide resources that enable governments to ease their short-term cash-flow problems and to generate long-term capital improvements. Moreover, given the changes in banking laws over the past decade, "scholars agree that financial capital is increasingly mobile . . ." (Horan 1991, 124). Accordingly, industries in a monopoly relationship with local governments and large financial interests are considered economic elites because of their inherent importance to local policy-makers.

Economic elites, therefore, wield influence as a result of the very nature of the urban political system. In an insightful analysis, Clarence Stone terms this type of inherent influence "systemic" and defines it as "that dimension of power in which durable features of the socioeconomic system confer advantages and disadvantages on groups in ways predisposing public officials to favor some interests at the expense of others" (Stone 1980, 980). According to Stone, systemic power relationships in American cities have four characteristics. First, they constrain, although they do not negate, the political autonomy of local public officials. Second, because they provide local officials with the means to achieve concrete accomplishments, systemic power relationships predispose these officials to favor upper-income over lower-income constituents. Third, because they lower the opportunity costs for political participation among upper-income groups, systemic power relationships facilitate the access these groups have to government officials. Fourth, systemic power relationships are based not only on economic factors but also on the associational positions and social ties of upper-strata interests (Stone 1980, 988–89).

The contextual approach builds on Stone's analysis. It accepts the idea of an overall systemic influence wielded by economic elites and assumes that such interests are relevant to local officials because of the nature of their positions and not because of any specific political activities in which they engage. However, the contextual approach takes the systemic power analysis a step further. It suggests that, although Stone's notion of the nondeterminant nature of systemic power is valid most of the time, there are cyclical and predictable periods in urban history when the systemic power argument actually understates the extent of economic elite influence. The contextual approach proposes that during periods of urban fiscal crisis and retrenchment management, the power of economic elites becomes overt and indeed determinant in the local political arena. Further, the increased power of economic elites directly leads to the reshaping of urban regimes in the wake of fiscal crises.

From the contextual perspective, then, periods of systemic power relationships between economic elites and local officials are the norm, and periods where economic elites wield directive power are temporary but defining events for city governance. Each set of circumstances is a function of the scope of local political concerns relevant to financial interests at any particular point in time. During periods of normal urban politics, the political concerns of economic elites are relatively narrow, focusing on their immediate desire to accumulate wealth and relating only to those public policies that might help or hinder that process. During periods of fiscal crisis, however, the concerns of these elites are much broader, focusing on the relationships between local economic stability and the entire range of local government activities.

Attentive Nonelites and Local Officials

Attentive nonelites are active participants in city politics who influence local officials to the extent that their participation translates into votes or into the potential for creating instability in the social system. Obviously, a wide diversity of interests exists under the rubric of attentive nonelites, ranging from middle-income homeowners, who desire minimal property tax assessments and basic public services, through municipal employees, who seek improved pay and work conditions, to lower-income claimants, who require extensive public social services. Diversity of interest aside, the distinctive characteristic of attentive nonelite influence is that it exists outside of the systemic context that defines the interactions of economic elites with city government. Consequently, attentive nonelites are dependent on overt political action to achieve their ends and may find themselves in conflict with each other for the allocation of scarce public resources. Indeed, it is precisely this characteristic of attentive nonelite influence, as compared with that of economic elites, that produces a great deal of the public misunderstanding about the nature of normal urban politics. Because the political activities of attentive nonelites are overt, public attention is usually focused on the demands of these groups and not on the systemic influence of economic elites. Consequently, whereas the political influence of the former is often exaggerated, the systemic power of the latter is frequently ignored.

In summary, local officials, economic elites, and attentive nonelites are the core interests in urban politics. To govern, officials require the resources controlled by economic elites; therefore, the influence of these elites over policy is more systemic than that of attentive nonelites. However, because of a democratic political culture and democratic political institutions, attentive nonelites can be important political actors in urban politics. To ignore their demands puts city officials at great political risk.

Urban Regime Analysis

The concept of a political regime is fundamental to the analysis of urban politics. Urban regimes establish the immediate structural and procedural constraints within which local officials develop public policy.[7] They incorporate specific cultural, socioeconomic, and political values within the interactions defining their mode of governance. As such, urban regimes represent a historically specific set of accommodations among the three major actors involved in urban politics—officials, economic elites, and attentive nonelites.

The political interactions and policy accommodations among the major actors in urban politics are guided by both formal rules and informal norms. The formal rules, defining city government's scope of responsibility, decision-making procedures, and points of access, are the institutional basis of a regime. These rules, found in state constitutions, state laws, and city charters, legally constrain a regime's modes of communication, cooperation, and conflict resolution. Regime interactions, however, involve more than formal rules and government institutions; they are also based on informal norms that develop over time. "Because local governmental authority is by law and tradition even more limited than authority at the state and national level, informal arrangements assume special importance in urban politics" (Stone 1989, 3).

The formal rules and informal norms defining urban regimes favor some interests at the expense of others. As a result, urban regimes, like all organized endeavors, represent what E.E. Schattschneider has characterized as "a mobilization of bias in preparation for action" (1960, 30).[8] The interests favored by a particular set of formal rules and informal norms represent a regime's governing coalition. To the extent that the rules and norms allow favored groups to enjoy greater access to decision-making power, they promote cooperative regime relationships. In that light, a regime is "a means for achieving coordinated efforts that might not otherwise be realized" (Stone 1989, 4). The various components of a governing coalition, however, do not have to agree on all issues all of the time. Indeed, specific tensions between economic interests and attentive nonelite groups reflect larger conflicts between local officials' governing and electoral coalitions.[9] Moreover, political conflicts sometimes break out within the economic elite and attentive nonelite coalitions that compose a regime. As long as these conflicts do not result in the replacement of the formal rules and informal norms holding the governing coalition together, they can be considered part of normal regime interactions. Indeed, these day-to-day political interactions among the actors in the governing coalition define normal urban politics.

To a much greater extent than at the state and national levels, urban regime politics concerns the allocation of highly visible and divisible resources. More-over, because "people live in neighborhoods and not in cities" (Massotti 1979, 62), the resources allocated by city government are usually evaluated by recipients in community, not individual, terms. Communities, therefore, represent more than just spatially defined collections of social and economic relationships for urban residents; they are, in a very real sense, the immediate political focus for the urban citizenry. Consequently, urban politics, focusing on the "authoritative allo-cation" of highly divisible, spatially defined, material resources, often involves conflict between citywide and community-based interests. Indeed, much as the balance between federal and state power remains a central constitutional ques-tion in national government, the issue of central-city versus community power is a source of continual tension in city governance.

During much of this century, the city–community conflict has had cultural, socioeconomic, and political implications. The conflict is cultural in that it juxta-poses the more traditional values of community politics against the more mod-ernist ideals of citywide coalitions; it is socioeconomic in that it pits the interests of small businesses and moderate-income residents against those of large corpo-rations and a coalition of upper- and lower-income groups; it is political in that it concerns clashes over what social values should guide the "authoritative alloca-tion" of scarce resources. With socioeconomic constraints and local regime evo-lution as context, the conflict is played out in the urban political arena. In the short run, it involves control of a particular city government; in the long run, the conflict goes to the heart of urban governance, political legitimacy, and regime change in American cities.

Urban regimes, then, incorporate four characteristics. (1) They comprise polit-ical interactions among local officials, economic elites, and attentive nonelites. (2) Regime interactions are guided by both formal rules and informal norms. (3) Regime interactions include both cooperation and conflict. (4) Regime inter-actions often involve the allocation of resources within urban communities.

The questions of regime evolution and change are also fundamental to the analysis. By the nature of normal politics, urban regimes must accommodate sufficient numbers of local political interests to remain in power. The nature of the regime itself goes a long way toward determining which interests are accom-modated by political officials. However, over time, the evolution of normal politics incrementally alters the initial set of accommodations through a process of group inclusion. Fiscal crises, on the other hand, abruptly change the nature of urban regimes by destabilizing existing governing coalitions and forcing decidely nonincremental adjustments in public policy. It is to this dynamic that we now turn.

Fiscal Crises and Regime Change

The influence that economic elites and attentive nonelites have on city officials affects and is affected by the local fiscal situation, that is, the balance between revenues and expenditures. Indeed, as mentioned above, the range of issues relevant to economic elites depends on the fiscal situation within which the issues emerge. The fiscal situation in any city is reflected in three possible budget scenarios. *Fiscal stability*, or relative budget balance, indicates revenue growth sufficient to address both incremental increases in existing demands and new claims on city resources with minimal political conflict. Satisfying existing demands reaffirms the position of the interests already included within the regime's governing coalition; addressing new demands represents an attempt by local officials to expand the coalition's reach. *Fiscal stress* results from temporary imbalances in a city's revenue–expenditure base. It is produced by economic downturn, an increase in the number or nature of group demands, or both. Although periods of fiscal stress are troublesome and generate political tension as well as economic uncertainty, they are not crisis situations as long as local officials appear to have some control of the situation and credit markets remain open to city debt offerings. *Fiscal crisis* is the closure of short-term credit markets to city debt brought on by continued budgetary imbalance and creditors' perceptions that local officials have lost control of the fiscal situation. The contextual approach suggests that such crisis periods are central to the dynamics of regime change that characterize urban political history.[10]

Periods of fiscal crisis and retrenchment politics reflect in stark terms the contrasting pressures emanating from the economic and political components included within local governing coalitions. During crisis periods, systemically disruptive tensions develop between the economic priorities of capital accumulation, governmental efficiency, and administrative centralization, on the one hand, and the political demands for resource allocation, public accountability, and policy decentralization, on the other. Because local governments are required to balance their operating budgets, they confront directly the conflict between the economic pressures for fiscal responsibility and the political demands for resource allocation. The critical nature of the conflict at the local level is reflected in the fact that whereas urban fiscal crises signal a long-term breakdown in economic constraints, retrenchment management is only possible with the virtual eradication of political constraints.

Periods of fiscal crisis result in dramatic changes in the interest group alignments that define the prevailing urban regime. These changes are reflected in the emergence of an active and unified coalition of financial interests seeking to restore the city's fiscal stability and in the increased segmentation of attentive nonelite groups, each of which is seeking to protect its own past political gains. Coupled with the active intervention of state government, these coalition realignments severely limit the autonomy of city officials and result in substantial policy changes. In the immediate crisis situation, these changes are evident as retrenchment; in the long term, they help to explain the regime upheavals that follow crises.

To understand these dynamics, periods of fiscal crisis and retrenchment politics must be considered as part of the larger cycles of regime stability and change. During periods of fiscal stability or even fiscal stress, local politics is characterized by relative openness to group demands, shifting coalitions among attentive nonelite groups, and incremental adjustments in public policy. However, during periods of fiscal crisis, a clear division develops between financiers, who are concerned with economic stability, and attentive nonelites, who are seeking to protect past political gains threatened by retrenchment. As the allocation of local public resources increasingly becomes a zero-sum game and as public policy issues are increasingly perceived as redistributive in nature, the control of municipal budgets becomes of paramount concern to economic elites, and the accommodation between socioeconomic and political constraints, embodied in the existing regime, breaks down.[11]

The breakdowns in regime coalitions occasioned by fiscal crises are not haphazard affairs; they result in predictable changes in the immediate context of urban politics. Fiscal crises unify, activate, and empower local financial elites at the same time that they segment and weaken attentive nonelite groups. During fiscal crises, financiers broaden their interest and increase their influence in city politics for three basic reasons. First, to protect their investments, now threatened by fiscal instability, these interests become involved with a wide breadth of local issues, such as union contracts and service allocation, which formerly were of minimal interest to them. Indeed, prior to the onset of crisis, such issues were dealt with in the political arena through the distributive policies characteristic of fiscal stability. Second, because of their expertise in economic matters and their professional standing with the city's creditors, financial interests can effect fiscal relief through their access to credit markets. The city's creditors are the proximate cause of fiscal crisis because of their decision to reject the borrowings intended to finance local cash-flow shortages. Convincing the creditors to ease the crisis by again purchasing a city's debt offerings is more effectively achieved by fellow financiers, who represent the larger socioeconomic context, than by local public officials, who represent the political sector. Third, the prestige of financiers in the community as a whole—a prestige nurtured by favorable media coverage, which understates their involvement in helping to generate injuriously high levels of debt while it emphasizes their "civic concern" during crisis—enables representatives of these interests to assume directive responsibility in local government, for which there are no discernible procedural rationales.

On the other hand, there are a number of reasons why the influence of attentive nonelites is minimized during periods of fiscal crisis. First, these groups operate exclusively in the political arena, where their activities and demands are subject to intense media scrutiny and public attention. Consequently, during periods of crisis, attentive nonelites' access to public officials appears more as part of the problem than as part of the solution. Second, these groups depend on local officials' receptivity to their claims. However, as explained more clearly below, the onset of fiscal crisis dramatically diminishes the influence that elected local officials have on public policy. Third, attentive nonelite groups, which are quite diverse during periods of fiscal stability, are further segmented during periods of crisis, as each group struggles to protect its own specific interests during retrenchment. As the coalitions between and among these groups break down in the face of crisis, the influence of attentive nonelites over city policy-making diminishes.

This transformed group alignment—unified and active economic elites, on the one hand, and weakened and fragmented attentive nonelite groups, on the other—ensures that fiscal crises are dealt with in a manner consistent with socio-economic exigencies while minimizing political constraints. Ironically, then, it is the political sphere, which adapts to and integrates the demands of attentive nonelites during periods of fiscal stability, that so completely stifles such input during periods of fiscal crisis.

Among the immediate consequences of group realignment during crisis is the restructuring of formal political power in the city. To understand this process it is important to remember that although periods of fiscal stress always precede periods of fiscal crisis, fiscal stress rarely leads to fiscal crisis. In most cases of fiscal stress, local public officials are uncertain whether budget imbalances are temporary or have longer-term implications. However, due to their understandable desire to avoid the political costs that service cutbacks or widespread revenue increases would incur among their attentive nonelite support groups, these officials have powerful incentives to treat situations of fiscal stress as temporary. During periods of fiscal stress, local officials strive to "survive each fiscal year by trimming costs in areas where citizens, especially voters, are unlikely to notice service deterioration" (Levine, Rubin, and Wolohojian 1981, 14). Accordingly, they tend to employ short-term strategies—such as selective tax increases, often aimed at business interests, increased short- and long-term debt offerings, and one-shot revenue enhancers—to address the immediate budgetary imbalance. "The first response to fiscal pressure is frequently to draw down existing fund surpluses, engage in interfund transfers, borrow to support operating revenues, and take other actions which at a minimum buys time and delays the necessity of choosing between revenue increases and expenditure-reduction strategies" (Wolman 1980, 234).

If fiscal recovery follows close on the heels of fiscal stress, these strategies are but footnotes to the balanced-budget requirements under which most local governments operate. If, however, budgetary imbalances deepen and threaten to become structural, these same strategies sharply exacerbate an already deteriorating economic situation and become the focus of negative media and public attention. Thus, the indeterminate evolution of fiscal stress, coupled with the incentives that local officials have to conduct politics as usual under conditions of stress, explains why, when a crisis initially develops, it is viewed by many officials as essentially a management problem, divorced from its larger socioeconomic and political roots. This perception among local officials, in turn, is a large part of the reason that fiscal crises are perceived by many as failures of political leadership or examples of poor management.

During the initial stages of a fiscal crisis, state government officials, concerned about the effects of local problems on their own fiscal situation, become increasingly involved with local issues. In union with financial interests, whose previously mentioned access to credit markets affords them de facto influence during crises, state officials, with de jure authority, assume a more active role in local fiscal policy. As the range of issues relevant to state officials and financiers expands and as their involvement in local politics becomes increasingly unidimensional and overt, the range of options available to local officials correspondingly contracts. In their need to reopen credit markets that have closed to the city, local officials are faced with a political Hobson's choice. If they accede to the financiers' demands for immediate and dramatic retrenchment, local officials alienate the attentive nonelite support groups constituting their political base; if they resist such pressure in order to maintain their base of political support, they risk municipal bankruptcy. Regardless of which strategy they choose—and there is intense and immediate pressure to choose the former—they soon become weakened actors on the local political scene.

The assumption of fiscal responsibility by state officials and financiers, two sets of actors who are relatively insulated from local political pressures, allows the service cutbacks and tax increases—the effects of which are felt most directly by attentive nonelites—to be implemented. The legal authority of state government, the economic power of financial elites, and the weakened political position of local officials assure that local policy is no longer a local matter and that public accountability is no longer a countervailing force to governmental efficiency during crisis periods. During periods of fiscal crisis and retrenchment politics, the socioeconomic constraints within which cities operate overwhelm political constraints as government temporarily becomes virtually a tool of financial interests.

Retrenchment, therefore, is controlled by interests and is constrained by socioeconomic exigencies that require that the expenditure cuts and revenue increases necessary to bring local budgets into balance be implemented at the expense of attentive nonelite groups. Achieving this goal requires the breakup of the ruling coalition that defined the precrisis urban regime. However, once the immediate crisis has been resolved, or appears to be heading for resolution, political constraints on local government, that is, attentive nonelite demands, once again emerge as relevant. State government and financier control of local decision making, possible because of group alignments and government failure during crisis situations, must be brought into line with the political constraints that promote representative institutions as the normal democratic arrangements at the local level of government.

Reformulating the precrisis method of addressing attentive nonelite interests then becomes the central priority of retrenchment managers following fiscal crises. In effect, the socioeconomic priorities of capital production, governmental efficiency, and administrative centralization, which are undervalued before and preeminent during periods of crisis, once again confront the political priorities of resource distribution, public accountability, and policy decentralization after a crisis. Because the institutional balance between these twin constraints defines an urban regime, the reformulation of the balance under conditions still more conducive to socioeconomic than political pressures sets the stage for the emergence of a new regime.

Therefore, after the initial adaptations to crisis, political issues are confronted anew in an environment that includes the active and overt involvement of financiers in local policy-making; the disaggregated and diminished influence of attentive nonelites; and a weakened formal political structure. The general regime changes produced by the confrontation over fundamental issues within a fluid political environment are revealed in patterned political ways, although the specific adaptations in urban governance are historically unique. First, the governing coalition, including all the political interactions that had defined the now discredited precrisis regime, is replaced by a new coalition directed by financial elites and including some of the more fiscally conservative segments of the attentive nonelite community. Because of its makeup, this new regime is committed to continuing policies designed to achieve fiscal stability through cutback management. Initially, there is no political requirement that the regime be at all representative of attentive nonelite interests since, at this point, the city is still hostage to the authority of state officials and the power of financial interests. Second, local government's role is redefined by the new leadership in ways acceptable to the new ruling coalition. This means the replacement of city officials whose loyalty is still divided between commitments to fiscal stability and commitments to political accountability, and the emergence of city officials willing to continue the politics of retrenchment, albeit in decreasingly harsh forms. Third, the new regime institutionalizes its presence through formal, structural changes in city governance, which directly affect the process of political legitimacy by redirecting attentive nonelite demands to channels more acceptable to the new leadership.

Fiscal crises are watershed events that occur periodically in urban history, wreak their devastation on individuals and institutions, and produce major realignments in urban politics. They are in part a function of economic downturn produced by exogenous forces over which urban government has no influence. However, there are indications that, in the evolution of urban regimes, choices are made and policies are implemented locally that make fiscal crises more likely or that at least make them more difficult to control once they occur. These policy options, although not determined, are patterned. It is to this intraregime pattern that we now turn.

Intraregime Evolution: A Life-Cycle Approach

Assuming that political regimes, like all human creations, are temporary allows us to employ a "life-cycle" focus when analyzing their evolution. In his classic study of the organizational behavior and evolution of government bureaucracies, Anthony Downs employed a life-cycle approach to analyze the birth, maturation, and decline of public agencies (1959, 5–23). Robert Waste applied Downs's life-cycle model to city politics by tracing the stages of the urban policy-making process from problem recognition, through triggering mechanisms, to policy evaluation, leading to either policy maintenance, reformulation, or termination (1989, 29–41).[12]

The life-cycle approach also lends itself to the analysis of urban regimes. According to Downs, "as a bureau ages, its officials become more willing to modify the bureau's original formal goals in order to further the survival and growth of its administrative machinery" (1959, 19). In similar fashion, as urban regimes mature, their survival rests increasingly with continuing modifications and adaptations in their existing political interactions. Such alterations are necessary to accommodate conflicting intraregime factions, pacify dissatisfied attentive nonelite interests, and incorporate new interests into the regime's governing coalition.

As governing mechanisms, regimes represent and coordinate diversity. This dual mandate requires them to adapt to and integrate change into their existing pattern of political relationships. Consequently, urban regimes modify their original policy emphases as they address new political demands. The evolution in regime behavior can be viewed as a series of stages representing a regime's life cycle, including periods of regime initiation, regime consolidation, regime fragmentation, and regime demise.

Each of these stages in a regime's life cycle has its own distinctive balance of economic elite and attentive nonelite influence, degree of local autonomy, and mix of public policy. As the life cycle evolves, a regime's stabilizing or centripetal components, which reflect the socioeconomic constraints on urban governance, are increasingly displaced by its adaptive or centrifugal tendencies, which reflect the political demands made on city governments. Although each stage in a regime's life cycle lends itself to an empirically satisfying analysis by the pluralist, the statist, or the stratificationist perspective, the contextual analysis addresses the dynamics of urban politics and thus provides analysis of local politics across time.

To examine the policy emphases of the various stages in a regime's life cycle, it is useful to refer to Paul Peterson's (1981) analysis in *City Limits*. According to Peterson, local public policy can be classified as either developmental, redistributive, or allocational in nature. "Developmental policies enhance the economic position of the city. Redistributive policies benefit low-income residents but at the same time negatively affect the local economy. Allocational policies are more or less neutral in their economic effects" (1981, 41). From Peterson's perspective, each policy type has its own implications, which are best measured by calculating "whether the marginal benefits [of that type of policy] exceed the marginal cost to the average taxpayer" (1981, 42).

Developmental policies assist cities in their competition with other local governments, bolster the local economy in the long run, and provide widespread trickle-down economic benefits. Therefore, they produce a net benefit for local taxpayers and should be pursued by city officials. Redistributive policies, on the other hand, should be the responsibility of higher levels of government because, in producing a net cost to local taxpayers, they damage a city's economic competitiveness. Allocational policies, which include the normal "housekeeping services" performed by most local governments, do not affect competitiveness, because they represent the typical costs of government and are fiscally neutral in their impact.

According to the contextual approach, periods of *regime initiation* closely follow fiscal crisis and reflect fundamental changes in precrisis urban politics. The political consequences of fiscal crises—the bifurcation of financial and attentive nonelite interests, the loss of local autonomy, and the appropriation of fiscal power by state officials and financiers—have dramatic impacts on local policy. Periods of retrenchment politics produce an almost singular focus on developmental policies designed to maintain existing and encourage future private investment in the city, thereby promoting urban growth. Although such policies are defended in a political context as generators of trickle-down collective benefits, they serve most directly the immediate interests of financiers and are the clearest indication of socioeconomic constraints on local government during retrenchment.

By defining the urban public interest during periods of crisis and retrenchment, financial interests are able to implement policies that assume what in more normal times is a highly debatable premise, namely that there exists a unitary city interest. As Clarence Stone notes in a reply to Peterson's argument that local government policy must be guided by the structural imperatives of a competitive public-sector market, "Structural constraints are real, but they are mediated through the political arrangements that enable a prevailing coalition to govern a community" (1987, 17). The argument is compelling and, from a long-term perspective, points to significant limitations in Peterson's overall model. However, during periods of retrenchment, the political arrangements mediating structural constraints are decidedly unbalanced and weighted toward developmental interests. Indeed, during these periods, structural constraints are mediated by political arrangements that are created and maintained only with the explicit acceptance of financial interests.

The virtual determinant influence of financial interests during these periods of retrenchment offers substantial empirical support for a stratificationist view of city politics. Retrenchment politics negates many of the political constraints under which local governments normally operate by consigning attentive nonelite demands for allocational and/or redistributive policies to the "back burner" of the urban political agenda. Regime initiation, which involves the redefinition and restructuring of political interactions, begins the process of reestablishing meaningful political constraints on policy. It accomplishes this by reaffirming the values and reinforcing the legitimacy of retrenchment managers, albeit in a less directive role than during crisis, and by redefining the process of political legitimation from that of the discredited regime to that which will characterize the emerging regime. Periods of regime initiation are characterized, then, by fundamental alterations in the interactions defining attentive nonelite involvement in city government. This period, which begins readdressing the political constraints within which local governments operate, is guided initially by the conservative fiscal policies of retrenchment managers and ideologically compatible elected officials.

As the most recent fiscal crisis fades from memory, as cyclical economic recovery produces urban revenue growth, and as financial interests become increasingly comfortable focusing on their normal profit-making pursuits, the socioeconomic constraints on urban regimes begin to weaken. Political constraints, in the form of existing and newly emerging attentive nonelite groups, become increasingly more competitive with socioeconomic factors in local politics. Adaptation to change, encouraged by intraregime political conflicts and implemented by the incorporation of new group demands into the governing coalition, becomes part of the process of increasingly normal city politics. *Regime consolidation* is a period in which the constraints of the socioeconomic and political contexts of local government attain relative balance. This period, the apex of regime legitimacy, sees the reintegration of old and the integration of new attentive nonelite groups into the regime's base of support, thus allowing both policy responsiveness and fiscal stability. The mix of public policy is, more than at any other time, a function of the balance of competing political forces.

During periods of regime consolidation, economic growth and manageable attentive nonelite demands produce relative local fiscal stability. During these periods, the allocation of services increases incrementally, with community winners and losers reflecting the balance of power defining the new regime; redistributive policies are a function of local political culture, that is, the general consensus on the role of government, and the degree of organization among lower-income groups and their allies; and developmental policies are a consequence of market conditions and regime-defined government involvement in economic issues. Allen Schick, who employs the term *relaxed scarcity* to describe such periods, notes the fiscal balance characterizing them: "The incremental rise in the cost of existing programs can be paid out of available resources with enough left over for significant program additions" (1980, 116–17). However, Schick also incorporates a warning in his analysis: "Relaxed scarcity can persist only when the tax structure possesses sufficient elasticity to produce steadily higher yields above the incremental growth of expenditures" (1980, 119).

The responsive and stable nature of local politics, as reflected in the relative balance during periods of regime consolidation, fits well into the pluralist paradigm of competitive and open group politics. However, the process is hostage to economic forces over which local officials have little control. Recessions decrease local revenues and place great pressure on local budgets. The effects of economic downturn, while always deleterious to some interests in the city, are largely dependent on the evolutionary stage of the current regime. A new set of political arrangements, close enough chronologically to the most recent crisis so that socioeconomic constraints are still in place, will weather an economic storm more readily than a long-standing regime with a history of the political accommodations and group inclusions necessary for regime survival politically.

The period of *regime fragmentation* is characterized by continued group incorporation, without the centripetal authority to hold coalitions together. The existing regime, in power for several decades, is more a conglomeration of diverse groups than a coordinated coalition. As such, its socioeconomic and political balance is weighted against fiscal stability and in favor of continued political responsiveness. Public policy is no longer a function of coordinated competition; rather, it is a consequence of group entrenchment. This period is modeled quite well by pluralism's statist critics.

Although regime fragmentation can lead to *regime demise* if the socioeconomic situation deteriorates, as mentioned above, the transformation does not have to be immediate. Periods of fiscal stress and fragmentation may last as long as local officials can manage the situation. "Rather than face budget realities and scale down their activities, local governments might prefer to intensify their muddling-through improvisations" (Schick 1980, 124). Indeed, local officials, with access to funds secured from financial interests, whose own profit motives may be served by continued government borrowing and spending, can continue the process of group incorporation for years. However, once structural decline sets in, or once financiers begin to fear the economic consequences of uncontrolled government borrowing and spending, credit markets close to city debt, fiscal crisis becomes the norm, and retrenchment politics begins the process of ushering in a new regime.

The contextual approach highlights the fact that fiscal crises are more than manifestations of either economic downturn or governmental weakness. These crises are, in fact, the products of those historical junctures when regime fragmentation coincides with economic weakness. Political and economic variables are each necessary but insufficient explanations of fiscal crisis. As interdependent phenomena, however, these twin sets of variables explain the onset of crisis, the adaptations that are selected to cope with crisis, and the long-term effects of such events on local politics.

Regimes in New York City: A Retrospective

New York City politics has been characterized by three distinct regimes, which are most readily recognized as machine, reform, and postreform styles of governance. As a consequence of adaptations to fiscal crisis during the 1870s, New

York City's era of "gang rule" was superseded by an extended period of machine rule under Tammany Hall.[13] The machine's functional centralization under the boss system assisted the large-scale business elites of the day by coordinating the mechanisms of city government; the machine's geographically decentralized political representation addressed the claims of newly arrived immigrant groups for the price of electoral support. Machine politics tended to be extragovernmental, characterized by informal negotiations and deals between actors, only some of whom were part of the formal government. The machine era in New York reached its apex of power at the turn of the century, under the leadership of Charles F. Murphy, and lost its political dominance during the fiscal crisis of the 1930s, at the hands of Fiorello H. LaGuardia and the local urban reformers.

The reform regime, institutionalized in New York as the "welfare city," geographically centralized authority in center-city government while functionally decentralizing service distribution among a host of relatively autonomous city agencies. The business interests of the period and attentive nonelite groups were both serviced by center-city governmental agencies, although distinctly different types of agencies handled the demands of business and of attentive nonelite groups. For both philosophical and political reasons, the reform era de-emphasized community issues in favor of a citywide perspective on policy. Reform governments changed the manner of dealing with citywide concerns by placing the responsibility for those concerns in the hands of professionals in specialized bureaucratic agencies. By so doing, reform governments provided the increasingly professional corporate sector with a comparably modernized public sector with which to do business.

Reform agencies interacted with their business constituencies directly and, in general, amicably. Reform government also changed the basis for political legitimacy in cities from one founded on the vote–service exchange at the community level to one based on the services available from the "welfare state" at a citywide level. Reform governments secured legitimacy by extending the reach of the public sector into the provision of social services delivered, not directly in exchange for votes (at least not crassly in exchange for votes), but as of right—with the right determined by the professionals serving in the new administrative state created by reform. The reform regime experienced its high point during Robert Wagner's years as mayor and began its decline during the second administration of John V. Lindsay, a decline culminating in the fiscal crisis of 1975.

Since that crisis, the welfare city has been transformed by a postreform regime that has functionally recentralized fiscal authority in quasi-public monitoring boards and has geographically decentralized land-use planning, local budgeting, and service-monitoring responsibility in a system of community boards. The postreform era in New York was initiated as a consequence of the need to reestablish central coordination of city finances following the fiscal crisis of 1975 and to address community-based demands for participation. Postreform involved the reemergence of the community as a basis of political legitimacy.

The postreform regime modified early demands for participatory democracy and community control by establishing formal community organizations with ties to city government. It was a response to both grass-roots political pressures and the fiscal pressures resulting from the increasing costs of legitimizing the regime through the welfare state. As a result, the postreform era involved the institution-alization of central-city and community conflict within the new regime's govern-ing coalition.

The three regimes had common historical roots in that each achieved political dominance in New York as a result of a fiscal crisis that destabilized prior political arrangements. Moreover, when in power, the three regimes had other commonalities. Each regime was defined by a unique set of formal and informal political interactions; each included its own perspective on the proper role of government; each developed its own particular source of political legitimacy; and each is defined by a distinctive balance between central-city and community power. Chapter two focuses on the political interactions evident in two of New York's regimes: one led by the Tammany machine, the other guided by urban reformers.

CHAPTER TWO

Community Politics in Context: Machine and Reform Governance

This chapter traces the evolution of two political regimes in New York City history: machine rule under Tammany Hall and the reform regime that replaced the machine. Although these two regimes were markedly different in their political orientations, they experienced quite similar evolutions: each was initiated in the wake of a fiscal crisis that discredited the previous ruling coalition and resulted in the rise of a fiscally conservative political leadership; each regime matured during a period of relative economic stability, which allowed the leadership to consolidate power by balancing the need for fiscal restraint and the demands for public spending; each was weakened by internal conflicts and external challenges that forced the leadership to broaden the regime's political base to maintain electoral support; and each regime lost dominance as a result of fiscal pressures with which the regime, fragmented by political conflict, could not cope.

The evolution of Tammany Hall is a classic illustration of the principle that organizations survive by adapting to their environments. Originally established as a social society, Tammany Hall evolved over the course of the nineteenth century into a powerful urban political machine. Tammany was far from being the political monolith of urban folklore, however; its longevity was a function of its continued accommodation of economic and political forces in New York City.[1] Even during its era of organizational maturity and regime consolidation, from the 1890s through the 1920s, Tammany's rule was continually challenged by internal conflicts and organized reform opposition.

Coming to power as a result of the "bankers' strike" of 1871, the machine was replaced by a reform regime in the wake of the depression of 1929. Prior to achieving power, reformers had challenged Tammany rule for decades, winning control of city government for brief periods. Like its counterparts in other cities, the New York reform movement was largely a creation of upper-income interests; it incorporated both socially progressive and elitist values, and it sought to implement those values through structural reform of city government.

Brought to power after the fiscal crisis generated by the depression, a reform regime ruled in New York for roughly three decades. New York City's administrative and welfare state developed under this regime and reached its apex in the 1950s and early 1960s as reformers consolidated power. However, during the 1960s, reform governments were pressured by increasing demands for participation and community control from forces that, for the most part, were outside of the regime's governing coalition. Reform governance was progressively weakened by political conflicts as competing regime factions sought political support from groups across the city. Following the fiscal crisis of 1975, the reform regime, unable to manage fiscal matters and hostage to a variety of attentive nonelite demands, was superseded by postreform governance.

The Urban Machine: Organized Self-Interest

From a socioeconomic and political perspective, the urban machine was a creature of its times. The fragmented public sector in the United States meant that, in the absence of an alternative mechanism of coordination, the urbanization that accompanied the Industrial Revolution and that produced dramatic physical, demographic, and socioeconomic changes in the city would have to proceed with little or no organization. Between 1860 and 1900, the United States experienced huge increases in its urban population. In 1860, slightly more than six million people lived in urban areas; by 1920, nearly fifty-five million people lived in cities. Over that sixty-year period, a nation with fewer than one-fifth of its population urbanized saw over one-half of the population living in cities. National urban population growth was more than reflected in New York City's population, which rose from slightly over one million to more than five and one-half million residents, increasing the city's share of the nation's population from 3.5 percent to 5.5 percent in sixty-years.

These dramatic changes, however, were not matched by equally significant changes in the political processes or institutions that governed cities. Despite the population increases and the corresponding increases in social interdependence and tension, American cities continued to be managed by fragmented and ineffective governments. City governments were hostage to a laissez-faire philosophy, which, although often violated in the interests of business, remained a powerful constraint on public authority in general. Moreover, malapportioned state legislatures, controlled by rural interests with little concern for cities, except as sources of state revenue, created a host of independent boards and commissions in urban areas, each with its own policy emphasis, which further fragmented the exercise of public authority. Describing state–city relationships during this period, Charles Adrian and Charles Press maintain: "The state has been most unwilling to allow its child, the city, to grow up. A theory of perpetual infancy was adopted by nineteenth century state legislatures in their attitudes toward their offspring" (1977, 142). In short, American cities, undergoing the fundamental transformations involved in industrial urbanization, were still operating with local governments designed to manage the commercial cities of the early and mid-nineteenth century. By default, then, as much as by design, the urban political machine became the one mechanism capable of coordinating public policy in the industrial city.

The urban political machine institutionalized direct quid pro quo politics in American cities.[2] The machine obtained and maintained power by organizing narrowly defined self-interest throughout the city. As a structured exchange mechanism, the machine relied on "inducements both specific and material" to secure internal political support from its members and external support from business elites and attentive nonelites (Banfield and Wilson 1963, 115–16). By employing incentives for participation that were both private and material, the machine transferred the operations of the private market to the public sector. Professional politicians secured authority over the allocation of highly divisible local resources and consequently the opportunity for personal advancement for the price of organizational loyalty. Business elites secured a relatively stable economic climate and access to public resources for the price of contributions to machine coffers. Attentive nonelites obtained services for the price of electoral support of machine candidates.

Although these overt functions were predominantly private and individual in nature, the machine's "latent functions" were decidedly public and social in effect (Merton 1967). An analysis of the machine's organizational structure clearly illustrates this point. The urban political machine of the late nineteenth and early twentieth centuries was characterized by *functional centralization* (i.e., the machine was hierarchically arranged under a boss or collection of bosses) and *geographical decentralization* (i.e., the machine's electoral support was located in a district system and was sustained by a largely extragovernmental set of community-based interactions).

Because the machine's functional centralization enabled bosses to coordinate the process of urbanization, it represented a major benefit to business interests seeking urban economic growth. Indeed, their coordinative function made machine bosses crucial to the business interests with a need for government contact, which, in turn, provided the bosses with a steady source of revenue in the form of campaign and personal contributions from these interests (Griffith 1974). As Eugene Lewis noted, "Industrialization and the expansion of municipal services meant increased opportunity for the politicians and the industrial owners and managers to find common, mutually profitable ground" (1973, 51).

The machine's geographical decentralization, by reflecting and eventually institutionalizing the spatial segregation of economic, ethnic, and racial groups in American cities, promoted personal and direct service–vote exchange at the community level.[3] Such decentralization created mediating structures between attentive nonelites and city government and acted to rechannel worker dissatisfaction with the inequities of the private market into the quasi-public realm of machine politics. Geographical decentralization was based on the need to secure popular support in a more or less democratic political order, and, as such, it served as the basis of the urban machine's political legitimacy.

Fiscal Crisis and the Fall of Boss Tweed

The machine era in New York City was ushered in by the combined political and economic effects of a financiers' strike in 1871 and the financial panic of 1873. The former produced a fiscal crisis as creditors closed markets to city debt and refused to pay local taxes; the latter acted to extend the period of retrenchment politics following the initial crisis. The precrisis period, characterized by Martin Shefter (1976) as the era of "rapacious individualism," had been marked by the rule of competing political gangs held together more by corruption and intimidation than by any discernible structured pattern of political interactions. The Tweed Ring, the most successful of the premachine gangs, ruled from 1866 to 1871.[4] Analyzing the ring's absence of structure, Shefter notes: "It was a combine within Tammany, whose membership was considerably narrower than the party's and whose corrupt activities did not serve to strengthen the party. . . . [T]he Ring did not command a disciplined party organization" (1976, 24).

The Tweed Ring provided a "piece of the action" to a variety of interests. It addressed business and financial interests by implementing infrastructure improvements on the city's docks and in its northern "frontier," thereby increasing the potential for commercial expansion; socializing business costs by changing a system of special assessments on property owners benefiting from improvements to a system where the costs of improvements were borne by general city revenues; and supporting stricter building codes promoted by fire insurance companies and large real estate developers interested in minimizing both claims and competition. The ring addressed attentive nonelite concerns by helping to naturalize, often illegally, hundreds of thousands of immigrants; providing aid to parochial schools, thereby appeasing a growing Irish-Catholic population; and increasing public assistance to local charities thereby addressing, at least symbolically, the interests of the urban poor.

The ring financed its programs through the sale of city debt. Between 1867 and 1871, the level of municipal debt in New York rose threefold from $30 million to over $95 million, with over 50 percent of that owned by state-chartered banks, many with connections to the ring (Durand 1898, 373). Although the debt levels rose with the acquiescence of financial interests who underwrote the offerings, questions concerning the city's ability to carry the vastly enlarged debt as well as its capacity to manage the funds raised eventually began to shake investor confidence in city offerings. By 1871, domestic and international purchasers of municipal securities were increasingly wary of the city's creditworthiness. In April 1871, for example, "the Berlin *Zeitschrift fin Kapital und Rente* noted that only the reputation of the city's underwriters, Rothschild and Discounts Gesselschaft, encouraged it to trust the soundness of the New York securities listed on the Berlin exchange" (Mandelbaum 1965, 77).

Denials of fiscal problems by Tweed's handpicked officials were as ineffectual as they were predictable. A series of exposés in the *New York Times* chronicled the corruption involved in the management of city funds.[5] By the summer of 1871, financial interests became openly concerned about the effects of increasingly expensive public amortization costs on the property tax rates affecting their mortgages and clients. To gain control over the city's fiscal situation, financial interests organized a "bankers' strike," refusing to underwrite any further municipal debt or to pay property taxes to Tweed's government. A Committee of Seventy, composed of representatives of the city's major financial institutions and wealthier families, was organized to force reforms on city government (Werner 1928, 204–32; Mandelbaum 1965, chap. 8). In September 1871, Judge George Barnard issued an order restraining any further sale of city debt (Mandelbaum 1965).

The bankers' strike and the court order dried up the Tweed Ring's sources of capital and turned a situation of fiscal stress into one of fiscal crisis. Indictments of political and governmental officials, resulting from legal inquiries into the use and misuse of city funds, undermined the formal authority of local officials. At the same time, state officials, Tammany reformers, and financial interests cooperated in appointing a special deputy comptroller for New York to manage the city's fiscal affairs. The power of the Tweed Ring, a power based on individual corruption and fiscal largess, was broken as fiscal authority was centralized in officials beholden to state government and financial interests. It was a pattern the city would see again. On election day, November 7, 1871, the Tweed government was swept from power.

Restructuring the Machine: Regime Initiation

Following the immediate period of crisis, politics in New York was restructured. The coalition of financial interests and Tammany reformers that broke the Tweed Ring succeeded in installing "Honest" John Kelly as the leader of Tammany Hall.[6] Throughout his tenure as county leader, Kelly maintained a conservative fiscal posture, thereby addressing the demands of financial interests for political and economic stability. At the same time, Kelly acted to restructure the Tammany machine by reorganizing its district operations.

Kelly's commitment to fiscal conservatism was evident in many of his actions. To decrease the costs and the visibility of corruption at the district level, he established central oversight of district operations. To improve the machine's reputation among wealthy financiers, Kelly recruited respected businessmen to serve as sachems of the Tammany society. Lastly, to reaffirm his commitment to "good government" and fiscal stability, Kelly secured the Tammany machine's endorsement for reform candidates in three of the six mayoral elections held during his tenure. David Hammack maintains that for most of Kelly's tenure, "Democratic affairs were managed by the wealthy merchants and lawyers who constituted Swallowtail Democrats" (1982, 114). Kelly's restructured Tammany Hall provided business interests of the day with both the fiscal restraint they desired to ensure economic stability and the functional centralization of public authority they needed to coordinate industrialization and economic growth. Indeed, the fiscal conservatism of Kelly and his immediate successors, by minimizing new and amortizing old municipal debt in the 1870s and 1880s, helped city government avoid a fiscal crisis during the financial panic of 1893.

However, Kelly's machine was more than just a conduit for upper-income interests. Under Kelly's leadership, the newly structured Tammany machine addressed the emerging political influence of immigrant groups in New York City by institutionalizing the Democratic party's presence in the city's ethnic communities. This was accomplished by transforming Tammany Hall into a hierarchically coordinated, community-based political organization (Werner 1928, 276–302; Connable and Silberfarb 1967, 181–85). Under Kelly's system, the leader of the Tammany machine was selected by and accountable to an executive committee composed of assembly district leaders who were themselves selected by and accountable to district committees composed of election-district (precinct) captains.

In this context, the notion of political accountability should be neither overestimated nor undervalued. Once selected, bosses wielded enormous power within the machine. Through extensive influence over the appointment of district leaders, they could enlarge their majorities on the executive committee. Through their control of campaign finance and patronage, they could reward friendly district leaders and punish internal opponents. Finally, through their influence over elected officials, Tammany bosses had access to the power of government. Nonetheless, however impressive, the bosses' power was based on the ability to generate continued majority support on the committees that originally selected them. Their control was rarely, if ever, as complete as theory and folklore suggest. Control was based on the political accommodations that the bosses, acting as brokers, could reach with the always diverse and frequently competitive factions within the machine. Throughout their tenure as leaders, John Kelly and his two successors, Richard Croker and Charles Murphy, engaged in frequent and often bitter battles with a variety of competing factions for control. The power they managed to exercise was not just a consequence of organizational reforms; it was also a function of their skill in exploiting their organizational position to overcome the internal divisions within the machine and to maintain and expand the political accommodations among the different factions composing the machine.

Kelly's machine formalized both the roles of assembly district leaders within their communities and the central control over these local leaders within Tammany Hall. Election financing and patronage dispersal, key elements of machine power, which had been largely ad hoc enterprises under Tweed, were coordinated by Kelly through Tammany's system of central councils. Under the new structure, Tammany's Committee on Organization was empowered to reject political nominations suggested by district leaders and to expel problem members, and the Committee on Discipline was mandated to oversee district patronage

(Shefter 1976). All of this meant that, under Kelly's leadership, district leaders became less political entrepreneurs and more local representatives of the larger Tammany machine.

Kelly maintained internal discipline partly by making such self-control worthwhile for district leaders and their election-district captains. He created a general campaign fund, collecting contributions from officeholders, city workers, and business interests, and he organized "dough days" before elections to allocate the funds raised among Tammany's district leaders. He established quotas for district patronage within city agencies to standardize the process of rewarding party workers with government jobs. "John Kelly had changed Tammany Hall from a disorderly and sociable political society for the development of the financial interests of its members into an efficient association for complete political exploitation" (Werner 1928, 303).

Tammany under Kelly traded services for votes in lower-income communities around the city, but the process was more structured than it had been under Tweed. Moreover, because of Tammany's newly acquired taste for, at the very least, the appearance of fiscal responsibility, the upper-income interests, which had organized to overthrow Tweed, left Kelly alone to pursue the business of politics. "By creating the modern Tammany machine, Kelly and his successors, Richard Croker and Charles Murphy, established a mechanism for incorporating immigrants into the city's political system in a way that was tolerable to, if not entirely to the liking of, the city's propertied elite" (Shefter 1977, 101).

District Leaders: The Machine in the Community

Geographic decentralization in New York was personified by two sets of political actors: district leaders and aldermen. District leaders, the most visible representatives of the Tammany machine in the local community, made operational the quid pro quo politics of the machine. Although they sometimes held elected positions as state legislators or city aldermen, their role in the machine hierarchy was to oversee the day-to-day concerns of their districts. With their cadre of precinct and block captains, district leaders were the level of the machine closest to the voters. Their primary job, getting out the vote for machine candidates, required them to address the voters' needs in their district, particularly in lower-income communities. George Washington Plunkitt, a Tammany district leader and state senator, explicitly noted the expected return for careful district work: "The poor are the most grateful people in the world, and, let me tell you, they have more friends in their neighborhoods than the rich have in theirs" (Riordan 1963, 28).

District leaders played a broker role between the substantial but finite resources of the machine, resources that had to be shared with districts all over the city, and the endless supply of demands made by residents. They also served as ombudsmen for community residents. "If the people of a ward were aroused about a local injustice, the district leader carried their complaints to the halls of the mighty, and often enough something was done to pacify his constituents" (Cook and Gleason 1959, 262). Much like that of their superiors in the machine hierarchy, the power of district leaders was based on their skills in brokering among the competing factions within their districts and in allocating scarce resources with minimum political friction.

The relationships developed in the community were direct and personal (Hayes 1967). Such community-based machine–constituent interactions had the effect of making politics a personal experience for millions of immigrants, most of whom were strangers to democratic government. As a result, the geographic decentralization of machine politics established the local community, early on, as the focus of electoral politics and public service delivery for the new immigrants. If the urban political machine fulfilled the "latent function" of political socialization, as Robert Merton (1967) contends it did, it fulfilled that function through the urban community, which became the identifiable center of political participation for millions of Americans.

Under John Kelly, Tammany Hall institutionalized a process whereby district leaders provided patronage positions for their successful election-district (ward) captains. In this manner, effective election-district work would be recognized formally by Tammany's hierarchy, and machine politics could serve as a source of upward social mobility for people locked out of private-sector advancement. Indeed, district-leader positions, which themselves often served as rewards to local party loyalists for previous service and as possible bases for even greater advancement within the machine, were almost always filled by people who, as individuals, were representative of the social, economic, and ethnic composition of the community in which they worked. "Local leadership was deeply rooted in the local community. . . . [P]olitical leaders had characteristics that closely resembled those of the community from which they were elected" (Hayes 1967, 164).

Machine largess through the district system has sometimes been romanticized beyond what it was—a system of services rendered for votes. With a few exceptions, machine politicians were not interested in the social reforms that might address more structurally the problems experienced by the residents of their districts, unless they were pressured to do so by organized, "populist" forces. Indeed, Tammany candidates made it a standard practice to run against the "radical ideas" of social reformers, until the organized pressure for such reforms became too potent to resist. Nor were machine politicians overly generous in their allocation of resources, tending, whenever possible, to provide symbolic rather than material incentives to their constituents (Wolfinger 1974, 69). Although much of the Tammany machine's electoral support was founded on the service–vote trade-off at the district level, much was also the result of the always cynical and sometimes violent corruption of the election process. Some groups were locked out of machine–constituent interactions because they were not essential players; that is, their votes were not needed. Other groups were excluded because of ethnic rivalries or racial prejudices. Nevertheless, the direct and material interactions between machine politicians and urban voters are of fundamental importance to an understanding of the machine's longevity in American cities. Indeed, these extragovernmental interactions at the community level were the primary legitimizing element of local government in the late nineteenth and early twentieth centuries.

City Legislators: The Machine in Government

Although much of the machine's operation was extragovernmental, it was essential for machine politicians to control government to maintain continual access to public resources, which they needed to succeed.[7] Tammany's electoral base of power was the city legislature, the Board of Aldermen, where members were elected in partisan, ward-based elections.

Legislatures have both a representative and a coordinative function. The representative function is a consequence of the fact that legislative seats are usually allocated on a geographic basis and districts are more often than not internally homogeneous. Because their coordinative function, that is, citywide policy concerns, may conflict with the representative responsibilities, legislators are often faced with difficult political choices.

However, as Jon Teaford points out, a confluence of forces in the late nineteenth century mitigated the conflict between district-based and citywide concerns by diminishing the role of city legislatures as policy-making bodies while increasing their district-based, representative function (1984, 16–17). First, there was a growing distrust of city legislatures by downtown business interests, who wished to deal with one representative of the machine and not be forced into the negotiations and accommodations inherent in legislative politics. Indeed, it was precisely the functional centralization represented by the boss system that made the machine useful to business elites in the first place. Second, an increasing tendency for state government to create administrative boards with responsibility for specific policies had placed a great deal of citywide policy-making authority in the hands of individuals accountable to state politicians. While this practice had, in some instances, increased the influence of the machine boss by further fragmenting the formal city government, it had decreased the influence of the city legislature over these citywide issues. Third, the growing heterogeneity of cities and the increasing homogeneity of urban neighborhoods resulting from the more culturally diverse immigration of the period meant that locally elected officials needed to expend more effort dealing with the specific concerns of the groups they represented and less effort dealing with issues of wider geographic significance.

The amount of diversity inherent in the industrializing city of the nineteenth century, coupled with the incentives for legislators to concentrate almost exclusively on district needs, could have produced legislative deadlock in the absence of some strategy to coordinate the different demands being made by all the diverse groups. Machine legislatures found such a strategy in logrolling, the practice whereby one member votes in favor of a colleague's program in return for support on his/her program. "In American municipal councils a form of 'aldermanic courtesy' often prevailed, which meant that the board as a whole deferred to the judgement of a district's representative(s) on any questions dealing solely with that district. . . . On many neighborhood questions the judgement of the district alderman was thus decisive" (Teaford 1984, 26). In New York, "by a custom called 'privilege,' the aldermen deferred to the decisions of individual members in matters relating to their respective neighborhoods" (Shaw 1954, 32).

As long as aldermen loyal to the machine controlled a majority of seats within the legislature, Tammany had a secure base of governmental power. However, consistent control was threatened by the high turnover rates that characterized city legislatures in the late nineteenth century. Between 1885 and 1892, only about 47 percent of the members of the New York board had served in the previous session; fewer than 20 percent had served in two previous sessions (Teaford 1984, 40). Turnover aside, the chances for machine maintenance of legislative control were enhanced by two factors: (1) the machine's cultivation of voters in immigrant wards and its willingness to employ corrupt methods of securing votes, and (2) the malapportionment of city legislatures, with districts containing lower-income voters, which formed the machine's political base, overrepresented, giving the machine a numerical advantage. Coupled with their opponents' political weaknesses at the community level, such practices helped ensure continued Tammany control of the Board of Aldermen and continued access to the public resources so critical to machine power.

Regime Consolidation under Tammany Hall

The years between 1890 and 1910 witnessed major transformations in New York City. Unprecedented levels of immigration produced dramatic demographic changes as the city's population nearly doubled and the number of foreign-born residents reached 40 percent by 1910 (Tobier 1984, 20). The city's export base grew impressively as the number of industrial workers more than doubled and the assets of major financial enterprises increased, in some cases more than exponentially (Hammack 1982, 47). And, in 1898, the city's geopolitical situation was altered fundamentally by the consolidation of the five boroughs, resulting in the creation of Greater New York City.

It was during this period of dramatic demographic, socioeconomic, and political change that the Tammany machine consolidated its power by successfully performing two functions. First, Tammany maintained, if not the active support, at least the passive acceptance of important business and financial interests in New York. Second, Tammany institutionalized the political structures within which its governing coalition interacted and was, therefore, able to integrate new interests without upsetting the fundamental rules of the game, which it had established.

Tammany and the Financiers: Coordination and Conservatism

Two strategies helped Tammany secure the passive acceptance of business and financial interests. First, Kelly's successors, Richard Croker and Charles Murphy, maintained the hierarchical structure he created. This enabled them to enforce the machine's commitment to control "excesses," which might impact negatively on the city's economy, and to routinize the mutually beneficial interactions between the machine and business interests. Second, Tammany acted as a political buffer between city government and the radical proposals of urban populists.

By all accounts, Kelly's successors maintained and expanded his system of hierarchical coordination. Although intended as a negative assessment, the Fassett Committee's conclusion about New York under Croker is quite direct on this point: "The one clear and distinct fact brought out by this investigation is that we have in this great city the most perfect instance of centralized government ever known" (cited in Connable and Silberfarb 1967, 198).[8] During Murphy's tenure, the machine remained under the control of a strong leader, by one account reaching "the zenith of its powers in the 1920's" (Shaw 1954, 141).

Croker used his power to assist the economic development priorities of business interests.[9] In exchange for monetary support to machine officials, financial syndicates realized large profits from contracts to construct street railway systems; insurance companies received lucrative policies; and public utilities were awarded exclusive franchises. Although each specific favor benefited a particular business concern, taken as a whole, these favors helped generate citywide economic growth, increase property values, and generally add to the assets held by financial interests in the city.

Charles F. Murphy, who succeeded Croker in 1902 and ruled Tammany until 1924, routinized his predecessors' interactions with the financial community.[10] "By the period when Charles F. Murphy became 'chief' the 'businessman' type of leader had evolved" (Myers 1917, 310). The *Evening Post,* commenting upon Murphy's "office" in Manhattan's Delmonico Restaurant, noted, "Nearly every important financier in the city is said to have entered it at one time or another" (quoted in Werner 1928, 486). Under Murphy, Tammany's interactions with the business community were defined by ever-increasing mutual benefits.[11] Machine politicians found that the rewards available from "honest graft" far exceeded those from corruption and that Tammany's business interests were sufficient to insulate it from occasional electoral defeats (Myers 1917, 556–58).

Aside from the mutual material benefits arising from machine–business interactions, Tammany adopted the role of the one major political force capable of keeping "radical elements" out of power. In 1886, during the first mayoral election after his ascendance to the position of leader, Croker's candidate, businessman Abram S. Hewitt, defeated Henry George, whose "radical" single-tax doctrine was particularly upsetting to real estate interests in the city. The campaign was notable for the intensity of Tammany's "red-baiting" attacks on George's proposals (Connable and Silberfarb 1967, 205). In the 1905 mayoral campaign, soon after Murphy's selection as leader, Tammany once again championed status quo politics in its campaign against William Randolph Hearst and his platform of public ownership of utilities. In the election, despite Tammany's victory, Hearst cut into the machine's traditional vote in lower-income districts, decreasing Tammany's normal two-thirds majority into plurality victories in these districts (Henderson 1976, 106–7). In the 1913 and 1917 mayoral elections against socialist candidates Meyer London and Morris Hillquit, Tammany employed "every political and legal mechanism to defeat the Socialists" (Henderson 1976, 225).

Tammany and Attentive Nonelites: Coalition Expansion

To secure its political base in the city's communities, the Tammany machine had to institutionalize the geographically decentralized organization originally crafted by John Kelly in the 1870s. That organization, which extended from the boss's office as county leader to the thousands of block captains in the thousands of election districts around the city, was based on the quid pro quo politics mentioned above. To institutionalize that process and protect it from temporary defeats, Tammany had to maintain its existing political base while integrating new factions into the framework of machine politics.

Both Croker and Murphy proved quite adept at the political maneuvering necessary both to maintain and to expand their ruling coalitions. After assuring financiers that Kelly's restructured machine would be preserved, Croker began loosening the most direct central controls over district leaders. To reward loyal district leaders and thereby reaffirm his support on the executive committee, Croker returned the allocation of local patronage to the district level. To strengthen the machine's electoral base, he extended the scope of Tammany's assistance to lower-income groups and brought the Board of Aldermen under Tammany control, while resisting the structural reforms in social service programs demanded by "radical elements" in the city. To solidify his own political power, Croker developed working relationships with the state Republican boss, Thomas Platt, and, following city consolidation in 1898, with the Brooklyn Democratic boss, Hugh McLaughlin. Although his relations with Platt were volatile, Croker's relationship with McLaughlin began the process of neutralizing the Brooklyn political organization, a potentially competitive political force in Greater New York.[12]

Commitment to Kelly's organizational reforms aside, Croker oversaw the evolution of the Tammany machine from an organization largely beholden to wealthy Democrats to one with an interdependent relationship with the city's financial interests. Croker, whose primary allies on the machine's executive committee included both leaders from the poorer districts on the Lower East Side and those from the wealthier districts in northern Manhattan, was able to straddle the political fence between Tammany's relationships with financiers and its interactions within lower-income communities. Pressured by his allies' demands for increased autonomy and by his opponents' manuevers to discredit his leadership, Croker acted to increase Tammany's political legitimacy in the city's communities and thereby increase its political autonomy in general. "Under Croker's leadership, . . . Tammany had successfully presented itself as the legitimate representative of, and broker among, the city's increasingly diverse lower- and middle-income ethnic groups" (Hammack 1982, 168).

Charles Murphy's term as leader saw both increases in the scope of machine power and new threats to its hegemony. In 1910, Tammany loyalists controlled the governorship and both leadership posts in the state legislature.[13] However, during this period, the machine was increasingly pressured by populist movements aimed at the heart of its political support in the city's lower-income districts. Murphy used the machine's newfound power in state government to address the populist challenge. To deflect the machine's growing chorus of social critics, quiet the increasing demands for radical change, address union concerns, and appease the growing liberal wing within the state Democratic party, Murphy allowed Tammany liberals, such as Al Smith and Robert F. Wagner, Sr., relatively free reign in their pursuit of social reforms. During Murphy's tenure, a Tammany-controlled state government enacted child labor regulations, workmen's compensation laws, and a code of quite progressive factory laws.[14]

Although such reforms represented a departure from previous machine practices, a continued exclusive reliance on the quid pro quo vote–service exchange mechanism to address unmet social needs would have resulted, given the emerging populist alternatives, in political setbacks for the machine. Indeed, Hearst's inroads into Tammany's lower-income support base in the 1905 mayoral election clearly illustrated the political danger of ignoring demands for social reform. "In the wake of the Hearst-induced working-class upheaval of 1905, Tammany embraced not only the candidate within a year, but also his issues, adopting a municipal ownership program" (Henderson 1976, 124). Considering the circumstances, it is not surprising that a utilitarian Tammany machine, under the direction of the astute and flexible Charles Murphy, would shift "political gears" and move in the direction of encouraging social reform. Nor is it surprising that the financial community, troubled by radical threats and wishing to avoid major political dislocations, would raise few objections to Tammany's newly discovered organizational social conscience. The progressive legislation passed during Murphy's stewardship served as much to quiet a rising and increasingly organized clamor for even more fundamental changes as to address social problems.

Populists were not the only threat to the machine's electoral base. Tammany, like all political machines, had opposition from urban reformers. During Kelly's tenure, reform opposition had been neutralized by Tammany concessions to the agenda of "good government" groups. However, Croker's and Murphy's attempts to reassert Tammany's autonomy reignited the machine–reform conflict in New York. At times, the reform opposition was relatively organized and temporarily threatened the machine's political hegemony; in general, however, its efforts during Tammany's consolidation produced only sporadic success.

Reform in New York appeared in the form of a *fusion* movement among the city's minority Republicans, members of "good government" groups, and social reformers in the "progressive wing" of the Democratic party. During the period between the 1890s and the 1930s, fusion coalitions managed to elect three reform mayors: William Strong, Seth Low, and John Purroy Mitchel, who together governed for a total of nine years.[15] Even during these periods of fusion control of the executive, Tammany usually managed to maintain control of the city's Board of Aldermen, which enabled the machine to check the process of reform from the inside.[16]

The reformers' inability to overcome Tammany control in New York was a function of their own political failings as well as Tammany's institutionalized control. The fusion movements that elected reform mayors were decidedly more adept at coalescing to defeat Tammany than at coalescing to govern. When in power, fusion administrations, composed of factions as likely to disagree as agree on public policy, found that the removal of the machine had erased the one external force that united them. Moreover, Tammany control of the Board of Aldermen meant that fusion mayors faced important policy roadblocks. Theodore Roosevelt, a reform candidate for mayor, spoke of the difficulties fusion faced:

> The difficulty seems to be inherent in the conditions. If a reform administration honestly endeavors to carry out reform, it makes an end of itself at the end of its term and insures the return of Tammany to power. If a reform administration fails or falters in carrying out the pledges of reform on which it was elected, it utterly loses the confidence and support of the reform forces, and that again means a triumph for Tammany at the next election. (Quoted in Werner 1928, 445)

Under Croker and Murphy, therefore, the Tammany machine, although under constant attack from internal dissidents, outside populist forces, and an increasingly vocal reform movement, strengthened its functional capabilities and its geographic base in the city's communities. Internal dissidents usually proved quite susceptible to either the political largess or the political sanctions available to Tammany's leadership, and those who remained in opposition represented a minority view on the machine's executive committee. Populist opponents were vulnerable electorally to liberal policy co-optation of their ideas, and reformers proved singularly incapable of sustaining power during this period.[17]

Urban Reform: Reversing Regime Patterns

The early urban reform movement was composed of two more or less organized groups—a moralist faction, led by Protestant church leaders, who condemned the machine's corruption, and the displaced WASP elite, who rejected immigrant ascendance in the cities and desired to reestablish their lost preeminence. By the late nineteenth century, however, a number of newly emerging and increasingly powerful interests had joined the original reformers and had succeeded in transforming the movement from an ethical and "nativist" reaction to one more reflective of the pressures for modernization in American life. This new reform coalition included a professional class, which wanted to rationalize local government operations; corporate interests, which sought a more positive and professional city government to subsidize urban economic development; and social reformers, who wished to create formal government programs to address urban pathologies.[18]

The new reform coalition emphasized cosmopolitan or citywide issues and disregarded what the reformers considered the parochial conflicts defining community politics. A cosmopolitan perspective addressed the needs of each of the components of the reform coalition. It provided the moralists and "nativists" with a method of countering the machine's community-based ties with immigrants; it gave the professionals the opportunity to restructure and restaff city government; it provided the corporate sector with the professional public sector necessary to underwrite production; and it allowed progressives to develop large-scale social programs.

Regardless of their primary motivation for participating in the reform movement, then, reformers needed to eradicate the decentralized base of machine power. To the reformers, the community emphasis of the machine fragmented government decision making, ignored citywide interests, and resulted in inefficient service delivery. Moreover, because spatial decentralization was the basis of the machine's legitimacy, it provided the machine with institutional power in city government.

To refocus city government on cosmopolitan concerns, two steps were necessary: the removal of those aspects of the urban electoral system that encouraged the consideration of community issues on the public agenda, and the creation of central-city centers for policy formulation and implementation, staffed with individuals who, because of their electoral base or their specialized training, were unresponsive to parochial concerns and attuned to citywide values. Political power in the reform city was to be centralized geographically downtown and decentralized functionally in professional, bureaucratic agencies—the organizational converse of the machine model. The immediate political intent of these reforms was to remove traditional machine politicians from power. The larger intent was to reformulate the urban policy agenda; redefine the relationship between citizens and their government; minimize the importance of parochial conflict; maximize the expression of the "public interest"; and recruit the new professional class into government.

Electoral Politics and Reform

In their views of political participation, reformers exhibited an intellectual paradox resulting from a commitment to democratic procedures coupled with an elitist distrust of the masses. The writings of Woodrow Wilson are indicative of this tension. True to a democratic perspective, Wilson believed that "wherever public opinion exists it must rule" (Wilson 1887, 23). Wilson was also beset by fears, however, that public opinion might prove "meddlesome" to the effective administration of government, either directly or more probably through an activist legislature. Accordingly, Wilson argued that public opinion should only constrain the formulation of general policy, and then only periodically through the election cycle, but that it should be silent on issues of administration, which were better left to the experts. This politics–administration dichotomy was to be the theoretical basis for many of the structural changes instituted by urban reformers.

Despite his view that public opinion should rule in the policy formulation stage, Wilson had doubts that the public was prepared for even this task. He argued that it was the responsibility of political leadership to "make public opinion willing to listen and then see to it that it listens to the right things" (Wilson 1887, 23). Wilson was particularly concerned about the task of guiding public opinion "to the right things" in cities so inundated with immigrants (Wilson 1887).

The electoral changes favored by the urban reformers reflected the paradox evident in Wilson's writing. The reforms were not designed to disenfranchise lower- and moderate-income voters, although some reformers suggested this as an option, but rather to ensure that the urban masses would have access to the "right information" in order to make the "right decisions" about political and not administrative issues. To the reformers, the electoral procedures of the machine city—frequent, partisan, ward-based elections—corrupted democratic theory while institutionalizing machine rule. By focusing on the immediate delivery of services rather than the larger policy issues with which voters ought to be concerned, machine politics served to concentrate voter attention precisely where it did not belong—on administrative matters. By emphasizing the service–vote trade-off, machine politics encouraged voters to consider only their short-term interests and ignore the longer-term implications of policy. By creating community districts and including national party labels in local elections, machine politics placed unnecessary intermediate steps between citizens and their local government.

From the reform perspective, the politics–administration dichotomy could only become reality by instituting procedures designed to focus voters' attention on larger policy issues, emphasize cosmopolitan values by making voters consider their "larger self-interest," and eradicate the unnecessary intermediate steps separating citizens from their governments. The primary mechanisms to accomplish this agenda were nonpartisan, at-large elections.

Nonpartisan elections negate the effects of party identification in municipal voting. By disallowing party labels, an important voting cue is removed, and the information costs of voting consequently rise. In the absence of such cues, citizens have to research candidates' positions on "the issues." Because such information costs are more likely to be paid by upper-income voters than by their lower-income counterparts, nonpartisan elections weakened the machine's political base (Alford and Lee 1968; Judd 1988).

However, the rationale behind this reform is more complex than mere political advantage. Nonpartisan elections clearly represent the reform perception that urban government is essentially an instrument of policy consensus and not a mechanism for mediating political conflict. To the reformer, urban government is an administrative entity charged with developing and carrying out the "one best policy" to deal with the variety of problems endemic to urban areas; it is not a political entity designed to accommodate diverse and often conflicting interests. Nonpartisan elections affirm the reformers' belief that urban government was essentially an exercise in administration, not politics.

Another electoral change favored by reformers was the substitution of at-large council elections for the community-based system used by the machine. The immediate political rationale behind this reform is to destroy the base of machine power by erasing the electoral boundaries that helped institutionalize parochial politics. City councils, elected at large, would not reflect the varied spatial interests of the city but would instead address the city as a unitary administrative unit. Once again, however, the rationale is more complex. Because reformers believed that citywide concerns were the only relevant policy issues facing urban government, it follows logically that the city's legislative branch should reflect citywide and not community values. Under at-large elections, the city legislature would no longer be the focus of community-based logrolling but rather the popularly elected center of the new citywide consensus.

The electoral changes recommended by urban reformers were intended to alter not only the politics of American cities but also the fundamental raison d'être behind urban government. City government, because of these reforms, becomes more distant from and uninvolved with community concerns. The electoral changes initiated by urban reformers meant that the level of government "closest to the people" became a forum for the representation of supracommunity concerns, precisely the concerns of those interests that formed the political base of the reform movement.

Government Structure and Reform

Reformers favored an activist public sector with a more direct role in the local economy and in citizens' lives. Although machine politics had emphasized each of these areas, such activity had been essentially extragovernmental and informal under the machine. Because of the reformers' desires to subsidize local economic growth, develop efficient service-delivery programs, and, given the progressive wing of the reform movement, address social problems, they required a government strong enough and independent enough to handle a new and expanded role.

As part of their policy aims, reformers subscribed to an approach that not only increased the formal authority of government but also structured that authority systematically and professionally. To the reformers, the optimal form of city government was the city-manager system, under which a council chosen in non-partisan, at-large elections selects a professional manager to implement policy and handle the day-to-day affairs of the city. The city-manager system met the structural requirements of the reformers in several ways. First, given its at-large, nonpartisan origins, the council is responsive to citywide concerns and not to community interests. Second, the city-manager system makes operational the politics–administration dichotomy. In theory, the manager and his/her fellow value-neutral professionals on staff are separated from the political process of formulating policy and are concerned only with implementing policy. Moreover, even if the manager does become involved in policy formulation, which has been the experience under such systems, his/her input will be that of a trained professional and will, therefore, help guide policy in the "right direction."

Under the city-manager system, power is directed toward officials who either are elected citywide or are appointed by officials who themselves were elected citywide. City-manager systems require a different class of administrators than do machine governments. The reformers' desire to establish central administrative agencies staffed by professionals in specific policy areas changed the resource pool from which they could recruit for government positions. From a reform perspective, merit selection, based on strict civil service standards, would ensure that the "best and the brightest" were brought into government and that the administrative responsibilities of running a city would be in the hands of well-trained professionals. Moreover, reformers realized that strict civil service systems would deal the patronage-dependent machine a severe political blow.

Reform initiatives were often characterized by their proponents as nonpolitical. However these changes were actually intended to enable city governments to address a different constituency from that emphasized by the machine, specifically, the emerging corporate sector in American cities, which actively supported the urban reform movement (Hayes 1964). Whereas the more traditional business and financial leaders of the nineteenth century found in the machine boss the public-sector coordination necessary for conducting business, the new corporate sector had outgrown the party system. The bosses, brokers among diverse functional and geographic interests, were primarily professional politicians. The party system, however friendly it might have been to business interests during early industrialization, was essentially a grass-roots organization dependent on community support for its political power. The corporate system was organized from the top down and was dependent on administrative efficiency for its influence. "While the party rested upon geography, . . . the corporate system rested upon the integration of different functional groups, often located in different geographical areas, into single systems of activity and under centralized control" (Hayes 1967, 169).

This emerging corporate sector, directed by managers rather than entrepreneurs, required a more professional government partner than that offered by the machine. Corporations needed predictable and enlarged government programs to socialize the increasing costs of production. Moreover, segments of the corporate sector understood that social legitimation in the industrial city required more than the service–vote exchange characteristic of machine politics; it demanded formal government programs to address social problems. In short, the corporate private sector needed a more corporate public sector with which to do business, and reform government represented such an entity.

Fiscal Crisis and the Emergence of the Reform Regime

By the beginning of the twentieth century, the efforts of the increasingly powerful reform coalition of financial interests in the rapidly consolidating sectors of the economy, the new professional class, and political "progressives," coupled with the general social pressures toward modernization, posed an ongoing political challenge to machines like Tammany Hall. Tammany leaders responded by attempting to co-opt reform candidates with the promise of machine cross-endorsements and co-opt reform's electoral base with programmatic changes. Adaptations notwithstanding, machine rule in New York, with its electoral base in urban communities, was continually challenged by the influence of the reform movement, with its base of functionally oriented, supracommunity interest groups. Indeed, as noted above, several times during Tammany's heyday, reformers running on fusion tickets had secured control of the mayor's office and initiated temporary changes in city government, only to be replaced by machine candidates after brief periods in power. In 1933, however, the change in city politics was more basic than in previous years, as reformers seized control of city government and began to institutionalize their regime in New York. Once again, as in the 1870s, the vehicle for fundamental as opposed to sporadic change in city political arrangements was fiscal crisis.

Charles Murphy's death in 1924 left the Tammany machine without strong central leadership. Murphy, coping with state and city political issues while attempting to maintain Tammany dominance during a period of extraordinary social and political change, did not leave an heir apparent. Murphy's successor, George Olvany, a compromise choice among the district leaders on a divided executive committee, was focused on using his newly acquired position as Tammany leader more to increase his law firm's contacts than to hold together the various factions that had selected him (Connable and Silberfarb 1967, 273–74). These diverse factions, which included party regulars, internal reformers, a politically progressive wing, and a collection of district leaders united only by their efforts to control the machine, eventually replaced Olvany with the notably unimpressive John Curry as county leader. Curry was as unsuccessful as Olvany had been in uniting the machine's increasingly diverse factions or in exercising decisive leadership.

In the years following Murphy's death, the Tammany machine was led by a series of people considered compromise choices among its competing factions, with the strongest potential leaders too closely associated with each faction to be acceptable to the others. Tammany's difficulties, however, were not just intraorganizational. World War I and the National Origins Act of 1924 had slowed to a trickle the flow of immigrants, who represented an important part of the machine's political base. Moreover, according to the 1920 census data, Brooklyn had surpassed Manhattan in population. Given its county's demographic preeminence in Greater New York, the Brooklyn Democratic machine, without a strong Tammany leader to restrain it, began to flex its newfound political muscle. In 1925, the Brooklyn machine openly broke with Tammany over James J. Walker's nomination for mayor and, along with the Democratic organizations in Queens and Staten Island, challenged the Tammany candidate in a primary campaign. Despite Walker's eventual victory in both the primary and the general election, the Tammany machine emerged from the 1925 elections more divided than ever and with an increased need to be responsive to the demands for a share of the wealth by its Brooklyn counterpart. Indeed, Walker's victory signaled the beginning of a six-year period in which a distracted and often disinterested mayor, coupled with incompetent county leadership at Tammany Hall, presided over a form of modern "gang rule" in New York City.

The worldwide depression of 1929 produced substantial shortfalls in anticipated city revenues while generating increased demands on city resources. Despite tax increases in 1931 and 1932, total revenues fell in New York City in these two years by nearly $50 million, while expenditures increased by more than $100 million (Beyer 1933, 164). By the end of 1932, debt service costs equaled nearly one-third of the city's expense-budget outlays. Tammany's ability to cope with the deteriorating fiscal situation was hampered by a number of factors: (1) The city's long-term debt obligations had risen markedly during the 1920s because of the extensive public-sector borrowing by an increasingly fragmented Tammany regime, which was addressing an increasingly fragmented collection of interests. (2) The depression had produced rapidly escalating demands for increased public assistance programs to aid the victims of economic downturn. (3) The machine had extensive commitments to honor in the city communities, where the vote–service trade-off remained the basis of its political support. "Since jobs were the fuel of Tammany's political machine, a disproportionate share of . . . the budget went to purchase that fuel" (Caro 1974, 326).

Twice in 1932, city officials were compelled to implement retrenchment measures, including layoffs and salary reductions among city workers, in return for the extension of further credit from the city's major financial institutions. Although these concessions staved off immediate bankruptcy, the fear of impending default frightened potential creditors and drove interest rates ever higher. Finally, in 1933, city officials were forced to "negotiate" the Bankers Agreement with financial institutions that had refused to roll over any more short-term debt without major concessions by local officials.

The Bankers Agreement was the culmination of three years of political activism by the city's major financial interests.[19] Throughout the period, a coalition of financiers, using their control of credit markets as a negotiating tool, had pressured the Jimmy Walker and John O'Brien administrations to cut back on city programs and on employee salary levels. By the summer of 1933, it was evident that in the absence of even further dramatic retrenchment, the financial community would close credit markets to the city. In a series of meetings, the financiers, assisted by the intervention of Governor Herbert Lehman and the state-run Municipal Economy Commission (MEC), forced local officials to relinquish effective control of the city's fiscal policy. On September 29, 1933, in the manner of heads of state, representatives of the city's major financial institutions and city officials formally signed the Bankers Agreement, which had been drafted earlier by the financial community and was subsequently ratified by the state legislature. The agreement confirmed William Beyer's analysis of earlier that year that in New York City "power is shifting from the political organization and its leaders to the financial interests of the community, especially the bankers" (1933, 162).

According to the Bankers Agreement, financiers consented to refund approximately $130 million of city revenue bonds, create a revolving fund to provide for city needs during the ensuing four-year period, and purchase an additional $70 million of serial notes to finance unemployment and home relief programs, $47 million of which would be used to repay past debts in these programs. In return, city officials agreed to segregate all taxes delinquent or in arrears in order to retire current and future bonds, freeze property taxes at the 1933 level with the exception of funds needed for debt service, and drop new taxes levied against stocks, savings banks, and life insurance companies.

The 1933 fiscal crisis and the period of retrenchment politics that followed were characterized by state officials and financial actors playing the very same roles others had played sixty years earlier. The banks, acting in light of economic pressures, and allied with state officials, pressured city government officials to retrench by threatening fiscal crisis. Local officials, already in a weakened political posture because of the fragmentation of their coalition support, responded by enacting severe retrenchment measures in order to regain access to necessary credit. As a result, machine officials seriously disrupted and in some cases severed their relationships with attentive nonelites who depended on government programs. Moreover, all of this occurred with a new political coalition, organized and preparing to govern for years, waiting impatiently in the wings.

Reform in Power: Rationalizing Government

The Bankers Agreement, the employee layoffs, and the salary decreases averted immediate bankruptcy. Damaged, however, by a decade of fragmented leadership, the forced resignation of Mayor Jimmy Walker to accommodate Governor Franklin Roosevelt's national campaign plans, the Seabury investigations, which had led to a series of embarrassing disclosures about the city government, and, most importantly, its general inability to respond to the scope of social needs produced by the fiscal crisis, the Tammany machine entered the 1933 city elections divided and weakened. These elections, coming as they did on the heels of fiscal crisis, produced a fundamental realignment in local politics that resulted in major structural changes in city governance. Tammany's preeminence in New York City politics, a preeminence achieved in the 1890s and threatened periodically by reform efforts over the next forty years, ended in the wake of the fiscal crisis of the 1930s upon the election of Fiorello LaGuardia's reform administration.[20]

LaGuardia's fusion administration inherited a city where many of the tough retrenchment decisions had already been forced on and politically paid for by the preceding mayor. Nonetheless, the economic situation remained precarious. LaGuardia addressed the continuing fiscal problems of the early 1930s by reaffirming the Bankers Agreement, although at renegotiated interest rates. Subscribing to the reform notion that urban problems were amenable to structural corrections, the LaGuardia administration addressed the demands of financial interests, "good government" groups, and state fiscal monitors for fiscal constraint and political stability by acting to rationalize city government. Political power was increasingly centralized in citywide offices and administrative agencies. Programs such as home relief, which were financed by Tammany through borrowing, were placed on a "pay-as-you-go" basis by the reformers. Efficiency became the watchword of the day as the reformers streamlined city government. The Economy Bill of 1934 initiated these changes; the charter revisions of 1938 institutionalized them.

The Economy Bill, submitted to the state legislature one day after LaGuardia's inauguration, proposed the institution of payless furloughs for many city employees, resulting in an average across-the-board salary cut of 4 percent; the requirement that borough officials reduce budgets by 10 percent, forcing pay cuts and layoffs at the borough level; and the provision to the mayor of full authority to reorganize the operations of mayoral agencies. The bill was a major effort to cut the city's 1934 budget deficit, which had grown despite the Bankers Agreement, and to impress the city's creditors with the reformers' seriousness in dealing with fiscal issues. It was amended by the Democratic state legislature so that the authority requested by the mayor, described as "full dictatorial powers" by Governor Herbert Lehman, was allocated instead to the city's Board of Estimate. However, because the Board of Estimate was controlled by reformers, the salary reductions and payless furloughs included in the bill were implemented immediately. The spending cuts made it possible for LaGuardia to seek an increase in revenues without generating a markedly negative reaction among financial interests. As Charles Garrett concludes, "With adoption of the LaGuardia financial program of 1934, the financial position of the city became basically sound" (1961, 150).

The 1938 Charter Revisions

The clearest indications of the reformers' intention to rationalize city government were the charter revisions, which went into effect in 1938. The proposals offered by the Charter Commission, created in 1935 and chaired by Court of Appeals Judge Thomas Thacher, altered city government in a number of important ways. First, the city executive was strengthened by increasing the mayor's powers and reaffirming the city's strong-mayor system. A strong-mayor form of government was the fallback position for reformers who realized that the city-manager system was often incompatible with the demographic characteristics and political realities of the older and larger cities of the Northeast and Midwest. Under a strong-mayor form, the city's chief executive was given administrative appointment and removal responsibilities, extensive budgetary authority, and substantial veto powers.

Extensive appointment and removal authority over upper-level municipal administrators allowed New York's mayor to coordinate the implementation of policy and made possible the short ballot in election campaigns. Such broad-reaching personnel authority theoretically addressed the problem of policy fragmentation by centering policy responsibility in one office. An executive budget system provided the mayor with the means to influence New York's economy through control of the fiscal agenda. To the reformers, the executive budget system meant that urban fiscal policy, developed by professionals in the executive branch, would codify the "public interest" rather than reflect the political accommodations inherent in legislative politics under the machine. Furthermore, because the executive veto represented a potent political deterrent to unwanted legislative action, it provided the mayor with influence over general policy formulation. Veto power helped ensure that even if Tammany controlled the city council, executive-branch reformers would still be able to dictate the city's policy agenda.

Second, the 1938 charter revisions transformed the city's sixty-five-member Board of Aldermen into a twenty-five-member city council elected by the Hare system of proportional representation employed on a borough basis.[21] As a result, the focus of council representation moved from a district to a borough level, and the average number of constituents represented by each council member increased over 160 percent from fewer than 114,000 constituents to nearly 300,000 people per member. Moreover, proportional representation was intended to increase minority, that is, non-Democrat, representation on the council. "The system institutionalized the representation of a wide number of political parties with differing viewpoints" (*New York Times*, August 11, 1991, sec. 4, 6). During the eight years the city council was selected by proportional representation, Democratic majorities were smaller and the mix of parties represented was wider than before or since (Sayre and Kaufman 1960, 618–19).

Increasing the scope of councilmanic representation through proportional representation accomplished several reform goals. (1) It disrupted established traditional political patterns by severing community ties to the council. Because these ties had served as the basis of the machine's control of the council, Tammany would be forced to reformulate its political operations. Moreover, the interactions between machine officials and voters at the borough level became necessarily more remote. (2) The change de-emphasized neighborhood concerns in the city council by deposing the traditional community as a mediating factor between city government and citizens. (3) Through proportional representation, reformers refocused the urban policy agenda on the concerns of supracommunity, functional interests and away from those of community groups, thereby establishing the primacy of cosmopolitan values in city government.

Third, the 1938 charter revisions transferred responsibility for several city services, including street maintenance and public works, from the borough presidents to mayoral agencies. As Robert Caro points out, this particular change "dealt a body blow to the small contractors who had played so vital a role in providing the jobs and campaign contributions that the machine needed" (1974, 744).

Fourth, the new charter required that most local bills be approved by both the city council and the city's Board of Estimate, which was composed of the mayor, the city council president, the comptroller, and the five borough presidents. Because the voting method employed by the board was weighted toward the three city officials, and because reformers were able to generate consistent majorities on the board, this particular revision further weakened the city council and borough presidents while further empowering officials elected citywide.[22] Finally, the charter revisions provided for the creation of a City Planning Commission to formulate and oversee the implementation of a master plan for land use in the city. Such a mechanism combined all the elements of reform rule: land-use planning would be done by a centralized bureaucracy composed of experts and beholden mostly to their sense of professionalism, good government, and the public interest.

In addition to the geographic centralization of government, recruitment and appointment patterns for public personnel were changed by reformers. Seventy-four percent of city workers took competitive civil service examinations for job entry in 1939 as compared with 55 percent in 1933 (Garrett 1961, 43). Fifty-two percent of LaGuardia's cabinet appointees came from "low-mobility," that is, middle- and upper-income, groups as compared with the previous high of 30 percent. Thirty-four percent of LaGuardia's cabinet appointees had no previous political party experience; the previous high was 24 percent during John Purroy Mitchel's short-lived reform administration (Lowi 1964, 47–49).

Reform's recruitment and appointment patterns therefore reflected the intent to include middle- and upper-class professionals in government service. From the reform perspective, government responsibilities had become too complicated and the stakes involved too high to have the public sector staffed through political patronage. Because administration was a profession to the reformers, it is not surprising that they wanted professionals as administrators. Reform recruitment and appointment patterns resulted in marked increases in the number of college-educated, professional, middle-class people employed by city government and a concomitant decrease in the number of their lower-income counterparts in government jobs.

Creating the "Welfare City"

Reformers came to power in New York during a period of active, occasionally violent, protest by groups adversely affected by the economic downturn. It was apparent early on that Tammany's manner of dispensing relief was inadequate to deal with the major economic dislocations caused by the depression. Faced with unprecedented attentive nonelite demands for assistance, reformers too were operating under severe constraints. To do nothing would not only invite a resurgence of the machine or even social upheaval but was repugnant philosophically to the progressives within the LaGuardia administration. To develop locally funded programs would threaten the precarious fiscal balance produced by retrenchment and shake the confidence of financial interests in the new government. Financial interests, pleased with the Economy Bill of 1934, had not blocked LaGuardia's sales tax proposal to finance home relief in that same year, but the money generated by that tax would not be sufficient to address the problem. The answer to the dilemma was found in Washington, D.C., and the social programs of the New Deal.

The availability of federal funds made possible by the New Deal served two purposes for urban reformers. First, it allowed an explosive social situation to be dealt with at minimal local cost. Second, federal programs enabled reformers to replace the machine's community-focused service system with one based in citywide agencies, thereby altering the relationship of attentive nonelites to government. Lower-income attentive nonelites would no longer be required to engage in quid pro quo politics to obtain needed services; instead, these groups would now receive services "as of right." The constituents of Tammany Hall had been transformed into the clients of reform's professionalized welfare bureaucracies.

Using federal money, the LaGuardia administration reformulated New York's entire social service delivery system. Working with federal agencies, it

- earmarked revenues for home relief to be allocated on a regular cash basis by the Emergency Relief Bureau which was 80 percent federally funded;
- used funds provided by the Federal Emergency Relief Administration, the Civil Works Administration, the Public Works Administration, and the Works Project Administration to finance capital construction projects and help ease unemployment; and
- used Public Works Administration financing to construct the city's first public housing projects. (Garrett 1961)

The reformers literally and figuratively brought the New Deal to New York. Following initial retrenchment measures, they increased the size and purview of city government. Using largely federal resources, city government undertook what was formerly a primarily extragovernmental function—providing assistance to the victims of economic downturn. As a result, political power was removed from machine politicians and their geographically decentralized base of support and gravitated to the functionally decentralized framework of the "new machines"—professionalized bureaucracies (Lowi 1967); furthermore, political legitimacy, once a function of community politics and parochial concerns, was to become the responsibility of citywide agencies, with their cosmopolitan emphases.

The changes in New York's government need to be considered within the context of reform values. Implementing these values changed city government by altering the relationships between citizens and public authority. New York avoided many of the "pure reform changes," such as nonpartisan, at-large elections and city-manager systems. Nevertheless, assisted by increasing federal involvement in local affairs, urban reformers in the city, centralized and professionalized governance. By augmenting executive authority, diminishing council influence and enlarging council districts, encouraging agency autonomy through rigid civil service systems, and developing professionalized welfare programs, reformers institutionalized their values in New York City to such an extent that even the formal return of Democratic mayors would not dramatically alter the regime.

From Machine to Reform: De-emphasizing Community

Machine politics helped legitimize government in American cities during a period when legitimation was difficult to achieve. Guided at first by a social Darwinist and later by a Taylorist perspective toward workers, industrialization threatened to destabilize the social order by alienating large segments of the urban population.[23] Machine politics mitigated the more damaging consequences of industrialization without hindering the overall process of urban economic development. In American cities, the functional centralization of the urban machine aided the industrial process by coordinating public authority on behalf of business interests. Coterminously, the geographic decentralization of the machine, necessary to maintain power, served as a mechanism for political legitimation among the working classes. By mitigating social ills and by socializing immigrants to the new world, the machine legitimized the political system, encouraged economic production, and helped stabilize the social order.

The machine accomplished its political functions through geographic decentralization. Services were delivered by and votes were cast for district representatives. In American cities, the spatial segregation of immigrants was reinforced by community-based politics. During the machine age, the urban community was more than just a place of residence or a spatially defined tie to ethnic culture. It was, in a very real sense, the focus of political life in American cities.

The structural changes in urban government introduced by reform removed many of the mediating factors linking voters with city government. Among the most important changes was replacing the community as a significant factor in city politics with processes and structures emphasizing cosmopolitan perspectives. Theodore Lowi (1967) contends that the increasing power of administrative agencies under reform in partnership with citywide interest groups produced "new machines" constructed around functional and not geographic concerns. Moreover, these agencies and their group constituents governed with substantial autonomy within their policy domains. Political influence within the reform city, therefore, moved to those whose interests were defined by functional rather than community boundaries.

As a result of reform initiatives, the process of allocating resources in cities shifted from the "institutions of popular control" to bureaucratic "decision centers" (Sayre and Kaufman 1960). The weakening of city legislative power was an important part of these developments. In reformed cities, nonpartisan, at-large elections changed the role of city legislator from that of community broker to that of representative of supracommunity interests. Concerns relevant to local and national business interests, good-government groups, professional associations, and, eventually, municipal unions, replaced concerns relevant to local communities on the political agenda. Even in less "purely structured" reformed cities, such as New York, the increased power of the executive branch, the growth in councilmanic district size, and the increasing autonomy of administrative agencies served to weaken the community focus of the legislative branch. Governance by a citywide consensus, based on the professional and cosmopolitan values inherent in reform bureaucracies, replaced governance by the accommodation of community interests evident in machine legislatures.

One of the effects of these changes was to lessen the political influence of lower-income groups on city officials. By their very nature, the professional administrative agencies created by reform do not reflect the diversity within the city. Rather, such agencies generally reflect the interests of the middle- and upper-middle-class groups, which form the bases of their support and the personnel pool for their recruitment and appointment. Reformers who consistently portrayed themselves as above politics were in fact responsive to different interests than those of the more overtly political, urban machine. Indeed, reformers did not abolish interest group power in urban government; they simply changed the interest groups to which government was responsive.

The rejection of community input under reform regimes left residents of lower-income communities with little opportunity to have impact on the agencies on which they depended for services or whose decisions greatly affected them. Over time, these changes in the structure of local government and in the perspectives of those who came to power because of these changes resulted in the grassroots protests and the changes in federal priorities that helped usher in the postreform era in American cities. It is to this reaction that we now turn.

CHAPTER THREE

Postreform Politics: The Reemergence
of Community

Postreform politics is the "open recognition that we are a society of diverse interests, that these interests should be represented, and that politics, the activity through which this representation is obtained, is an inescapable part of modern life" (Stone, Whelan, and Murin 1986, 134). Postreform, termed "new reform" by some, "accepts and embraces the political nature of big city government" (Benjamin and Mauro, 1989, 12).

In cities, postreform politics is a reaction against the diminution of community power by reform governance; it is a rejection of reform's claims to ethical and administrative superiority; and it is a repudiation of the reform ideal that professional, central-city governments are best suited to formulate and implement policies to address urban problems. Postreform politics is not an attempt to reinstitute the geographic decentralization inherent in machine politics; it is, however, an effort to reassert community values and interests in the urban policy process. "The movement represents an effort by powerless groups to become part of the system and, at the same time, *to make the system responsive to their needs*" (Fantini and Gittell 1973, 7; emphasis added).

The emergence of community-based organizations in American cities in the 1960s was the clearest manifestation of postreform politics. Janice Perlman (1976, 6) notes that these organizations took many forms and pursued diverse political strategies. Direct-action groups employed confrontational tactics, such as protests, sit-ins, and demonstrations, to draw official attention to community concerns; grass-roots electoral groups sought to develop intra- and inter-community coalitions in an attempt to "enlarge the base committed to policies for a restructuring of American society from below"; and alternative institutions, such as community development corporations, involved themselves in helping to generate economic development, housing reconstruction, political organizing, and service-delivery reform. These organizations, focused on the problems of specific urban communities, represented the vanguard of the postreform reaction against reform governance.

Although community activism dates as far back as the social settlement movement of the 1880s, the evidence suggests that during the 1960s community organizing changed as activists adopted more definitive goals and confrontational tactics.[1] "If conservative neighborhood organizing was the dominant style of the fifties, the radical organizing efforts responding to the contradictions of life in the 'affluent society' characterized the succeeding decade" (Fisher 1984, 91). Prior to the 1960s, the listings of community-focused stories in the *New York Times Index* refer almost exclusively to neighborhood settlement houses or drug rehabilitation centers. However, since the 1960s, articles about politically active community groups are indexed frequently. One observer, chronicling the spread of community groups in 1979, noted that "local authorities were not sure whether the local groups, *which began forming and multiplying a decade ago*, would last" (*New York Times,* June 18, 1979, 1; emphasis added). In another piece, two urban scholars, specializing in neighborhood organizing, noted "a growing interest in local government control by white middle-class Americans in the 1970s and of blacks since the 1960s" (Warren and Warren 1977, 152).

A review of the social science literature prior to the mid-1960s found few articles concerning community activism. Articles on metropolitan government, the benefits of a strong-mayor system, and the strengths of council–manager and/or commission governments reflected the prevalent academic view of the time that centralization and professionalization were sound, if not exclusive, approaches to city problems. However, during the 1960s, research on the issues of participatory democracy, community control, and geographic decentralization of service delivery began to emerge. Indeed, a content analysis of urban research conducted in 1988 found that over the prior forty years: "Articles written in the 1960s and early 1970s reflect the popularity of the community-saved concept of neighborhood role as articulated in the black power and locality control movement" (Schmandt and Wendel 1988, 12). It is also during this period that urbanists first applied the term *urban crisis* to the social problems in American cities and began connecting these problems with the failures of reform policies.

Postreform Values: Decentralization and Participation

The tension between reform governance and postreform values centers on two distinct factors: the scope of geographic authority, that is, a community-based versus a citywide focus, and the nature of political decision making, that is, a reliance on a participative versus a professional approach. In their "pure forms," reform and postreform politics are polar opposites, with reform emphasizing a citywide scope of authority and a reliance on professional norms in decision making, and postreform focusing on a community-based scope of authority and a participative approach to decision making. Considering the significant spatial and decision-making differences between the two perspectives, the consequences for urban governance of the shift from one perspective to the other are dramatic.

Postreform and the Community

To reestablish the political salience of geographic diversity, postreform politics required the decentralization of the reform city. Historically, the movement for urban decentralization included diverse strategies. Borrowing from Alan Altshuler's (1970) classification, we distinguish between political and administrative decentralization. Political decentralization involves the transfer of authority over a range of local public issues from central-city to community-based officials; administrative decentralization is a managerial concept involving the delegation from superior to subordinate officials within a bureaucracy (1970, 64).[2]

In its pure form, political decentralization is synonymous with *community control*, which incorporates the idea of local governance over a specific territorial unit, that is, community decision-making authority over some range of public policies, as its operational definition of decentralization. From this perspective, only local autonomy is a meaningful response to the centralization of authority institutionalized by reform regimes. An alternative conceptualization of political decentralization as community integration, however, is broader and, in the final analysis, more empirically based than that of community control. *Community integration* does not require local control over policy, only the inclusion of community interests in decision making. Because it represents less of a threat to the reform status quo, community integration has been favored by some central-city elites as well as by those local politicos who are more "comfortable" with accommodational as opposed to confrontational tactics (Altshuler 1970, chap. 3). From this broader, integrative perspective, political decentralization includes any formal governmental attempt to channel community-based input into the formulation of policy on issues relevant to a community. "It implies, at a minimum, creating ground rules that establish a new basis for *negotiation* between citizens in their communities and the public agencies that affect them" (Mudd 1984, 33).

Whereas political decentralization refers to policy formulation, administrative decentralization focuses on policy implementation. There are two dimensions to administrative decentralization. The first, command decentralization, is defined as the devolution of decision-making authority to agency field offices. Under this intraorganizational decentralization, field employees exercise authority over some aspects of policy implementation within their areas of spatial responsibility. It represents "the attempt by a service agency to grant its own district officials greater discretionary authority to be more responsive to neighborhood needs" (Yin and Yates 1975, 35). The second dimension, community-based administrative decentralization, takes the process a step further by requiring that the devolution of authority to the field level be coupled with a degree of accountability by field employees to community interests. In its most dramatic form, then, community-based administrative decentralization incorporates three dimensions: the inclusion of a range of service agencies in a decentralization program, a high level of command decentralization, that is, a degree of autonomy to community-based agency representatives, and a formal community-based mechanism at the community level empowered to monitor and coordinate local service delivery (Barton et al. 1977, 5–8).

The diversity of decentralization proposals prompted a variety of arguments. Political decentralization as community control was defended by some intellectuals as a reflection of the inherent community right to self-determination. To these advocates, reform governance was the end result of a historical dynamic that began with municipal annexation of surrounding communities and culminated in the consolidation of political control in "downtown" elites. Milton Kotler argued that a system of "neighborhood governments" would permit communities to assert their interests with greater political legitimacy (1969, 89–93). In its most radical incarnation, the ideological commitment to decentralization justified strategies of community independence and self-sufficiency, pulling the plug, as it were, on central-city contacts (Morris and Hess 1975; *Chicago Tribune,* November 17, sec. 7, 1, 1977).[3]

Critics raised a number of philosophical and empirical objections to community control. Some suggested that communities were ill-equipped to handle the complicated issues of urban governance. These analysts argued that many of the urban problems emphasized by proponents of postreform politics resulted from metropolitan fragmentation and could be addressed most efficiently not by further decentralization but by consolidating metropolitan areas and creating regional governments (Wood 1961; Lineberry 1970; Hawley and Zimmer 1970).[4] From this perspective, community control would lead to even less coordination of urban policy and generate even more negative externalities as community organizations made decisions with little regard for their impact on neighboring areas. Moreover, increased centralization has its own larger, democratic rationale. Because it is more effective and responsive, metropolitan centralization "is likely not only to be better managed in the professional sense but more democratically managed as well . . ." (Wood 1959, 297).

Other critics suggested that community control would result in a strengthening of class-based inequities in urban areas as wealthier communities secured their already substantial advantages at the expense of their lower-income counterparts. Some research has indicated the validity of this concern (Lipsitz 1970; Parenti 1970). Middle- and upper-income communities have proved more capable of exploiting the opportunities offered by decentralization than have lower-income areas. From this perspective, decentralization does not mitigate the larger socioeconomic inequities that characterize American cities but, rather, acts to reaffirm them.[5] "We must face the fact that without a significant restructuring of national priorities, without altering our social system, much local work will be in vain" (Lipsitz 1973, 56).

Postreform advocates, who were themselves hesitant about the feasibility of community control, suggested more moderate forms of decentralization. They argued that either community integration approaches or administrative decentralization were more useful strategies for increasing service-delivery efficiency than was community control. Howard Hallman suggested that communities be equipped to organize and deliver services like police patrols, refuse collection, and traffic control, while other services requiring large-scale capital investment, such as mass transit and police training, be maintained under central-city control (1974, 52–53). Others argued that the increasing complexity of urban life and the growing heterogeneity of urban populations made decentralized service delivery a cost-effective strategy, particularly in the area of social programs (Kochen and Deutsch 1969; Bish and Nourse 1980). Still others suggested that, at the very least, moderate decentralization would be useful for improving the feedback mechanisms between citizens and city government, thereby helping to make city government more directly accountable and responsive to residents' concerns (Zimmerman 1972). This consumer argument is founded on the notion that as recipients of city services, community residents are policy experts to the extent that they experience the consequences of central-city decision making (Cahn and Cahn 1968).

Reform-minded critics countered that even the moderate decentralization plans emphasized parochial issues at the expense of professionalism and efficiency. Reform governments centralized political authority in city-manager or strong-mayor systems in order to formulate public policy based on the public interest. Reformers instituted strict civil service regulations so that the policies formulated would be implemented as efficiently as possible. This was all predicated on the notion that because the formulation and implementation of policy were concentrated in central-city authority, economies of scale could be maximized, service redundancies minimized, and the entire policy process rationalized. Accordingly, even moderate decentralization threatened a primary raison d'être of reform governance because it "would disperse departmental expertise and reduce the economies of scale in the department" (Ross and Stedman 1985, 117).

Moreover, moderate decentralization challenged another central tenet of reform governance. Urban reformers emphasized the need to separate politics from administration, maintaining political accountability through periodic elections. "The politics–administration dichotomy . . . virtually prevented analysis of the environmental relationships of public agencies" (White 1970, 118). From a reform perspective, the emphasis on decentralization to secure resident feedback would connect administration much too directly to "the consumers" in the political environment and might very well interfere with the professional delivery of urban services.

Because even moderate forms of geographic decentralization threatened the political position of important interests in the reform city, there were substantial practical hurdles facing advocates of postreform. As we saw in chapter two, reformers were careful to construct electoral systems that strengthened the political position of citywide, functional interests while weakening that of community groups. Moreover, once in power, reformers created government structures that centralized authority geographically and insulated it functionally within administrative agencies. Accordingly, to decentralize the reform city, postreform proponents would have to overcome the resistance of powerful groups including the finance, insurance, and real estate interests (FIRE), which supported the creation and benefited from the continuation of growth-oriented, reform governments; the established municipal bureaucracies, whose personnel valued the autonomy secured by reform's emphasis on civil service rules and professionalism; and organized municipal employees, whose primary interests involved functional issues, such as salaries and benefits, and not territorial concerns. All of these interests shared the fear that decentralization would have negative repercussions on the political standing they enjoyed under reform (Altshuler 1970).

With the powerful administrative and political obstacles to decentralization, it is not surprising that the early literature indicated that the initial community-empowerment experiments met strong resistance and produced mixed results. Several analysts found that, although decentralization tended to increase activists' feelings of political efficacy and satisfaction, it did not result in significant transfers of political power from central-city to community-based interests (Strange 1972; Cole 1974). In a review of 269 studies of urban decentralization conducted in the late 1960s and early 1970s, Yin and Yates (1975) concluded that, although decentralization improved the flow of information to the public and resulted in the upgrading of service delivery, it had not substantially increased client control. In another study, Yates (1973) found that decentralization did not generate increased community influence because community leaders rarely attempted to expand their political bases beyond the neighborhood level.

Postreform and Participation

The geographic focus of city government was only one of the major distinctions between reform and postreform politics. In contrast to reformers' emphasis on the professional administration of government, proponents of postreform politics advocated widespread citizen participation.[6] Although conceptually vague and at times more a rhetorical than a substantive demand, citizen participation was generally thought of as an increased amount of involvement by active residents in policy decisions affecting their communities. Citizen participation has been defined as a "redistribution of power that enables the have-not citizens, presently excluded from the political and economic processes, to be deliberately included in the future" (Arnstein 1969, 216). From a postreform perspective, resident participation was the antidote to increasingly distant and insular governance in the reform era.

Studies have distinguished several types of resident participation. One differentiates between modes of resident participation within neighborhood organizations: "Procedural participation has as its central value the accountability of organizational elites to general membership. . . . Substantive participation is characterized by the direct involvement of nonelites in organizational decision making" (Pecorella 1985, 20–22). Another suggests a typology of levels of participation ranging from participation as "manipulation" by center-city forces to participation as actual "control" by community organizations (Arnstein 1969). The latter makes it clear that postreform participatory mechanisms vary widely and can be employed both to empower and to co-opt community residents.

Advocates suggested that widespread participation included many positive implications for urban politics. First, proponents argued that resident participation improved policy-making by increasing the number and the variety of actors involved in the policy process (Goodman 1971; Boyte 1980). By introducing new actors into the process, resident participation increased the breadth of policy options considered on the urban political agenda. Such an argument, a clear assault on the reform notion of professional government, represented an increasingly popular view during the postreform period: that the objects of public policy and the recipients of public services were in a uniquely qualified position to evaluate and improve those policies and services.

Second, advocates defended a participatory approach as psychologically beneficial to the involved individuals, whose sense of personal worth and political efficacy would be heightened by such participation (Altshuler 1970, 210). From this perspective, because community organizations combined direct participation by residents with concrete signs of community improvements, involvement with these organizations would renew an individual's "sense of identity" and "experience of competence" (Hampden-Turner 1974). Moreover, the experience would help develop an indigenous leadership class in the community (Alinsky 1946; Fisher 1984, 133–38).

Third, citizen participation was defended not only as a source of more effective public policy and/or increased self-worth for the participant but as a more general public good. Proponents suggested that community residents, experiencing the personal and collective satisfaction of effective participation in issues of immediate concern to them, would develop into more capable and more informed participants in the political process as a whole (Cahn and Cahn 1968). Furthermore, political participation lessens individual alienation, which can only result in increased social stability (Cole 1974; Fainstein and Fainstein 1976).

Several studies suggested that resident participation was more than a rhetorical component of postreform politics in some community organizations. In research on community development corporations (CDCs), Rita Mae Kelly concluded that, in spite of difficult obstacles, citizen participation in and even control of community economic development "are not only feasible, but also positive factors contributing to the success of CDC organizational goals" (1977, 145). Another study found that the executive directors of CDCs valued resident participation on matters of organizational policy formulation, while tending to disregard resident input concerning day-to-day management (Pecorella 1985).

A study of rural grass-roots organizations concluded that by employing a "learning process approach" such organizations can broaden political choices, demystify social science jargon, and even enable residents to participate in the more complex areas of public policy (Korten 1980). A case study of two community organizations in East Los Angeles found that one of them regularly used a form of the "learning process approach" to increase resident information and to generate increased participation in organizational decision making (Ventriss and Pecorella 1984). Two recent studies of community politics in Birmingham, Alabama, found evidence of active participation in that city's community organizations, particularly among lower-income groups (Hutcheson and Prather 1988; Haeberle 1989).

Much of the research, however, has not been supportive of the contention that widespread participation in community organizations is a feasible alternative to reform professionalism. In fact, to the critics, a participatory strategy in urban communities was an idea whose time had passed. To some analysts, such participation was inherently antithetical to the kind of economic decision making crucial for community growth and development (Hetherington 1972); to others, meaningful participation was especially problematic for lower-income residents of inner-city neighborhoods and only tended to increase intracommunity conflicts (Peterson 1970); to a third group, participation was an empty process without the inclusion of specific rewards based on the concrete self-interest of the participants (O'Brien 1975); and to another group of analysts, focusing on participation emphasized a peripheral concern at the expense of substantive issues like reducing poverty and improving housing (Davis 1970, 71). Indeed, one analyst, characterizing the institutional emphasis on citizen participation as "repression by inauthentic participation," wrote: "Citizens may be invited to participate in an institution in ways that do not challenge the distribution of power and which in fact may reinforce the inequality of choice possibilities." As a consequence, "there is no meaningful opportunity for participants to shape conditions which affect their lives . . ." (Katznelson and Kesselman, cited in Katznelson 1972, 329).

One of the more compelling arguments raised against a participatory strategy reflected the basic rationale for reform governance: citizen participation cannot be revived at the community level because it has already been negated by the ubiquitous forces of modernization. According to this argument, the social complexity of modernization displaces the traditional values of holism, participation, and accountability with the modern values of specialization, professionalism, and efficiency. Indeed, the overriding feature of modern society is the "overtowering power" of bureaucracy, the institutional manifestation of modernization. "Bureaucratization offers above all the optimum possibility for carrying through the principle of specializing administrative functions according to purely objective considerations" (Weber 1968, 975). Because community organizations must interact with and generate resources from the larger society, they are forced to sacrifice traditional values (i.e., participation) in favor of modern norms (i.e., professionalization). Accordingly, despite the initial intentions of organizers, postreform's participatory ideals inevitably succumb to the professionalized exigencies of the larger reform environment.

In a case study of the Pico-Union Neighborhood Corporation (PUNC) in Los Angeles, Terry Cooper (1980) illustrated how, over time, that organization abandoned its initial commitment to resident participation as it became increasingly more like the bureaucratic agencies with which it interacted in the larger society. Cooper concluded: "Community groups which manage to survive and engage public agencies for a prolonged period of time tend to assume the major organizational characteristics of those agencies" (1980, 412). The transformation of organizational emphases, more subtle than overt, involves "cognitive, structural and operational changes in the organization and its leadership" (1980, 413). The result of this transformation was a decrease in resident interest as PUNC displaced its original participatory goals and adopted increasingly professionalized norms of behavior.

Other studies also found evidence that modernization hindered widespread participation. Marilyn Gittell (1980), in an analysis of community organizations involved in educational issues, noted a discernible pattern for once "politically active groups" to move from "advocacy" to "service" roles with a consequent increase in organizational professionalism and a decrease in citizen participation. She concluded that "advocates of citizen participation have more reason to despair than they did ten years ago" (1980, 241). Harry Boyte, a strong supporter of decentralization and citizen participation, noted that extensive interactions with elements of the larger society can impose "great pressure toward bureaucratization" among formerly participatory community organizations (1980, 131). In an analysis of New York's Office of Neighborhood Government experiment, Barton et al. noted: "The program changed during its planning phase from one emphasizing community representation and outreach to one emphasizing the strengthening of local administrative capacity" (1977, xiv). Ernest Alexander (1976) warned that the need to generate external support meant that community organizations must modify general participation by restraining residents' demands. John Mudd lamented the fact that, in many cases, "political decentralization took place alongside continued administrative centralization—an organizational formula that frequently produced conflict, frustration, and disillusionment on all sides" (1984, 35).

Other analysts noted that the role distinctions that follow from modernization separate the interests of organizational leaders from those of the general membership. Robert Michels's (1947) "iron law of oligarchy" is the classic formulation of this process of interest division. From this perspective, broad-based participation in organizational decision making is difficult because organizational leaders attend to agendas that are reflective more of interorganizational leadership priorities than of intraorganizational membership demands. Harry Berndt's (1977) case study of the Union-Sara Economic Development Corporation (USEDC) in St. Louis highlights the negative effects of elite-member role differentiation on participation within community organizations. Echoing John Kenneth Galbraith's earlier analysis of private corporations, Berndt concludes that, because USEDC embodied a corporate rationale to maintain its organizational relationships, it became a "creation in the service of its own bureaucracy" and "serves the purpose of its own management" (1977, 126).

The Evolution of a Concept

While the academic studies and intellectual debates on the merits of decentralization and participation proceeded, the concept of community power evolved from a radical idea to a fact of governance in many American cities. The nature of the evolution reflected those studies and debates as well as the fervor and commitment of postreform activists, the acuity of postreform's critics, the social relevance of reform values, and the political power of reform governance. As a result of these diverse pressures, community power has been institutionalized in many cities, although less radically than in its original form (Hallman 1984; Pecorella 1984).

From a geographic perspective, the development of community power has been characterized by an evolution from an emphasis on community control and self-sufficiency to one on community influence on and integration with central-city government. This evolution was a consequence of two factors. First, there were modifications in postreform demands as the intense conflicts around community-control experiments weakened the position of the ideologues, while the more flexible attempts at moderate decentralization strengthened the position of the politicos. Second, decentralization strategies had to adapt to the exigencies of modernization reflected in reform emphases on central-city authority.

The evolution from an emphasis on participatory democracy to one on representative forms of participation was also a function of postreform moderation in light of central-city pressures and political realities. Such moderation was a consequence of the fact that although the bureaucratic institutions of political modernization were highly susceptible to rhetorical attack, they proved difficult to counter operationally. Proposals for participatory democracy often appeared quaint, and participants sometimes appeared naive and unfocused in the context of the established bureaucratic procedures of reform governance. Moreover, community-based elections, whether for general neighborhood councils or specific service-delivery agencies such as school boards, were frequently characterized by embarrassingly low voter turnouts. In fact, community-based organizations tended to involve the active interest of relatively few area residents. Indeed, it became increasingly clear that if mobilizing large numbers of residents was a difficult task, keeping large numbers mobilized and active for extended periods of time was even more problematic.

By the 1970s, with moderation the key concept, postreform values had been institutionalized in a number of city governments. Virtually every city that had adopted geographic decentralization and resident empowerment since the 1970s emphasized an integrative and representative approach to such reforms (Hallman 1977; Pecorella 1985). As in previous years, the classic integrative reform involves allocating to community representatives an advisory role in local policy-making. Many observers still saw this type of local empowerment as an example of co-optation of community interests or an indication of victory by the "metropolitan establishment" over local interests (Kraus 1984). Others, however, contended that political realities had changed since the early decentralization period and what was once a co-optive reform might no longer be so. In analyzing the evolution of community politics since the 1960s, Howard Hallman wrote: "Since that time, many citizens have learned to use the advisory role as an entry point for bargaining and exerting influence, and there are public officials who genuinely seek participation and respond to what they hear" (1984, 65). Moreover, even assuming that co-optation was the original intent of reform, manipulators often lose control of the legitimation mechanisms they devise, a point illustrated in Piven and Cloward's analysis of the institutionalization of entitlement programs in the welfare state (1982, 100–124).

Considering the social and political obstacles in their path, the postreformers' success in achieving even modified forms of decentralization and resident participation is impressive. To sustain a challenge to the values and power of an existing political regime requires an opposition movement with two characteristics: (1) It must have a working, if often tense, balance between movement ideologues who "keep the faith" and politicos who accommodate feasibility. (2) The movement must have as its base a multifaceted coalition of committed groups whose own agendas are served by the success of the larger whole. It is to an examination of this multifaceted coalition that chapter three now turns.

Historical Antecedents of Urban Postreform

With the review of the fundamental tenets and the clarification of the basic terminology of postreform politics complete, it is now useful to examine the historical forces underlying the postreform reaction. Postreform politics had its roots in reform governance in much the same way that reform politics was a reaction to the political machine. Moreover, like the reform movement before it, the postreform movement resulted from the historical confluence of several distinct forces, including community-based grass-roots organizing in opposition to reform government policies, the northern black power variant of the southern civil rights movement, and federal initiatives from the Kennedy and Johnson administrations. Each of these forces pressing for community empowerment represented a direct threat to reform regimes because each emphasized, for its own particular reasons, the parochial concerns of local communities. Moreover, by establishing its own unique parameters for community involvement, each also influenced the eventual institutional nature of the postreform regime.

Many of the grass-roots political organizations that emerged during the 1960s reflected community dissatisfaction with the policies of reform administrations. Local activists saw community empowerment as a strategy for challenging both the political hegemony of progrowth forces in reformed cities and the administrative power of reform bureaucracies. To these activists, only indigenous political organizations had the potential to provide community residents with the capacity to counter the center-city policies that they saw as destabilizing to communities.

African-American leaders, who saw community activism as means to organize their constituents in northern cities, brought a related but distinct perspective to postreform politics. The civil rights movement had succeeded in raising national public consciousness about the plight of southern blacks. In northern cities, the black power movement, a regional variant of national civil rights activities, sought to organize black communities socially, economically, and politically. Subscribing to what Fainstein and Fainstein (1976, 906) termed a "race-conflict" perspective, these community-power proponents argued that white "colonial power" in the black community could only be countered through organized resident activism leading eventually to community control of local economic and political development (Hampden-Turner 1974; Carmichael and Hamilton 1967). To many African-American leaders, community control was a means to institutionalize racial representation on the urban political agenda.

The demands for community empowerment in the African-American community spread to inner-city white ethnic neighborhoods in the 1970s (Warren 1975). Residents of these communities often perceived themselves as the victims of the liberal "social engineering" programs of the 1960s. Accordingly, white ethnics organized for the most part not to promote community control or fundamental political and social changes but to protect their neighborhoods against external threats, usually defined in terms of liberal politicians in general and minority groups in particular (Fisher 1984, 47–49) Fainstein and Martin 1978, 461–63). As opposed to the often radical genesis of community empowerment among intellectuals and black activists, therefore, community organizing in white ethnic communities tended to emphasize utilitarian and conservative values from the start.

By emphasizing the relevance of community concerns and by encouraging the creation of community-based organizations, the federal social programs of the 1960s also helped relegitimize the value of community input on the urban political agenda and, consequently, helped usher in the postreform era. Government-sponsored community-empowerment experiments of the 1960s often incorporated the rhetoric of community control while offering at best integrative mechanisms for participation. Generally, neighborhood residents were allocated advisory responsibilities within programs formulated and implemented by the federal government (Fox 1972; Sundquist 1972; Donovan 1967) or by "progressive" central-city administrations (Mudd 1984; Barton et al. 1977). Attempts by community elites to assume more direct control of these federally subsidized programs, such as those that occurred in several of the War on Poverty's Community Action Agencies, were usually thwarted by coalitions of central-city interests.

As a consequence of these internal conflicts and the ways that they were resolved, some analysts concluded that these federal initiatives were ill-conceived (Moynihan 1969), whereas others argued that they simply served to co-opt community interests and reaffirm central-city power (Piven and Cloward 1971; Arnstein 1969). Regardless of their intended purpose or degree of effectiveness, however, these federal programs helped promote a reemphasis on community empowerment in the 1960s.

Grass-Roots Organizing and Community Power

Much of the grass-roots organizing that occurred in the 1960s was a political reaction to reform policies that destabilized, and in some cases destroyed, urban communities in the name of a citywide public interest. Progrowth coalitions, consisting of "central-city politicians, a new breed of bureaucrats, large corporations, central-business-district real estate and merchant interests, and the construction trades" (Mollenkopf 1978, 123), sought the revitalization of downtown urban centers partly to counterbalance the suburbanization that had been encouraged by federal mortgage and highway subsidies. Operating under the classically reform notion of a unitary city interest and using the substantial subsidies available through federal urban renewal and highway programs, these progrowth coalitions initiated revitalization programs resulting in the dislocation of inner-city residents and the replacement of much of the low- and moderate-income housing stock with commercial facilities. Robert Salisbury characterized this "new convergence of power" in American cities: "They identify the problems, they articulate the alternative actions that might be taken, and they themselves take most of the relevant actions" (1964, 791).

The Housing Act of 1949 included a proposal for urban renewal, a program theoretically intended to produce improved housing by demolishing substandard housing in "blighted areas" (*U.S. Statutes at Large* 63, 23). In practice, however, urban renewal efforts increasingly reflected market pressures rather than commitment to affordable housing. As a result, the program was responsible for destroying low-rent housing in scores of inner-city communities, thereby decreasing housing options for inner-city residents. As a case in point, Martin Anderson (1964) reported that neighborhoods such as Boston's West End were selected for urban renewal not because of their blighted condition but because they offered optimal sites for luxury housing.

The Housing Act of 1954 amended the original urban renewal program by allowing local governments and private developers more leeway in selecting the type of facilities that would replace demolished housing in blighted areas. Under the 1954 amendments, the amount of nonresidential, replacement development permitted within urban renewal projects increased from 10 percent to 35 percent. "Areas being cleared were only required to be 'predominately residential,' and even this link to the goal of improved housing was interpreted flexibly to favor commercial revitalization" (Marcuse 1982, 104). Indeed, by the early 1960s, some local authorities were manipulating federal requirements for minimum residential replacement and allocating almost two-thirds of the available funds for commercial projects (Judd 1988, 271). As a consequence of the commercial revitalization and residential gentrification effects of the program, urban renewal replaced less than 25 percent of the housing it demolished, and much of the replacement housing constructed was out of the price range of those dislocated by the demolition (Anderson 1964, 65).

Similarly, in the hands of progrowth factions, federally subsidized highway programs displaced thousands of residents and destroyed dozens of communities in cities around the nation. The Works Progress Administration "spent 38 percent of its budget on roads and highways and almost nothing on other forms of transportation"; while the Public Works Administration allocated ten times as much money for highway construction and maintenance as it did for subways (Sawers 1984, 236). Robert Caro (1974) describes how the functionally decentralized spread of responsibility inherent in reform governance empowered public authorities in New York, under the control of Robert Moses, to build miles of limited-access highways while displacing hundreds of thousands of residents from their homes.

In the early 1960s, these progrowth coalitions were "virtually the only unified political interest that spoke for the inner cities," and they "dominated city politics" (Judd 1988, 372). They exercised extensive influence in city government at precisely those geographic locations and over precisely those issues that had been the focus of the reform movement. Their power base was citywide; their policy interests were dealt with largely by the central-city agencies of reform cities; and their emphasis on economic development was considered by much of the local media as being in the common interest (Molotch 1976). Moreover, because the progrowth coalitions included the building trade unions and some progressive politicians, their political support base was often populist in character. In the absence of a significant citywide coalition to oppose central-city development strategies, the only place where effective opposition could emerge would be from within the affected communities themselves.[7]

Community mobilization against these coalitions did indeed take place (Davies 1966). Chester Hartman's (1974) analysis of the attempts by powerful downtown interests to "revitalize" San Francisco by constructing the Yerba Buena Convention Center chronicles the evolution of community mobilization in that city. The pressures from the coalition of corporations, financiers, central-city politicians, and local media pushing for redevelopment generated organized resistance among the low- and middle-income residents of the "South of Market" community slated for renewal. The reaction in San Francisco is a classic example of how the land-use programs initiated by reform governments led to counterorganization by community groups who used the federal courts, federal agencies, and street protests to delay plans for redevelopment. Similarly, Danielson and Doig (1982) attribute the decline of Newark's Housing Authority, which coordinated urban renewal projects in that city, to the increasing pressures from community opponents, particularly those in the African-American community. Robert Goodman (1971) reviews how opposition to Boston's urban renewal plan was responsible for extensive community organizing in that city. Nancy Kleniewski, who examined the evolution of community opposition to urban renewal plans to relocate residents of North Philadelphia, concludes: "These initial protests against urban renewal formed the basis of an urban social movement among community activists in the city which is still challenging and protesting the city's housing and community development programs" (1984, 217). This local organization in reaction to the plans of urban reformers, the product more of community desperation than of long-term design, became a crucial component of postreform politics in the 1960s.

A second incentive for grass-roots community organizing was provided by the service-delivery agencies of city government, which, as reconstituted by reform, were bureaucratic in every sense of the term. Indeed, postreform advocates argued that reform government's reliance on professionalism had resulted in a bureaucratic isolation that could only be countered by a renewed emphasis on local democracy. Reform agencies were hierarchically ordered; they were staffed by specialists who were, for the most part, hired on the basis of merit; and they were structured in theory to treat all clients in basically the same manner. Indeed, from the democratic and egalitarian perspectives, there is much to be said in support of such large-scale efforts to deliver government services efficiently and equitably to mass populations.

Benefits notwithstanding, there are also many problems with bureaucratic service delivery that are inherent to the very nature of such organizations. Research on reform bureaucracies has uncovered a pattern of defining client interests within a framework that emphasizes bureau needs even when they clash with client concerns (Scott 1969; Lipsky 1980, 1984). Task specialization, so necessary for the division of labor that allows an agency to operate in an informed and efficient manner, can be viewed by clients as the tendency of agency personnel to avoid responsibility or as another strategy for passing them along a seemingly endless chain of lines and windows. Standard operating procedures, allowing agencies to function with predictability and with a minimum of internal confusion, are often viewed with hostility and suspicion by clients who neither understand them in the abstract nor see the relationship of the procedures to their particular cases. The extensive paperwork mandated by bureaucratic rules, necessary for the preservation of bureaucratic memory and the effective disposition of individual cases, is often seen as unnecessary red tape by clients who may be frustrated or even intimidated by all the forms they are required to fill out and all the personal information they are required to provide.

Other problems with bureaucratic service delivery are more a consequence of socioeconomic and political inequities than of bureaucracy per se. Merit selection, theoretically intended to ensure that "the best and the brightest" secure administrative positions in reformed government, may be viewed simply as biased hiring by lower-income clients who find themselves interacting primarily with white, middle-class personnel in government agencies. Indeed, the civil service system includes a number of class-based problems. "Civil service, once an instrument for improved standards and performance, was now seen instead as protecting agencies from outside review and demands for accountability and as creating administrative rigidities that prevented adaptation to service demands of clientele" (Rogers and Chung 1983, 6). Furthermore, when civil service was coupled with the widespread and increasingly militant unionization of municipal employees, a double-edged insulation between service providers and recipients was created. "The civil service system and unionization protected public employees not only from the vagaries of the political whim but from the need to respond to new direction" (Mudd 1984, 22).

Moreover, the individuals appointed under reform-style merit selection may harbor or develop cultural biases against the clients being served, particularly in the social service agencies in big cities. For example, provider–recipient tensions can develop as the written culture of the bureaucracy interacts with the oral culture of many lower-income clients. An agency paternalism, based on the professional training of personnel, and especially infuriating to clients dependent on agency programs, may well develop. The personnel reward systems of large-scale government agencies encourage internally focused behavior by civil servants while discouraging all but the most routinized interactions with clients or with other agencies that could be of help to clients. Furthermore, external political pressures on social service bureaucracies to cut costs and trim welfare rolls may well create intimidating anticlient behavior designed to discourage potential applicants from receiving benefits.

These problems, some endemic to bureaucracy, others the consequence of class-based bureaucratic politics, result in client alienation from service-delivery agencies. Such alienation, combined with a more general dissatisfaction with public services and the threats to the physical integrity of the community arising from progrowth coalitions, helped generate organized community opposition in the 1960s. The rise in community dissatisfaction and pressure increased the organizational defensiveness of service-delivery agencies. As community activists became more demanding and more militant, agency personnel, often with little understanding of the cultural divide between themselves and their clients, responded by reinforcing their bureaucratic norms of behavior. In turn, the increasing rigidity of organizational behavior increased the alienation of grassroots activists. As William Tabb notes, "The failure of city officials to respond adequately gave rise to further demands for community control of schools, civilian review boards, co-ops, and other institutions" (1984, 374). By the late 1960s, reform and postreform forces were locked in a political and cultural struggle over the basic nature of urban governance.

The particular causes notwithstanding, the fact that extensive grass-roots community mobilization occurred at all is testimony to the depth of frustration felt by community residents. Such movements are difficult to initiate and very difficult to maintain. First, they require not only a common understanding of the problems facing a community but also some communal agreement on strategies to address those problems. Second, grass-roots mobilization demands a commitment on the part of residents to volunteer time and effort to deal with the issues, including perhaps long and often frustrating meetings with frequently defensive agency representatives and city officials. Third, such mobilization requires continuing attention by indigenous leadership in order to maintain the organized political pressure on public officials.

Black Power and Community Control

Because many of reform government's urban renewal and highway projects had negative impacts on lower-income neighborhoods, much of the grass-roots organizing in opposition to these programs occurred in black communities. However, postreform organizing in the black community included the additional sociopolitical dimension of black power, which afforded the notion of community empowerment even more legitimacy than it had as a generic defense of spatial integrity. The black power movement can be considered both a derivative of the civil rights movement in the South and, given its spatial emphasis, a reflection of postreform politics.

The civil rights movement was generally successful in challenging de jure desegregation and in obtaining legal rights for African-Americans in the South. Martin Luther King's strategy of nonviolent confrontation was both philosophically and politically focused. It was based philosophically on the notion that integration of the races was possible when the majority of American society, confronted with an immoral and patently unconstitutional system of segregation in the South, responded by doing essentially what was right. King's strategy was based politically on the premise that the national government would be forced to respond to the internationally embarrassing scenes of southern state officials employing brutality to maintain the anachronism of segregation.

However, King's strategy, useful in the legally segregated but spatially integrated southern states, encountered major problems in the North. In the large cities of the North, de facto segregation, resulting in black spatial concentration, was the norm. Northern racism was more institutional than legal. In northern black communities, children often lived in substandard housing while attending substandard schools equipping them for substandard jobs. Indeed, the black community was in a unique position in northern cities. Unlike other urban neighborhoods, black communities were "artificially created geographical units; . . . a product of legal and de facto discrimination" (Warren 1975, 31). Spatial segregation, therefore, disguised the social and economic heterogeneity of the black neighborhood and made the community a particularly important focus of individual and collective status vis-à-vis the institutions of the larger society (Warren 1975, 92–93). Northern racism, unencumbered by law and brutal stereotypes, was perhaps more ingrained and certainly more insidious than its southern counterpart. It proved more difficult to combat through a strategy of nonviolent resistance than de jure segregation because the "enemy" was less clearly defined and the "external allies" less willing and, in the case of the federal courts, less able to act.

The black power movement was designed to combat the institutional nature of northern racism by mobilizing the residents of the economically heterogeneous black community. Black power was a call to racial pride and cultural consciousness among individual African-Americans as well as a call for organizing the black community. The "developments in the Civil Rights Movement leading to the breakdown of the myths of assimilation and 'one culture' . . . have led to demands of Black Americans for 'local control' of all institutions in the neighborhoods where they live" (Moore and Johnston 1971, 423). The black power movement was, therefore, a strategy to unify the black community politically on two distinct but interrelated levels: one based on cross-sectional racial identification, the other based on the realities of the African-American experience in northern cities, that is, the urban community. Consequently, the concept of community control, a clear manifestation of postreform politics, became an integral part of the black power movement.[8]

Much of the writing among black intellectuals of this period reflected a distaste for and a distrust of the reform notion of a cosmopolitan, citywide interest. Carmichael and Hamilton referred to the need to "challenge Anglo-conformity and other prevailing norms and institutions," and expressed the view that "reform politics groups . . . frequently are not tuned to the primary goals of black people" (1967, 62–65). Roy Innis, the head of the Congress of Racial Equality, was also disdainful of the reform ideal of policy consensus developed by disinterested professionals: "As to whether we are seeking consensus, no we are not. No place, no time . . . has anything important in society been done by consensus" (quoted in Hampden-Turner 1974, 153).

In terms of the day-to-day issues, studies consistently showed very high dissatisfaction with city service agencies among black respondents. For example, the National Advisory Commission on Civil Disorder, known popularly as the Kerner Commission, reported that African-American respondents rated school adequacy in their neighborhoods significantly lower than did their white counterparts (*Report of the Advisory Commission on Civil Disorders* 1968). Thomas Pettigrew (1971) highlighted some of the distinctions between whites and blacks in assessing urban police services, an issue that generated intense racial divisions in a number of American cities. However, it was not only the operational aspects of city services that were called into question by the black power movement but the very legitimacy of the agencies and of the governments providing those services (Hamilton 1969). Katznelson, Gille, and Weir conclude: "Black struggles, like urban struggles elsewhere, were struggles against the providers of government largess" (1982, 216–17).

As an integral part of the black power movement, community control became a strategy for organizing black self-interest; with this organization, the black community could begin to interact with the majority society from a position of strength. Whereas Dr. King's southern strategy was focused on achieving the racial integration of individuals through a politically sophisticated strategy of moral persuasion, community control pursued a collective-action strategy focused on the development of communal economic and political resources. The philosophy of community control is founded on the notion that collective equality must precede individual integration. Consequently, the urban community became the central organizational focus of the northern African-American activists. As such, the black power movement reinforced and added another dimension to the notion of spatially focused postreform politics. As one analyst of the period put it, "The trend towards localism, with some reality and more appearance of black control of black communities, seems irreversible" (Marshall 1969, 203).

Federal Initiatives and Community Politics

Indigenous resistance to reform governance in cities was coupled in the early 1960s with dissatisfaction among some federal officials with urban social policy in general. There were several reasons for official disquiet during this period. From a policy perspective, Michael Harrington's book, *The Other America,* had surprised many with its portrayal of the extent of postwar poverty in the United States. At the same time, taking cues from the social sciences, some members of the Kennedy administration were reassessing the nature of American poverty and considering changes in the way the national government dealt with the problem (Donovan 1967; Moynihan 1969). However, policy considerations about the extent and nature of poverty were not the only forces impacting on the federal social agenda. From a political perspective, the electoral alliance between Democratic administrations and African-American voters required some action on the part of the federal government to deal with the growing signs of black frustration in northern cities (Piven and Cloward 1971).

Historically, poverty has been viewed in the United States from within the conceptual framework of the Protestant work ethic. From this perspective, individual success or failure reflects the extent of individual initiative. Accordingly, the problem of poverty and its possible solutions were considered as inherent, except in extraordinary circumstances, to individuals. Moreover, any efforts to mitigate poverty's social consequences should to be undertaken largely by the private sector. Indeed, it was believed that government's attempts to mitigate the effects of poverty would only serve to weaken both the poor and society in general. As a consequence of this worldview, charities and churches were the primary sources of assistance for the poor in many parts of the country until the 1930s. (Of course, for the price of their support at the polls, the poor could receive some forms of assistance from the community representatives of the political machine in a number of cities.)

The initial development of federal efforts to assist the poor took place during the New Deal and were a consequence of the severity of the Great Depression and of Franklin Roosevelt's attempts to solidify his electoral coalition. Although New Deal initiatives did not represent a rejection of the accepted view of poverty as an individual problem, they did establish temporary measures to assist the "worthy poor" and help them return to the labor and consumer markets. Indeed, far from being revolutionary, the New Deal's relief programs reflected clearly the basic values of the market economy and the work ethic. Programs were designed to ensure basic survival while providing benefits meager enough to encourage people to get off the public dole as quickly as possible. Relief included "the degradation of a pariah class that serves to mark the boundary between the appropriately motivated and the inappropriately motivated" (Piven and Cloward 1971, 149).

These punitive attitudes, internalized within the social service administrative agencies, helped create a relief system in the United States that was professionally distant from and often hostile to its clients. Furthermore, in more than passing interest to the overall analysis in this book, the development of the federal administrative state under the New Deal, of which relief programs were only a part, also acted to reaffirm reform governance in American cities. By providing federal assistance to those cities that showed themselves structurally capable of professionally delivering services, federal programs encouraged reform-style urban governance.

As mentioned above, the traditional attitudes toward poverty, incorporated within New Deal social programs, changed among some government officials in the early 1960s. One contemporary assessment of the change saw in the Kennedy administration a decidedly different and more activist approach to the issue: "An important aspect of the new attitude was that poverty became for the first time a subject of scientific investigation and intellectual inquiry. The methods of the social sciences and the new statistical techniques were called upon to aid political leaders and social reformers who were seeking to solve the age-long problem by means of governmental action" (Robson 1964, 65).

The new approach to poverty manifested itself in a number of program initiatives. Influenced by the Ford Foundations's "gray areas" projects, which were designed to address youth problems through community-based programs, and by research on the causes of juvenile delinquency conducted at the Columbia School of Social Work, which emphasized the socioeconomic antecedents of such behavior, federal officials began to address social problems as a collective rather than an individual phenomenon. President Kennedy's Committee on Juvenile Delinquency and Youth Crime, headed by Attorney General Robert Kennedy, was an early example of such policy initiatives, and President Johnson's War on Poverty represented the culmination of such efforts.

The officials who adopted the new attitudes toward social problems—the self-styled "urban guerrillas" of the Kennedy and Johnson administrations—increasingly saw poverty as both a cause and, more importantly, an effect of larger structural constraints beyond the control of individuals. To these new poverty activists, the poor were caught in a structural problem not of their making and certainly not within their control. Moreover, poverty produced alienation, despair, and resignation, which, in turn, acted to reinforce poverty. Policy changes were needed to empower the poor to break the "cycle of poverty." Many of these officials, however, had come to believe that existing bureaucratic agencies at all levels of government were inflexible and consequently incapable of implementing the necessary changes in policy.

The attitudinal change toward social policy in general and toward the capabilities of the existing service-delivery agencies in particular was clear in Attorney General Robert Kennedy's testimony before Congress in support of the Economic Opportunity Act of 1964. Kennedy, whose office included many of the officials committed to the new structural interpretation of poverty, offered his assessment of the relationships between modern bureaucracies and their lower-income clients: "The institutions which affect the poor—education, welfare, recreation, business, labor—are huge complex structures operating far outside their control. They plan programs for the poor not with them. Part of the sense of helplessness comes from the feelings of powerlessness to affect the operations of these organizations" (U.S. House of Representatives 1964, 305).

Kennedy's testimony reflected the desire on the part of the new poverty activists to avoid traditional policy responses and develop instead innovative program implementation techniques. To that end, they sought to reorganize both the supply and demand sides of federal social policy. On the supply side, the Office of Economic Opportunity, charged with coordinating the overall poverty effort, was designed as an independent agency directly accountable to the president and consequently insulated from the traditional federal bureaucracies. On the demand side, the new poverty activists wanted to help organize urban communities so that the residents might "exert pressure on local bureaucracies, to encourage them to innovate and to challenge them to create new institutions" (Donovan 1967, 41).

In this context, the War on Poverty was an attempt to bypass existing social service agencies at all levels of government. The strategy, which combined an emphasis on local empowerment with a focus on avoiding bureaucracy, was to aim federal initiatives directly at the community level. To achieve this end, the communities would have to be organized to manage the federal programs. The Community Action Program, included in Title 2 of the Economic Opportunity Act of 1964, addressed this need directly. The program encouraged, indeed required, the development of community-based associations to represent local residents and to coordinate federal programs within city neighborhoods.

By organizing communities in this fashion, the Community Action Program helped redefine, at least theoretically, the relationship of urban citizens to their governments. The low-income citizen as an individual client dealing with distant city agencies, a relationship initiated and continually reaffirmed by reform bureaucracies, was to be replaced by the citizen organization articulating the interests of organized community residents. Community concerns and community organizations, dismissed as parochial annoyances by urban reformers, were to serve as the basis for the allocation of federal funds under the War on Poverty programs. As a result, the Community Action Program represented direct federal encouragement of postreform values at a time when those values were already emerging indigenously in urban communities throughout the nation.

Through the War on Poverty, social activists in the Kennedy and Johnson administrations sought to address what they perceived as the structural nature of poverty in the United States. However, despite their initial success in creating a community-based poverty program, their worldview was not widely shared in government. Indeed, it was the strategic positions occupied by the activists within the administration more than their numbers that explain their influence on the poverty effort. The willingness shown by President Johnson in 1965 to back away from the Community Action Program when it was under attack by Democratic mayors is a clear indication that the commitment to community empowerment was neither widely shared nor deeply held within the administration as a whole. In the final analysis, the War on Poverty was not the watershed program in American social policy that it had the potential to be. Ira Katznelson observed: "These innovations provided some change in the generally bleak picture of public policy toward the poor, particularly with respect to the punitive aspects of poverty programs. However, they remain grossly inadequate, and remain essentially paternalistic" (1972, 323).

At the local level, experiences with the Community Action Program were often frustrating. General confusion existed about what the phrase "maximum feasible participation" meant and how it was to be implemented. Consequently, a wide variety of community action programs (CAPs) emerged—some controlled by city hall, others more broadly representative of the residents of the communities from which they arose, and still others reflective of more radical elements within the community. "At the risk of oversimplification, it might be said that the CAPs most closely controlled by City Hall were disappointing, and that the ones most antagonistic were destroyed" (Moynihan 1969, 131). Moreover, the CAPs were often isolated from the other agencies of city government and were frequently unable to coordinate their own efforts with those of existing programs (Mudd 1984, 36–40).

In 1966, in an attempt to standardize the procedures for and moderate the nature of community-based representation in federal programs, Congress passed the Demonstration Cities and Metropolitan Development Act, which established the Model Cities Program. The local policy committees (LPCs) created by this legislation were designed to address some of the political and administrative problems experienced by the CAPs. By uniting community associations under neighborhood directors appointed by the mayor, the LPC program sought to coordinate community organizations while keeping them accountable to locally elected officials. To achieve this end, the neighborhood directors, appointed by and accountable to the mayors, were given far wider discretion over LPC operations than had been the case with CAP leadership.

Despite the changes, lack of program coordination continued to hinder community efforts under the Model Cities Program. For example, in New York City, Mayor Lindsay insisted that no individual could serve on both a CAP and an LPC. Although Lindsay's intention was to encourage widespread participation in community-based programs, the effect of the policy was to institutionalize rivalries between the two federally sponsored efforts (Viteritti and Pecorella 1987, 10–12). Moreover, in New York, as in other cities, the segregation of program efforts which hindered the CAPs also hampered the coordination efforts of the LPCs (Mudd 1984, 41–44; Washnis 1974, 11–12).

The overall problems with the War on Poverty and Model Cities Program aside, these initiatives had fundamental implications for urban politics. Unquestionably, a reassessment of the traditional interpretations of the causes of and solutions to poverty did take place at the highest levels of the federal government in the 1960s and was reflected for a short time in public policy. Moreover, these federal policies emphasized the value of community input and the validity of community activism and therefore encouraged postreform politics in cities. This was particularly true in African-American communities. "Very possibly, the most important long run impact of the community action programs of the 1960s will prove to have been the formation of an urban Negro leadership echelon at just the time when the Negro masses and other minorities were verging towards extensive commitment to urban politics" (Moynihan 1969, 129). Much as the New Deal programs of the 1930s had provided political support and programmatic incentives for the ascendance of reform values in urban governments, the federal antipoverty initiatives of the 1960s helped reaffirm the legitimacy of community-based organizing at the beginning of the postreform era.

From Reform to Postreform

In the three decades prior to the 1960s, reformers had institutionalized their regime by centralizing city government and reinforcing bureaucratic prerogatives. Reform consolidation was a function of two broadly defined policy emphases: city government's active involvement in local progrowth coalitions, which addressed the interests of economic elites, and reformers' support for increased social services to address attentive nonelite needs. During this period, there were notably few bases of viable citywide political opposition to the reform regime. The criticisms by fiscal conservatives, who were concerned about extensions in government responsibility, were neutralized by regime support among economic elites with interests in urban growth. Progressive assaults on the inadequacy of urban social programs were often hostage to co-optation by reform's welfare city. Indeed, reform's only organized citywide opposition, the political machine, had been discredited during the 1930s, and party politicians had adapted to changing circumstances by incorporating reform policies such as merit selection and social service programs into their platforms.

In the 1960s, however, a variety of political forces emerged to challenge reform hegemony. Representing less a political coalition than a confluence of separate but interrelated forces, the postreform challenge was based in the urban neighborhoods that reformers had left behind. Some of the opposition groups were the direct consequence of reform policies and their negative impacts on lower-income, urban communities; others represented urban variants of the larger social movements sweeping the nation; still others were products of federal initiatives.

Despite the disparate nature of its political base, postreform politics in American cities has consistently emphasized two primary values. First, postreform is founded on the principle that the public interest, which was defined in the reform city as a cosmopolitan common interest best discovered and managed by professionals, is better characterized as the aggregation of particular interests, which emerges through participative political conflict. Indeed, what reformers defined as the public interest was seen by postreform activists as simply the preeminence of progrowth coalitions seeking to maximize their own economic and political advantage at the expense of other interests in the city.

Second, urban postreform was founded on the notion that geography matters. The twin reform emphases on centralization of political authority in citywide agencies and decentralization based on bureaucratic specialization had raised the interests of supracommunity groups to the apex of the urban agenda. Reform regimes addressed the demands and secured the support of financiers, developers, large corporations, and trade unions, each of which had functionally, not geographically, defined interests in the city. Indeed, community interests had been dismissed by reformers as parochial in content and untutored in practice. To postreformers, however, community politics represented the legitimate mobilization of community concerns, and these interests deserved a place on the urban agenda.

As is to be expected in any social movement with such a diverse support base, postreform politics in practice meant different things to different practitioners. Postreform incorporated emphases on both political and administrative decentralization; demands for either community control or community integration; and proposals for either participatory or representative democracy. To evaluate these different postreform emphases and trace each of their unique contributions to the development of the postreform regime, the next chapter narrows our focus and analyzes early postreform politics in New York City.

CHAPTER FOUR

Reform Consolidation and the
Postreform Reaction in New York

The wide variety of community organizations that emerged in the 1960s and 1970s reflected political conflicts within the postreform movement over the nature of urban decentralization and the feasibility of widespread citizen participation. While ideologues remained committed to community control and participatory democracy, other, more accommodative, proponents of decentralization sought to expand the territorial scope and qualify the strict adherence to citizen participation among postreform activists. As with many movements for social change, the demands of ideological purists offered the more pragmatic activists an opportunity to secure concessions from public officials and helped make some forms of community power feasible options within reform regimes.

As community empowerment became a more common demand in cities, reform officials attempted to address the demands for urban decentralization. At times, such attempts represented preemptive and co-optative strategies designed more to preserve reform centralization than to address a postreform agenda. At other times, however, community-power experiments were initiated by mayors who, in seeking to extend their personal political bases, sought electoral alliances with community-based interests outside of the reform regime's traditional governing coalition. In these latter cases, community-power experiments were often legitimate, sometimes quite radical, efforts to satisfy postreform demands.

The evolution of postreform politics from its radical origins to its more moderate institutionalization is exemplified by the New York City experience. Indeed, New York's current community board system, the most far-reaching community-empowerment program in the nation, reflects the overall evolution of postreform politics. This chapter examines several examples of New York's early decentralization efforts and is intended as an immediate historical and conceptual backdrop to the analysis of the community board system, which, in the wake of the 1975 fiscal crisis, helped institutionalize postreform politics in the city. The chapter examines the range of grass-roots organizing in New York City from community self-help groups, which were exclusively locally focused and politically participatory, to community development corporations, which adopted a territorially interactive approach and were less committed to the notion of widespread participation.

Chapter four also analyzes two major postreform experiments sponsored by city government during the period: community control of schools and administrative decentralization through the Office of Neighborhood Government. Each of these experiments directly influenced the eventual structure of the community board system in New York. The school decentralization experiment of the late 1960s was, in its initial phase, a classic community-control experiment. The evolution from the demonstration school districts created in 1967 to the state legislature's school decentralization plan in 1969 is a case study of how intense political conflicts around community control led to the modification of political decentralization plans. The chapter then examines community-based administrative decentralization through the Office of Neighborhood Government. This short-lived Lindsay administration experiment, one of the most comprehensive efforts undertaken in any city to coordinate the delivery of public services at a neighborhood level, had a direct impact on the service-monitoring responsibilities eventually allocated to the city's community boards.

Before examining these early manifestations of postreform politics in New York, however, it is important to explore the reform regime's consolidation in the city. After all, the postreform movement toward participation and decentralization only makes sense within the context of the institutionalization of reform values. Accordingly, the chapter begins by analyzing the evolution of post-LaGuardia governance in New York City. The analysis focuses on two basic issues: the eventual emergence of functional decentralization as the primary constraint on the political interactions characterizing normal politics in the city, and the influence of reform values on the behavior of the Democratic party.

The Consolidation of Reform Governance

The post-LaGuardia period in New York witnessed the election of three consecutive Democratic mayors who governed the city for the next two decades. In 1945, Brooklyn District Attorney William O'Dwyer was elected mayor and served one full term before resigning at the beginning of his second term. O'Dwyer was succeeded by two Manhattan Democrats, City Council President Vincent Impellitteri in 1950 and Borough President Robert Wagner in 1954.[1] The three consecutive Democratic administrations coupled with the ascendance of Tammany leader Carmine DeSapio to a preeminent position among the five Democratic county leaders appeared to signal the reemergence of machine politics in New York. In terms of party control of local political nominations and judicial patronage, that is indeed what occurred.

The city governed by O'Dwyer, Impellitteri, and Wagner, and the party organization headed by DeSapio, however, had changed dramatically in the wake of reform. By the 1950s, New York's reform regime had consolidated its political power. In chapter one I pointed out that urban regimes are defined by political interactions guided by mutually reinforcing formal rules and informal norms.

The formal rules that served as the foundation for reform's hegemony in New York were found in the 1938 charter revisions, which had codified both the geographic centralization and the functional decentralization of government authority.[2] Geographic centralization had altered political interactions in the city by weakening the city council, with its traditional community base, and strengthening the executive branch, with its more modernist, cosmopolitan perspective. Coterminously, functional decentralization had redefined the policy emphasis of city government by weakening the impact of generalists and enhancing the influence of specialists and professionals. As a result, in the post-LaGuardia years, the reform regime, with its governing coalition in relatively insulated "downtown" administrative agencies, had achieved institutional preeminence in city government.

To fully understand the manner and implications of reform consolidation, however, it is necessary to examine the evolution of political interactions resulting from reform government's formal rules and informal norms. Unlike the compatible and mutually supportive geographic-functional balance inherent in machine politics, reform incorporated a contradictory political dynamic. On the one hand, geographic centralization of authority, a centripetal political strategy focused on citywide concerns, led to the creation of a strong executive. On the other hand, functional decentralization, a centrifugal force emphasizing expertise, promoted the development of politically insulated bureaucracies as the institutional channels for increased specialization. As the reform regime matured, its centrifugal forces overwhelmed its centripetal tendencies.

The ascendance of specialization over centralization in New York's reform regime was a function of several interrelated factors. First, reform-sponsored legal mandates, including the 1938 charter revisions, codified in detail specialization and professionalism within city government. Second, as specialization and professionalism made expertise a defining institutional value in the reform city, public policy increasingly reflected the influence of city agencies, which, given their bureaucratic organization, most directly embodied this value. Third, the policy influence of the bureaucratic agencies was enhanced even further by their interactions with issue-specific interest groups. All three factors acted to diminish central control over city agencies and their interest group allies as the reform regime matured.

Agency autonomy in New York was codified by the 1938 charter revisions and by civil service regulations encouraging professional administration of city government. The 1938 charter specified the professional credentials for deputy commissioners in several city agencies, including the Departments of Finance and Housing. The charter also required that members of the City Planning Commission be appointed by the mayor for eight-year overlapping terms and be removable only for cause. Such a stipulation, characterized by Sayre and Kaufman as "a coup d'état by the planners," ensured relative autonomy on land-use issues for Planning Commission members (1960, 372).

By the 1950s, regulations adopted pursuant to civil service laws had insulated more than three-quarters of city workers in New York from direct political control. Moreover, the reach of competitive positions, that is, positions protected by civil service, extended even to policy-making slots in some city agencies. Bureau chiefs, for example, could only be appointed in some agencies from lists of eligibles composed of upper-level agency personnel, thereby ensuring bureaucrats' internal control over organizational advancement within these agencies. In the reform city, administrative advancement was reserved for those with organizational rather than party loyalty. As Theodore Lowi noted about this period in New York City history, "it is the exceptional party leader whose influence at City Hall continues for long after an election, and even then such influence is limited to a certain few agencies" (1964, 121).

In a modern polity, the expertise arising from specialization and professionalism often structures decision situations. In a stark characterization of this process, Max Weber wrote: "Under normal conditions, the power position of a fully developed bureaucracy is always overtowering. The 'political master' finds himself in the position of the 'dilettante' who stands opposite the 'expert,' facing the trained official who stands within the management of administration" (Weber, quoted in Gerth and Wright 1946, 232). This imbalance is particularly acute given the fact that most professional politician–bureaucrat interactions occur on the bureaucrat's "home turf." Political leaders seek out bureaucrats whose specialities lie in the areas of immediate concern. Consequently, in the great majority of their interactions, bureaucrats have a strategic information advantage over politicians.

The institutionalization of specialization in the reformed city was also bolstered by the political relationships city agencies developed with the city's interest groups. "It is essential to every agency's power position to have the support of attentive groups whose attachment is grounded on an enduring tie. The groups an agency provides tangible benefits to are the most natural basis of such political support, and it is with these interest groups that agencies ordinarily establish the firmest alliances" (Rourke 1976, 46). In their analysis of agency–group relationships in New York, Sayre and Kaufman point out that city bureaucracies sought alliances with a variety of external forces, including organized state bureaucracies and bureaucracies representing other local governments, labor unions, the organized professions, the communications media, and occasionally even party leaders (1960, 407–10). Such agency–group relationships were defined by an emphasis on functional concerns and were based on mutually beneficial interactions. For the interest group, the relationship provided a point of access to government policy; for the agency, the relationship offered one more source of political insulation from central-city control.

As a consequence of these interactions, interest groups became important alternatives to the political party's geographically based access to city government. In analyzing the relative importance of professional groups in the selection of officials for policy-making positions, Lowi noted: "That professional groups compare extremely favorably to the party is to be expected since these groups are virtually organized around skill. . . . By and large they remain insulated from the party and, in the context of Cabinet appointments, competitive with the party" (1964, 117).

The mutual benefits evident in agency–group alliances in the city were reflected in other reform-era interactions. Interest groups in New York also developed mutually supportive relationships with the public authorities created by state legislation. "Public authorities are corporate subsidiaries of government, each established by legislative statute or charter to operate to some extent outside the regular structure of executive departments, usually, but not always, to finance, construct, or operate revenue-producing enterprises" (Walsh 1990, 197). Generally speaking, such authorities have responsibility for either transportation, commerce and development, or finance (Henderson 1989). Structurally, public authorities are classically reform institutions in that their boards are composed largely of professionals insulated from direct political control by an appointment process that affords them fixed and usually overlapping terms. The increasing number and variety of public authorities in the reform city further decentralized government functionally and made policy coordination even more difficult.

As Annmarie Hauck Walsh notes, however, "removing agencies from the traditional electoral structure does not end their involvement in the essence of politics, for decisions by their managers affect the stakes of politics: who gains and who loses" (1990, 196). Indeed, in the reform city, the interests coalescing around these authorities understood fully the stakes involved in their policy decisions. Financial interests, particularly bondholders or underwriters of authority debt, were quite interested in the decisions of the Port Authority of New York and New Jersey and the Triborough Bridge and Tunnel Authority. Developers and contractors were equally concerned with the policies pursued by the New York City Housing Authority. Such interest group–public authority coalitions, like those evident in interest group–city agency coalitions, saw the public good in quite specific and decidedly functional terms.

As the reform city evolved, then, there was the absence of an integrative force to tie the various agencies into a coherent whole, even with the increase in executive power arising from reform's centralization of government structure. The city became "well run but ungovernable" (Yates 1977). Reform's consolidation in New York was evident in the increased influence of issue-specific policy coalitions, composed of downtown bureaucratic agencies and their interest group allies, and the concomitant decrease in the influence of more generalist forces within city government. The capacity of city executives to coordinate administration policy is inversely related to the autonomy of line agencies. As Donald Haider noted, "The creation of additional 'elitelike' islands of power . . . reduced the ability of the overhead, centralizing forces to contain the separate islands of power" (1970, 135). Theodore Lowi, terming the policy coalitions built around bureaucratic agencies in the reform city "the new machines," characterized them as "relatively irresponsible structures of power" whose leadership was "not readily subject to the controls of higher authority" (1968, 8). Therefore, even the reemergence of Democratic mayors and a reinvigorated Tammany leadership did not signal the end of reform governance in New York because the regime's base was not controllable from the top.

Moreover, there is some question of just how much the newly empowered Democrats wanted to reorder reform governance even if they could. By the 1950s, the Democratic party in the city had changed markedly since the days of machine dominance under Tammany Hall. More than ever in its history, the party was a loose coalition of five diverse county organizations.[3] An internal reform movement had further fractured the party system in the city (Wade 1990). In many districts, insurgent factions of the Democratic party organized their own political clubs and contested with the regulars in primary elections. During the 1950s, the insurgents within the Democratic party, inspired in part by the emergence of Adlai Stevenson as a national Democratic force, made continual gains in district primary elections (Costikyan 1966). In addition to the pressure from intraparty reformers, the ever-present fear of a reemerging fusion movement uniting Republicans, Liberals, and disaffected reform Democrats served to temper the politics of regular Democrats.

Given the constraints of law as well as the system of formal and informal political interactions that had developed under reform in New York, the Democratic party was forced to adjust to reform values rather than contest them. Unlike the era of machine dominance, when party leaders structured the political game, reformers now defined the rules, and party officials had to adapt to a hostile political environment. The Democratic party's adaptation efforts were numerous. Carmine DeSapio's reign as New York County leader from 1949 to 1961 was marked by a consistent effort to sanitize party operations.[4] "By any accounting, Tammany had become under DeSapio the best publicized and least corrupt political machine New York City had ever seen" (Connable and Silberfarb 1967, 300). For example, reform's emphasis on professionalism had changed the Democratic party's recruitment and appointment patterns for city positions. Appointment based on merit had largely replaced patronage hiring from the city's lower-income neighborhoods, and this became evident in the type of individuals who were appointed city commissioners. Prior to LaGuardia's administration, 32 percent of the commissioners appointed by Democratic mayors were from lower-income groups. However, in the post-LaGuardia era, only 18 percent of Democratic commissioner appointments were from these groups (Lowi 1964, 113).

Democratic party officials "defused opposition by accommodating its major organized interests" (Shefter 1977, 103). Growth-oriented financial interests had unimpeded access to the city agencies and public authorities relevant to their land-use plans. Professionals in city agencies were free to increase their influence over bureaucratic decision rules impacting public policy in their areas of specialization. Municipal employees, protected by unchallenged civil service regulations, were left alone and at times were encouraged to organize for increased salaries and job-related benefits.

In 1961, in an election characterized by Lowi as "one of the most significant . . . in American urban history," Democratic party reformers engineered a major coup, which removed even the formal appearances of machine leadership from the party (1968, 11). Incumbent Mayor Robert Wagner decided to seek reelection to a third term by rejecting DeSapio's leadership and embracing a new political coalition based primarily on the support of organized city workers and the insurgent factions of the party. Wagner's decision completed the transformation of the Democratic party in the post-LaGuardia years. During the 1961 campaign, Wagner became "possibly the first mayor in the country to organize the bureaucracy as a political force" (Morris 1980, 17). In the election, Wagner was returned to office with the backing of party reformers and city workers. As a result, "most of the larger city bureaucracies had political representation in the inner core of the new administration" (Eichenthal 1990, 70). Moreover, twenty-eight of Manhattan's thirty-three districts elected reformers as district leaders. Within the New York County Democratic Committee, "reform had triumphed, and the bosses were dead" (Costikyan 1966, 29).

In 1965, the city witnessed what appeared at first to be an even more fundamental reform victory with the election of John Lindsay as mayor. Lindsay, a progressive Republican member of Congress from the "silk-stocking" district on Manhattan's East Side, ran and won a classic fusion campaign uniting the Republican and Liberal parties to defeat the Brooklyn organization's candidate, Democrat Abraham Beame. Ironically, Lindsay, the quintessential reform candidate, was to be the mayor whose search for ways to cope with the urban crisis as well as for a personal political base led him to a focus on community politics that encouraged the postreform reaction in New York. As mayor, Lindsay presided over the political destabilization of reform governance and the emergence of a viable postreform alternative in New York City.

Wagner's and Lindsay's approaches to the Great Society's poverty programs provide clear examples of their diverse political styles and of the evolution toward postreform values under Lindsay.[5] As noted in chapter three, the War on Poverty and the Model Cities Program included federal mandates for resident participation in community-based organizations. As borough president of Manhattan, Wagner had not been unfriendly to the general idea of community involvement in city politics. Indeed, while in that office, he had supported the development of a boroughwide community planning board system. As mayor, however, Wagner resisted federal pressures for decentralization and maintained tight central-city control over poverty funds. Charles Morris argues that federal proposals for political decentralization were both philosophically and politically problematic for Wagner. "Radical community organization was alien to

Wagner's concept of government, and community control was antithetical to his instinct for controlling patronage" (Morris 1980, 62). Wagner was one of the many mayors to appear before the House of Representatives in 1965, arguing that federal funds should be channeled to cities through elected officials and not directly to community-based groups.

To maintain control of the poverty program, Wagner put his long-time ally, City Council President Paul Screvane, in charge of the Council Against Poverty, the city's clearinghouse agency for federal poverty programs. The mayor's centralized approach resulted in Washington officials rejecting several city-sponsored funding proposals because the city's poverty agencies did not include sufficient representation of the poor (David 1971). Wagner's approach to the poverty program also generated open hostility from African-American community activists, notably Congressman Adam Clayton Powell of Harlem. Community-based youth groups, such as Harlem Youth Opportunities Unlimited (HARYOU), Mobilization for Youth (MFY) on the Lower East Side of Manhattan, and Youth in Action in Brooklyn's Bedford-Stuyvesant, protested Wagner's centralized control of poverty funds and demanded increased community control of antipoverty programs. "In 1963 and 1964, New York City Hall municipal government was increasingly defined by MFY as the enemy" (Moynihan 1970, 113).

Mayor Wagner responded to the increasing community-based and federal pressures for community participation and local representation within the city's Community Action Program (CAP) by increasing the proportion of community representatives from poor neighborhoods within the city's CAP. In 1965, the New York City Council Against Poverty was enlarged to one hundred members, one-third of whom were required to be representatives of the poor. However, it was clear that neither Wagner nor Screvane was comfortable with the community emphasis of the federal program. "We have been in the process over the past few years of doling out pieces of the City of New York to various groups such as Mobilization for Youth, HARYOU-ACT, Youth in Action. . . . I am not confident at all that we would be able to solve all the problems we have with this kind of approach" (Screvane, quoted in Savitch 1990, 248). Joseph Viteritti summarizes the Wagner administration's approach: "Under Mayor Wagner the Community Action Program was administered in a way which protected the interests of the established power structure of the city. While some participation of the poor was allowed, the program itself concentrated on the improvement of service delivery rather than on the promotion of political action" (1979, 73).

It was John Lindsay who acted to decentralize New York City's poverty program. By unifying the city's social service programs within one "super-agency," the Human Resources Administration, Lindsay attempted to maintain some degree of centralized control over the antipoverty program. However, unlike Wagner, Lindsay radically reformulated the city's Community Action Program: He recast the city's Council Against Poverty so that one-half of the members would be representatives of the poor; he expanded the size of the poverty program from sixteen to twenty-six districts, encompassing a total population of over three million people; and he instituted the practice of selecting local board members through community elections. Under Lindsay, then, the poverty program was decentralized to the community level, thereby addressing the demands of black community activists for participation in programmatic decision making. As H.V. Savitch concludes concerning Lindsay's efforts: "The new structure for poverty was the modus operandi for Lindsay's two terms in City Hall. That structure served two ends: first, the desire to motivate the poor and bring them into power and second, the hope of building a new coalition of blacks, Latinos, and white liberals" (1990, 250).

If Lindsay's response to the War on Poverty's mandates for community participation indicated a commitment to postreform values, the implications of his actions regarding the Model Cities Program were less clear. Of the 150 Model Cities Programs in the nation, 3 were set up in New York: 1 in the South Bronx, 1 in Harlem, and a third in Bedford-Stuyvesant. As discussed in the previous chapter, the Model Cities Program allowed mayors broad discretion in determining the nature and the extent of community involvement. Mayor Lindsay responded initially by decentralizing the administration of New York's Model Cities Program. He divided program responsibilities fairly evenly between a central-city Model Cities Committee and three community-based local policy committees (LPCs). The LPCs were empowered to determine the program priorities for their communities. In 1970, however, in reaction to increasingly bitter intracommunity political conflicts, Lindsay backed away from extensive community participation in Model Cities. He appointed a citywide Model Cities coordinator with ultimate responsibility for the program in New York. In turn, the coordinator appointed an assistant administrator responsible for the day-to-day management of each of the city's three LPCs. The changes significantly reduced the role of community forces within the Model Cities Program in New York.

Lindsay's antipoverty policies reflected the persistent tensions in his administration between the postreform pressures for decentralization and the values of reform governance. Lindsay sought to counter bureaucratic inertia by creating superagencies, a functionally focused reform concept, and by encouraging community-based organizing, a decentralizing postreform concept. In the end, pressured by intense political forces and conflicts that threatened to destabilize the city (one of which was the furor over community school boards, discussed later in this chapter), Lindsay became a hesitant proponent of decentralization. But, hesitant or not, it was the Lindsay administration that did the most to internally legitimize postreform values in New York City.

The period of reform consolidation in New York, characterized by the ascendance of semiautonomus administrative agencies that were staffed by area-specific professionals and allied with equally area-specific interest groups, produced two fundamental changes in city governance. First, as reformers codified the change from geographic to functional representation, the relationship of citizens to city government changed. Second, as the centrifugal pressures of functional decentralization overwhelmed the centripetal force of geographic centralization, government policy-making became increasingly fragmented.

By changing the relationship of citizen to government, reform consolidation also altered the group balance in cities. Under the machine, the citizen was a consumer–producer (voter) within a political community; under reform, the citizen was merely a consumer within an administrative apparatus. This had particularly noteworthy effects on lower-income groups, which relate to government bureaucracies differently than most other groups. Eugene Lewis's (1977) distinction between a *constituent* relationship and a *client* relationship with bureaucratic agencies is instructive in this regard. Lewis describes a constituent group as one whose relationship with a city agency is in some way reciprocal; the group and the agency are interdependently connected. Such a relationship is clearly exemplified by the interaction between business interests and city economic development agencies. The client, on the other hand, is dependent on the agency for some necessary service, but there exists no reciprocity in the relationship. The relationship of lower-income groups, particularly minority poor, to city social agencies is an example of a client relationship. Charles Hampden-Turner argues that in its relationships with lower-income clients, "the organization always has the strength to impose its own requirements upon the applicant" (1974, 140).

Consequently, the functional decentralization inherent in reform devalued many interests in the city while providing others an important, often decisive, role in policy-making. Indeed, public policy in New York was increasingly the province of functionally defined coalitions organized around city agencies and public authorities. City government was best characterized as a collection of downtown interests without a central policy focus except for its overall commitment to the reform values that kept these interests separated in the first place. Moreover, as elected officials seeking to bolster their own political bases incorporated new groups into the regime's governing coalition, reform's fragmentation increased. When reform's increasingly fragmented political sphere was coupled with economic slowdown, the regime evolved from pluralist to interest group liberal politics.

It was during this period of reform consolidation that the postreform revolt took shape in New York. As in many cities across the country, postreform pressures on city governments were evident in grass-roots community organizing, particularly among urban blacks. In New York, however, postreform pressures were especially salient because of the Lindsay administration's policy and political commitment to decentralization. As Jewel Bellush suggests, "The most extensive community participatory effort took place in New York City. A host of community-based systems was created and placed alongside traditional institutions . . ." (1990, 304). Each element of early postreform in New York, grass-roots mobilization and city-sponsored decentralization experiments, forms a significant part of the backdrop to the creation of the community board system in the city.

Community Organizing and Postreform Politics in New York

Community organizing in New York City incorporated the range of postreform options reviewed in chapter three. Community self-help groups arose to address neighborhood service deficiencies by developing local alternatives or supplements to central-city service priorities. Community activist organizations emerged to block central-city redevelopment plans and to protest inadequate service delivery. In several New York neighborhoods, notably Brooklyn's Bedford-Stuyvesant, community development corporations combined local economic and political concerns under one organizational umbrella. In particular, African-American neighborhoods throughout New York were sites for local political activism founded on notions of racial pride and community control.

Community Self-Help Groups

Community self-help groups are associations of local residents mobilized to address specific community concerns. To the extent that such organizations are exclusively community-focused and highly participatory, they can be classified as ideologically pure examples of postreform politics. At their most basic political level, these groups are ad hoc ventures focused on one community problem, as, for example, when residents organize to secure a traffic light at a dangerous intersection. At a more developed political level, self-help groups attempt to broaden and institutionalize their efforts within a community by meeting regularly and monitoring a range of local concerns. Lastly, at their most developed political level, these groups establish ongoing programs such as crime patrols, park maintenance, and sweat-equity housing improvement projects.

Self-help groups provided early models for community organization and leadership development (Yates 1973). By mobilizing and directing residents' efforts and energies around strictly local problems, they supplemented, circumvented, or even countered central-city policy and service priorities for their communities. Considered individually, each community self-help group was a minor problem for reform governments; considered collectively, they represented a major threat to the reform status quo.

Community self-help groups were quite evident in New York City. One observer estimated that during the early postreform period, more than fifteen thousand block associations, at least two dozen community-based direct-action groups, and more than one thousand organizations involved with neighborhood housing issues were organized within the city (Perlman 1982, 28). Another study of New York noted: "By 1970, block associations existed throughout the city—in middle-class neighborhoods as well as poor ones" (Yates 1973, 36). There is evidence that at least some of these self-help organizations in New York had positive impacts on community life: they helped to secure local tenants' rights in disputes with landlords; they cleaned up and then beautified abandoned properties and garbage-strewn lots in several of the city's poorer neighborhoods; and they organized social projects such as summer youth programs for poor children (Yates 1973, 35–39).

The successes experienced by community self-help groups in New York were important for a number of reasons. From an immediate perspective, they represent concrete, beneficial changes in residents' quality of life in city neighborhoods. Moreover, success is an effect with discernible causes; understanding such causal connections is important to further empower self-help groups. From a longer-term view, the success experienced by self-help groups in the city reinforced the act of local participation and made it more likely that neighborhood residents maintained their involvement in city politics.

Community Political Groups

Other community activist groups in New York adopted more confrontational political strategies than self-help groups and directly challenged the policies of the city's reform regime. Such confrontational strategies were designed to counteract the disenfranchisement of community residents qua community residents in reformed cities by reasserting a particular community's input on the urban policy agenda. Many of these political activist groups in New York contested central-city land-use plans for their communities, particularly those involving urban renewal projects (Fisher 1984; Havelick and Kwartler 1982; Goodman 1971). For example, Francis Piven chronicles the struggle of Manhattan's Cooper Union neighborhood to fight an urban-renewal designation. She shows how persistent opposition within the Cooper Union community delayed the implementation of the original urban-renewal plan for over ten years (Piven 1972).

Other groups, such as the Congress of Racial Equality (CORE) in Brooklyn and the East Harlem Tenant's Council in Manhattan, organized rent strikes within their communities: "Activists of various persuasions moved in to canvass the tenements, blending the language of the building codes with the language of direct action. In a short time some 500 buildings were on strike" (Piven and Cloward 1972, 151). Whereas some groups confronted landlords, including the city, directly in rent strikes, others organized and implemented housing rehabilitation projects in lower-income neighborhoods of New York City (Olstein 1982).

Still other community activists in New York concentrated on the apparent inability of reform professionals to either address the causes or mitigate the effects of the urban social pathologies impacting their neighborhoods. The creation of Mobilization for Youth (MFY) on the Lower East Side represented that Manhattan community's effort to combat juvenile delinquency. MFY, which became a model for later federal community organizing efforts, was an early attempt to employ community-based agencies to coordinate a variety of programs dealing with the problems experienced by lower-income youth. On one level, MFY organized community residents and sought federal funding to support occupational, educational, and recreational opportunities for teenagers on the Lower East Side (Brager and Purcell 1967, 17–26; Moynihan 1970, 43–59). On another level, however, MFY was itself a community activist organization. In fulfilling their initial service function, full-time MFY staffers often found themselves in conflict with political-activist community organizers. As the pressures for local activism mounted, MFY increasingly adopted a more confrontational posture with city agencies. In this latter role, MFY evolved from an organization addressing individual residents' problems with city bureaucracies to one seeking to represent the community's collective interests in direct confrontation with city agencies (Piven and Cloward 1971, 290–95).

In other policy areas, grass-roots community organizing in New York presaged citywide and even national political movements. As mentioned above, MFY became the model for the Community Action Program of the War on Poverty. Charles Morris traced the origins of the welfare rights movement in New York City to community organizing efforts in the East New York section of Brooklyn in 1964 (1980, 69). John Theobald reported how CORE, the Council Against Poverty, and other community groups developed a People's Board of Education in 1967 in Brooklyn's Ocean Hill–Brownsville school district, which formed the organizational base for community control of the district's schools during New York's school decentralization experiment (1970, 189). George James argued that "disenchantment with the establishment" and demands for community participation regarding health care issues in New York as a whole was strongest in lower-income areas where "the ethnic composition of the population [was] rapidly changing and community traditions [were] few" (1970, 225).

During this period, the postreform rhetoric in New York was often pointed, as minority activists organized to contest what they perceived as the paternalism and colonial mentality of police, teachers, and welfare workers. In 1961, the city government awarded a contract to the Jewish Board of Guardians to develop a youth program in Harlem. In response, representatives of civic and church groups in that black community protested the "social work colonialism" of the project and "insisted that any program involving Harlem youth should include those agencies and groups within the community responsible for ongoing work with the youth" (Day 1987, 12). Using federal assistance from the President's Committee on Juvenile Delinquency, this community coalition subsequently organized Harlem Youth Opportunities Unlimited (HARYOU).[6]

One of HARYOU's founding principles was that a deprived community was capable of internally unifying its residents to overcome diversity and develop community-based opportunities for its youth. By establishing neighborhood boards to act as local service centers and the Community Action Institute to organize residents and to research community problems, HARYOU acted on its principles. However, internal divisions within the organization hindered the full realization of its aims. Political conflicts developed between the professionals hired under federal grants and community residents over program priorities and organization strategies. As discussed in chapter three, such intraorganizational conflicts were not uncommon in postreform organizations and often resulted in diminished resident participation within these groups. In the HARYOU case, these somewhat typical divisions were reinforced by other more overtly political conflicts. Organizational conflict between Congressman Adam Clayton Powell, a powerful political figure in Harlem, and Kenneth Clark, a professional educator and a well-respected social scientist, eventually resulted in Clark's departure from the organization and the merger of HARYOU with Powell's Associated Community Teams (ACT). Following the merger, HARYOU-ACT became more a tool serving Powell's political interests than a community activist group. Nevertheless, in its origins, HARYOU was a classic example of race-conscious community organizing.

Community Development Corporations

Grass-roots activist groups were not the only manifestations of indigenous community organizing in New York City. Community development corporations (CDCs), operating under a more broadly defined but nevertheless essentially postreform framework, were also evident in the city. CDCs have been characterized in a variety of ways. A CDC "operated programs aimed at both immediate relief of severe social and economic disadvantages and eventual restoration of its community" (Ford Foundation 1973, 5). Another characterization compares CDCs with private corporations, noting one major distinction: "Their [CDCs'] stated objective is not the enrichment of private stockholders but the enrichment of the people of poor neighborhoods" (Faux 1971, 27). Still another characterization defined CDCs as "permanent local institutions, owned and operated by the local community, in and through which, the local community decides and determines its own destiny" (quoted in Hampden-Turner 1974, 110–11). For our purposes, CDCs are defined as community-based organizations that use political empowerment to encourage the economic development of their communities.

Because CDCs emphasize both the economic development and the political empowerment of their communities, they are classic practitioners of community-integrative postreform politics. As economic organizations, CDCs proceed on the assumption that even poor communities include substantial collective wealth, which is continually drained through redistribution to "outsiders." CDCs seek to enhance a community's financial base by encouraging intracommunity capital circulation. However, to initiate the kind of economic development projects in lower-income neighborhoods that encourage intracommunity capital circulation requires outside assistance. To secure such assistance, CDCs, in their role as political organizations, must employ integrative strategies linking them to private-sector and government sources of support (Pecorella 1985). In a report on the Greater Jamaica Development Corporation, which sought to revitalize a deteriorating Queens neighborhood in the 1960s, Barry Jacobs chronicles the classic integrative approach adopted by that CDC in New York City (1982, 52–54).

CDCs were designed to slow the flow of capital out of the community, increase the resources coming into the community, and encourage the intracommunity exchange of wealth. The theory is simple: If residents owned the housing and commercial establishments serving a particular community, then the circulation of local wealth in rents and retail purchases would be more narrowly focused and more likely to impact positively on the community as a whole. "The objective of economic power in the community development effort . . . is such that the poor community can ultimately achieve a favorable economic base of its own, for all the residents of the community" (Blaustein 1970, 69). Although the end may be community-based, the means to that end must be interactive.

As political entities, CDCs were intended to do more than be conduits for outside economic assistance. They were designed to represent the interests and policy priorities of increasingly self-sufficient communities. They were organized to help develop community economic power and then to interact politically with organizations in the larger society from a position of economic viability (Pecorella 1985). In short, they are classic operational manifestations of black power and its idea of collective integration.

The Bedford-Stuyvesant Restoration Corporation in New York was one of the earlier and better-known CDCs in the nation. Indeed, it "became the national model for community-based economic development" (Gibbs 1982, 3). For more than five decades (1940–1992), Bedford-Stuyvesant has been one of the poorest communities in New York City. It is an area of approximately four hundred blocks in central Brooklyn containing more than 250,000 people.[7] Over 90 percent of the residents are African-American, with the remaining population largely Latino. Bedford-Stuyvestant has all the problems associated with poor urban communities, including high rates of poverty, large numbers of families living on fixed incomes, substandard housing, and disturbingly high crime, school dropout, and infant-mortality rates.

In an attempt to construct a community-based approach to these problems, a coalition, including existing community activist associations such as the Central Brooklyn Coordinating Council, professional institutions such as Pratt Institute's Urban Planning Department, local business interests, and Senator Robert Kennedy, established the Bedford-Stuyvesant Restoration Corporation in 1966. In a speech announcing the project, Kennedy made its purpose clear: "What is given or granted can be taken away and what is begged can be refused. But what is earned and kept is inalienable, and what you do for yourselves and your children can never be taken away" (quoted in Gifford 1970, 427). The Bedford-Stuyvesant Restoration Corporation was intended to address community priorities, assist in community economic development, and be the coordinator for community interactions with the larger society. The corporation was not intended as an experiment in community control but rather was "designed to serve as a conduit for government and private funds aimed at the neighborhood" (Gifford 1970, 427).

Early on, corporation leaders chose efficiency of operation over mass-based participation. Reflecting the values of the center-city agencies, federal bureaucracies, and private-sector corporations with which it maintained constant interactions, the corporation opted to avoid the extensive commitment of time and effort necessitated by widespread resident participation in community organizations.[8] As a result, the Bedford-Stuyvesant Restoration Corporation has helped bring discernible physical improvements to the community by securing governmental and private-sector investment, but it has not encouraged political participation among area residents.

Community Organizing in New York: A Summary

The extent of grass-roots community activism in New York during the 1960s was impressive. Community self-help groups, political activist associations, and CDCs were all in evidence in the city, particularly in lower-income, minority neighborhoods. Coupled with the community associations spawned by federal social legislation, such widespread indigenous local organizing made the city a center of the postreform reaction.

The scope and intensity of the local activism aside, New York's enormous size made it difficult for community-based organizations to capture the attention of city officials. Jane Jacobs addressed this problem of urban and community size differentials in her early proposal for the creation of local administrative districts in cities. She argued that these districts must be small enough to be representative but large enough to be politically viable (1961, 405–26). Community-based grass-roots organizations in New York were generally not large enough to exercise meaningful influence over city policymakers. Daniel Moynihan spoke to this point when analyzing the overall policy impact of MFY:

> In a city of eight million, Mobilization for Youth represented an area of 100,000 persons and was actively concerned with only a third of these. Almost all the principal "institutions" that affected the residents of the Lower East Side—the school system, the labor market, the housing, the police force—were at least city-wide in their organization and scope, and most had state and national ties. A neighborhood would sense little leverage in such situations. (1970, 108)

Despite their lack of immediate policy impact, grass-roots community organizations in New York were important because of their long-term political and organizational legacy. Their very existence spoke to what reform government in New York was *not* accomplishing and, given the value orientation of reformers, could not accomplish—the representation of community-based interests on the city's policy agenda. Their successes, however minor they might appear within the larger context of New York politics, convinced thousands of community activists that they could indeed "fight city hall." Moreover, community organizations provided vehicles for the emergence of the indigenous leadership so necessary for the eventual development of the postreform alternative in New York. In discussing community action in New York, Janice Perlman contends that "nowhere else is there such attention to the slow process of building people's capacities for political action by building their self-esteem, their ability to see their personal struggles within the larger context of their lives, and their feel for community participation" (1982, 34).

City-Sponsored Decentralization Experiments

Although the concept of community empowerment is most closely associated with the postrefrom era, there is a tradition of community involvement in New York that is independent of the Tammany machine and dates back to the consolidation of the "greater city" in 1898. Under the 1898 charter, local improvement boards were established in twenty-four districts in the city (Viteritti and Pecorella 1987, 15–17). These local boards, composed of the borough presidents and the members of the municipal assembly residing within the respective districts, had two primary responsibilities: they rendered advice regarding proposals for public improvements to be paid for by assessments before they were submitted to the city assembly and to the Board of Public Improvements, and they heard complaints from residents concerning service-delivery problems. However, their ability to respond to these complaints was severely limited.

New York City's early experiences with local improvement boards influenced community politics in the city seven decades later. The boards established the legitimacy of a community-based advisory role in city policy-making by separating that responsibility from an exclusive identification with machine politics. Moreover, they set the precedent for borough presidents having an important role in community politics.

Local improvement boards aside, it was in the 1960s and 1970s that Mayor John Lindsay experimented with the largest number and greatest variety of community-empowerment programs in the city's history. On the one hand, these programs were the administration's policy responses to postreform demands for decentralization. On the other, they helped a fusion mayor establish an independent political base. This section of chapter four examines two such experiments: school decentralization and the mayor's Office of Neighborhood Government.[9] They were selected for two reasons. First, whereas the former represents an effort at community control, the latter is a classic example of administrative decentralization. Second, each experiment directly influenced the development of the city's community board system.

Community Control and School Decentralization

The school decentralization experiments of the 1960s in cities like Detroit, New York, and Washington, D.C., were, in their emphasis on community control and parental participation in education, clear examples of postreform ideals (Gittell 1967; Rogers 1968; Moore and Johnston 1971). Indeed, New York's 1967 demonstration school district experiment was arguably the city's only direct experience with community control. Although the experiment was limited to three school districts, community control of schools in New York generated more intense political conflict than any other attempt at community empowerment in the city's history, mostly because of the wide sweep of issues and the high stakes involved in urban education policy. As Moore and Johnston note, school decentralization "is one issue in an urban polity which touches all the other issues: race division, group population boundaries, . . . economic class divisions, fear and favor of mass participation in democracy, professionalism, . . . versus relevance in education, elitism versus pluralism—whether in an educational or political sense" (1971, 422).

Educational policy-making in New York had been centralized and professionalized decades before the emergence of the reform regime in the city. Indeed, education in New York served as a prototype for reform policies generally, as control over the schools was centralized geographically (in downtown Brooklyn) and decentralized functionally in a professional, bureaucratic agency. Since 1902, a central Board of Education and a Board of Examiners had, for all intents and purposes, controlled curriculum, budget, and personnel matters in the city's schools (Theobold 1970, 168–69). The centralized educational system, much like reform government institutions in general, was theoretically intended to replace "a particularistic 'private-regarding' ethos of immigrant life . . . with a more universalistic 'public-regarding' one of Protestant 'native' Americans" (Rogers and Chung 1983, 5). During the first half of the century, the central education bureaucracy established virtually total control over the city's school system while becoming increasingly insulated from external accountability.

By the 1960s, as a part of the overall postreform reaction, the pressures for decentralizing educational policy-making in New York City were growing. As with postreform pressures generally, they emanated from a variety of sources. A number of academic analysts criticized, sometimes in unusually harsh language, the central bureaucracy at the Board of Education (Gittell 1967; Rogers 1968). One study, terming the education bureaucracy "sick" and "incapable of reforming itself," concluded that it "is a system that is strangled in red tape; mired in inertia, incompetence, and corruption; insufficient; insulated from its clients and from outside institutions; and fragmented into power blocs" (Rogers, quoted in Surkin 1971, 409).

Another source of pressure for school decentralization arose from within the city's African-American communities. Few issues were as important to black power advocates as that of education. To those who considered the black community a victim of white colonial power, the school system was the first step in socializing minority children to their subsidiary roles. "The schools are being focused upon as all important to the fostering of the ethic of black pride and black self-determination since a people who seek their liberation from a colonial system must control what is being taught to their young" (Maynard 1970, 102). Indeed, it was the perception among many African-American and Latino parents that the school system had failed to educate their children, had institutionalized racism, and had been unresponsive to their demands that galvanized that population to demand community control of schools (Lyke 1970). "People—black people—want control over their schools for self-determination, for building of a strong self-image, for individual and community development, for restoration of confidence in education, for economic stability, for recognition and survival" (McCoy 1969, 171).

The arguments in favor of community control of education were classically postreform, both in their attacks on the existing educational system and in their participative alternatives; conversely, the arguments against local control were classically reform in their defense of professionalism and their rejection of the values inherent to community control. Moreover, the larger political context within which the experiment was debated, enacted, and eventually assessed was intensely conflictual. It included segregated neighborhood schools, racial differences between the providers and the recipients of educational services, the institutional nature of the service providers' political power, and the backdrop of black power as both a rallying cry and a social philosophy among service recipients. Consequently, community control of schools in New York was initiated within a highly charged social and political environment. "There were clearly several sets of goals—economic, political, community development, as well as education. And the threat the pursuit of them by community control advocates posed to groups already holding jobs and bureaucratic power soon helped to escalate the conflict over the issue that became citywide in scope and that *tore the city apart*" (Rogers and Chung 1983, 3; emphasis added).

The vast cultural and political separation between the professionals within the educational system and the community activists seeking access to that system is obvious in their writings. Attacking community control as "an ideology of separation" and a reaffirmation of segregation, Harold Pfautz wrote: "If a democratic polity is to be upheld, neither national nor local community institutions (least of all the schools) can be permitted to espouse a policy of segregation, nor can a minority collectively waive its right to free and equal participation in the common life" (1970, 39). Conversely, a report from Washington, D.C.,'s Adams-Morgan Community School argued: "The school should take its character from the nature of the people living in the community and from the children utilizing the school rather than rigidly defining itself as an institution accepting only those people who already fit into a set definition" (quoted in Fantini 1970, 49). As part of the official reaction to the academic critics of the central educational bureaucracy and to the black community's demands for community control, several city- and state-funded studies of the educational system were conducted. One of the most prominent, the Ford Foundation's Mayor's Advisory Panel on Decentralization of the New York City Schools (the Bundy Report), came out strongly in favor of increased involvement by center-city parents in educational decision making. Indeed, the report contended that community control of education in the center city could be modeled on that which existed in the nation's smaller cities and suburbs (Bundy 1967). The Bundy Report served as the basis for the creation of three demonstration school districts in New York in 1967.

A major difficulty with the school decentralization experiment in New York was that none of the parties involved—the United Federation of Teachers (UFT), administrators at the Board of Education, and community activists—agreed either on what decentralization meant or what the experiment implied for control of the schools. The UFT, whose own recognition in 1961 was the first major break in the Board of Education's monopoly control of education in the city, advocated decentralization in the abstract while fighting the particulars in court and in the media. The UFT feared that many of the professional protections they had secured over the years would be threatened by community control.[10] Reacting to the Bundy Report, for example, a UFT report noted: "Under the Bundy Report, charges could be brought against a tenured faculty member by a *community board of laymen with no professional experience*" (United Federation of Teachers 1967, as quoted in Surkin 1971; emphasis added). The UFT also expressed concerns that community control would empower local groups with no real interest in education; that it would increase racial segregation in the school system; and that it would prove inherently inefficient in practice (Rogers 1990, 150).

The Board of Education favored only the most qualified form of administrative decentralization, with the school boards acting as local executors of board policy. "The board spoke of involvement, not decision-making power or influence; decentralization, not community control" (Surkin 1971, 409). The board's refusal to provide operational meaning to its intentions only added to the confusion. "For whatever reason, the board simply never defined the powers of the local governing boards of the experimental districts" (*New York Civil Liberties Union Report*, cited in Surkin 1971, 410). Indeed, during the tense and often angry debates of 1966 and 1967, the board was reluctant to make its proposals for school decentralization public (Cronin 1973, 183–85). The board's indecision, reflecting either a strategy of delay, a situation of internal confusion, or both, meant that administrators lost the opportunity to help shape the initial community school decentralization proposal.

While the UFT battled to stop decentralization and the Board of Education proposed only a vague form of administrative decentralization, members of the three demonstration school districts, particularly those from the Ocean Hill–Brownsville district in Brooklyn, demanded community control of the schools in their districts. "The agenda of the leaders in the community-control of education movement was to transfer political power, not just from the staff at headquarters to those in the local district offices, but rather from the professional staff to elected lay or citizen boards at the local level" (Rogers 1990, 148). To the advocates, community control of education included the interrelated demands for local control of district boards, accountability of educators to the local boards, and the overall debureaucratization of the educational system in the city (Seeley 1981).

The demonstration school districts experiment resulted in a major setback for community control in New York. The ambiguity of purpose and the diversity of perspectives among the actors involved quickly transformed a difficult situation into an explosive problem. A series of strikes by the UFT, indecision by the central board and the mayor's office, and an adamant community-control stance by the local boards resulted in policy deadlock; meanwhile, militant and often intemperate statements by teachers and community activists resulted in the polarization of the African-American and Jewish communities in New York. The apparent relationship between local empowerment and unmitigated racial conflict placed the notion of community control outside the range of acceptable political options in the city.

In 1969, in reaction to the pressures for educational accountability from minority communities and the continuing crisis surrounding the demonstration school district experiment, the New York State Legislature passed and the governor signed into law a school decentralization bill. The legislation divided the city into thirty-one (eventually thirty-two) school districts and created a modified form of administrative decentralization. Under the law, the seven to fifteen members of each community school board are chosen in district elections by a system of preferential voting. The school boards, responsible for the elementary and junior high schools in their districts, have the power to appoint district superintendents and school administrators. However, the legislation left the authority over high schools and special education programs with the central Board of Education, which also retains critical budgetary and personnel powers.[11] The schools' chancellor, an appointee of the central board, has the authority to establish and enforce educational standards for all city schools.

The 1969 compromise legislation was more an attempt to quiet social turmoil than an effort to implement a system of community-based education. Indeed, early critics of the legislation argued that the local boards lacked important powers within their districts, particularly in relation to personnel decisions (Cronin 1973, 195). Several analysts were quite blunt in their initial assessments: "New York City is the prime example of how decentralization was implemented to prevent local control" (Fantini 1970, 48). Others noted that the proportional representation system for electing school board members favored organized educational interests, such as that of UFT members, at the expense of less organized parents and community activists (Rogers 1970).

However, other assessments, although not glowing, were less critical of the plan and less pessimistic concerning the future direction of community school boards. Although cognizant of the plan's limitations, Joseph Cronin viewed the community school boards as mechanisms capable of opening the educational process in New York. "The new boards offered additional outlets both for testing ideas and absorbing hostility and for more immediate action by policy-makers who if not fully responsible by statute increasingly seized the informal power to shape central school headquarters decisions" (1973, 196).

In the years since the 1969 legislation was enacted into law, school governance has remained a controversial issue in New York City. Because of the moderate form of decentralization provided in the legislation, the system has never had the full support of community-control advocates. Indeed, many of the original advocates of community control encouraged local boycotts of the first school board elections (Rogers 1990, 151). However, in recent years, the debates over the system are no longer framed in the kind of racial antagonism that existed at the outset (Viteritti and Pecorella 1987, 27–32).

There are two common conclusions in most analyses of school decentralization in New York: the decentralization created was limited in scope and the level of participation has been disappointing. On the former point, most analysts agree that the 1969 legislation resulted in a limited and highly constrained form of administrative decentralization (Rogers 1990 and 1977; Rogers and Chung 1983; State Charter Revision Commission [SCRC] 1974). The limitations on community involvement are particularly striking when they are considered within the context of the demands for community control that drove the early reformers. New York State legislators, wishing to avoid involvement with the intense racial, religious, and ethnic conflicts that had developed around the demonstration school district experiments, enacted broadly worded and quite ambiguous school decentralization legislation. Such legislative ambiguity provided the Board of Education with substantial implementation discretion. Because of internal resistance and bureaucratic battles, the board moved only hesitatingly to allocate responsibility to the local school boards and to provide the training and assistance necessary for them to carry out their responsibilities.

Limitations of policy formulation and implementation notwithstanding, some of the local school boards have proved adept at influencing education in their districts. In their summary comments to a case study of four school districts in the city, Rogers and Chung concluded: "A community school-district system has come into existence in New York City as a result of decentralization. It has provided for enough social peace, local-level flexibility, and openness so that schools can be more effectively responsive and accountable to their local constituencies" (1983, 207). Other observers have noted that in recent years student reading and mathematics scores have risen, although few cite decentralization as a primary causal factor (Viteritti and Pecorella 1987). Still others have concluded that the system has resulted in increased social peace in the schools (Rogers 1990).

On the second issue of participation, there is also broad agreement. Participation rates in school board elections have been embarrassingly low. Turnout in the seven school board elections that have taken place since 1970 has averaged about 10 percent (Viteritti and Pecorella 1987, 29); in 1989, turnout reached a new low of 6 percent (Rogers 1990, 158). Moreover, by 1987, nearly one-quarter of the candidates elected to local school boards were employees of the school system. There is some evidence that, despite the fact that minority representatives on the local school boards have increased since decentralization was enacted, local boards do not always reflect the interests of the parents or children of the school districts they represent (Viteritti 1983, 215–66).

More broadly considered, school decentralization in New York had negative implications for postreform values. Despite the limited mandates of the 1969 legislation and the relatively quiet evolution of the system since then, school politics is often associated with the turmoil in the three demonstration school districts, most notably the one in Ocean Hill–Brownsville. Accordingly, the lessons arising from school decentralization, particularly in the 1970s, when other community-power experiments were being considered, pointed to the dangers of community control. After the school experiments, the term *community control* incorporated visions of racial and religious conflict, confrontations between community residents and service providers, and the empowerment of radical elements of the black community. In general, then, the experience with school decentralization became a warning to city officials of what to avoid.

Administrative Decentralization and the Office of Neighborhood Government

While the political decentralization of the demonstration school districts was being transformed into the current system of modified administrative decentralization, alternative forms of decentralization were being explored in other policy areas. Mayor Lindsay's emphasis on community empowerment dated back to the beginning of his administration when he proposed that a system of little city halls be opened in communities throughout the city. The halls, which would be supported through local tax money, would act in an ombudsman role for the communities, theoretically overcoming bureaucratic red tape by referring feedback and complaints about city services directly to city officials. They were intended more as outreach efforts by the administration than as attempts at political or administrative decentralization.

Lindsay's plan for local city halls was defeated by a Democratic city council concerned that the mayor, having been elected on a fusion ticket, was attempting to overcome his lack of a party base in the city's neighborhoods by creating a series of political clubhouses throughout the city at public expense (Viteritti and Pecorella 1987, 19–20). Indeed, in other cities, little city halls had served the dual role of centers for community feedback about urban policy and service delivery and political bases for big-city mayors (Nordlinger 1972; Mudd 1984).

The Lindsay administration also experimented with the Urban Action Task Force (UATF), which was intended to act as the mayor's "eyes and ears" in inner-city neighborhoods where the potential for racial disorder and violence was particularly high. The UATF program represented an attempt to carry Lindsay's storefront campaign strategy into the governmental process (Gotterher 1975; Morris 1980, 74–80; Mudd 1984, 57–64). As was the case with the mayor's proposal for little city halls, the UATF was not intended as a decentralization experiment per se but more as an outreach effort by central-city administrators to establish lines of communication between city hall and leaders in the city's most volatile communities. At its peak, the UATF operated twenty-two community-based offices under the direction of administration officials. Despite its limited decentralization mandate, the UATF program succeeded in helping city officials identify community leaders, isolate specific community concerns, and avoid the kind of urban racial violence that plagued other cities during this period. Moreover, "the task forces had an indirect impact by pulling high-level departmental commissioners out of their downtown offices and into the communities, where they would be exposed to citizens' feelings about the operations of municipal service agencies" (Mudd 1984, 61).

One of the Lindsay administration's more comprehensive decentralization proposals involved the Office of Neighborhood Government (ONG), which was established as a mayoral agency in 1971. The evolution of the ONG concept, from proposal to enactment, reflected the changes in the social and political forces influencing postreform politics in New York in the early 1970s. The ONG program, which appeared in the mayor's 1970 *Plan for Neighborhood Government,* was envisioned initially as an experiment in political decentralization that would merge the existing community planning board system with the UATF. Under the mayor's original proposal, local boards, representing community planning districts (CPDs) of approximately 150,000 people and composed of volunteer members appointed jointly by the mayor, the borough presidents, and city councillors, would form the community base of the ONG program. In addition to a local board, each CPD would also have a full-time director, appointed by the mayor, who would chair a district service cabinet (DSC) composed of local service officials (Lindsay 1970).

The original ONG proposal emphasized political decentralization and included three innovations in New York City government. First, it gave the mayor a direct role in community-based governance in the city. Previously, representatives in community-level organizations in New York were either appointed by and hence accountable to borough presidents, as with the local improvement boards, or were largely ex officio members of community organizations. However, under the mayor's original ONG proposal, not only would some board members be mayoral appointees, but the community-based district managers would have equal status with deputy commissioners in city government. Second, the proposal emphasized the concept of community-based service coordination. Such a postreform notion, by acknowledging the relevance of recipient input into the service allocation process, was a direct challenge to the authority of the central-city administrative agencies created by reform governance. Third, by providing for the eventual election of local board members and therefore democratically institutionalizing the legitimacy of community-level officials, the original ONG proposal sought to establish, through a step-by-step process, a level of community government in the city.

The ONG program was but one of many proposals for sweeping political decentralization that were offered during the second Lindsay administration. During this period, several quite radical proposals for decentralization were suggested by more or less politically conventional groups in the city. A Special Committee of the Bar Association of New York City produced one of the most ambitious plans for political decentralization in city history (Viteritti and Pecorella 1987, 25–27). The Bar Association plan called for a two-tier governmental system in the city including a central-city government and forty community-level governments of approximately 250,000 people with wide-ranging discretionary authority over a variety of urban services. The city's expense budget would be allocated among the community-level governments on a formula basis that took into account each service function assumed by the district. For the short term, the Bar Association proposal emphasized administrative decentralization and community control of service allocation. In the long run, however, the proposal envisioned a system of political decentralization where each of the forty communities would elect a chief executive who would serve with a community-based legislature composed of representatives elected from community subdistricts of fewer than 20,000 residents. A similar plan for two-tiered government, based, however, on the existing councilmanic districts, was offered by a state study commission for New York City appointed by Governor Rockefeller (Costikyan and Lehman 1972).

However, despite the wide-ranging and sometimes radical proposals for decentralizing New York's government, the political context of the decentralization debate in New York had changed dramatically by the early 1970s. Three interrelated factors help explain why proposals for significant political decentralization were less viable than they had been in the late 1960s. First, the political backlash to the nature and the intensity of the conflict that had accompanied the early school decentralization experiments had hardened the opposition of organized service providers to such proposals and had made the white middle class wary of the concept of community control. Second, having been denied renomination by the Republican party in an open primary and having barely won reelection as the Liberal party's candidate in a three-way race in 1969, Mayor Lindsay's political position was, to say the least, precarious. The lack of effective mayoral support for radical decentralization proposals, including those generated within his own administration, was a consequence of Lindsay's difficult political position. Indeed, the mayor's *Plan for Neighborhood Government* could not be approved in the city council. Third, political feasibility issues aside, the increasing sophistication of the advocates of postreform politics led them to realize that systems of administrative decentralization must already be in place before effective political decentralization, let alone community control, could become a reality (Barton 1977; Farr, Liebman, and Wood 1972). In the absence of command decentralization among service-delivery bureaucracies and areal coordination of city services, attempts at political decentralization would be doomed to the frustration that arises from political stalemate, as community-based organizations sought to influence centralized administrative agencies over which they had little or no control. In a succinct characterization of the change in the political context of the period, Barton wrote, "The deemphasis on community representation resulted from the political, racial, and union confrontation over community control of schools . . . as well as the realization that administrative capacity was a necessary condition for any further political decentralization" (Barton et al. 1977, xv).

Given the negative political climate around political decentralization programs and the emphasis on command decentralization among postreform advocates, officials in the Lindsay administration began to focus on the politically less threatening notion of administrative decentralization. Moreover, administration officials sought ways to ease the tensions associated with even administrative decentralization by making the accountability of service providers to service recipients indirect, that is, by working around the type of direct provider–recipient relationships that had generated such tensions in the demonstration school districts. "The city administration certainly wanted to avoid any more shattering confrontations between the unions of municipal employees and community militants" (Rogers 1990, 160). Accordingly, the ONG program, which originally had been part of a comprehensive political decentralization proposal, evolved into a plan designed to avoid the political battles associated with community-control experiments. It focused on command decentralization of the service-delivery agencies while avoiding any call for widespread community participation. As redesigned, ONG was to be a program "for" the community; it was not designed to be "of" the community.

The modified ONG program included a number of components that remain part of the modern community board system in New York (Mudd 1984, 70–92; Heginbotham 1977; Lindsay 1970). First, it designated eight experimental community planning districts (CPDs) of approximately 125,000 people, which were to serve as the focal points of areal efforts to coordinate service delivery.[12] The CPDs were varied demographically so that white middle-class communities would be part of the experiment and it would not be focused, as was the school decentralization experiment, exclusively on minority areas (Rogers 1990, 162; Heginbotham and Andrews 1973). Second, the program provided that each CPD was to have a district manager, appointed by the mayor, who was to serve as the ONG community representative responsible for coordinating service delivery within that CPD. In that capacity, the district manager was empowered to chair a DSC composed of the field representatives of a number of city line agencies serving the district.[13] Third, the ONG program mandated that the service-delivery agencies included in the program designate field personnel to represent them at DSC meetings. In addition to this mandate for command decentralization, the ONG program required that the relevant city agencies conform their service districts, as much as possible, with the boundary lines defining the experimental CPDs. Fourth, the program gave to central ONG the responsibility to monitor compliance among relevant city administrators, to supervise the district managers and the DSC operations, and to evaluate periodically the program's effectiveness (Mudd 1984, 70–92; Heginbotham 1977, 30–31).

ONG represented a classic example of command decentralization with two important additional components. First, the ONG experiment moved beyond a focus on a single agency providing a specific service and attempted to coordinate the operations of a variety of city agencies providing a variety of services within a community district. As such, the ONG program was designed to be less of a community advocacy mechanism and more of a community-focused service device. "Unlike other efforts to improve the delivery of services in a given neighborhood by adding substantial new resources, this program is aimed at increasing the productivity of existing resources" (Lindsay 1977, 262). Moreover, by institutionalizing interactions among agency district service representatives and ONG's district managers, the program was intended to be a focal point for other community-based organizations. Accordingly, the ONG program would be able to avoid the isolation problems that had so hindered the operations of the federally sponsored Community Action Program Corporations and the local policy committees (LPCs). Second, by creating the post of mayorally appointed district manager to coordinate service delivery within each CPD, the ONG program sought to hold city service providers accountable to community-based recipients through the mayor's office without directly involving the recipients in the program. Such an indirect approach to accountability was designed to avoid the direct service provider–recipient clashes that had characterized the school decentralization experiments. "The ONG program essentially created a weak city manager for districts within a large city to improve service delivery by encouraging cooperation between local officials of existing departments within existing budgets" (Barton 1977, 9).

ONG had troubles from the very beginning. Although the mayor accepted the scaled-back version of the ONG program, his support was tepid. Lindsay's commitment to the program was not helped by an investigation of ONG's primary proponent and financial manager, Lewis Feldstein, who was charged by City Comptroller and mayoral hopeful Abraham Beame with misusing program funds. Although Feldstein was not indicted for wrongdoing, his decision to step down left ONG in the hands of a capable but inexperienced deputy, John Mudd. "At this point in time, the program was clearly a political liability for the mayor, and he made no serious attempt to rescue the office" (Heginbotham 1977, 37).

Aside from immediate political difficulties, the ONG program also experienced structural problems. Although the district managers' positions were comparable to that of deputy commissioners, their formal authority was only vaguely defined. Moreover, their status as mayoral appointees, which was intended to increase their political leverage in dealing with agency field representatives in the DSCs, was compromised by the lack of a strong political commitment to the program by the mayor. Any influence that the district managers did achieve under the ONG program was more a reflection of their individual political skills than of a formal allocation of authority. For example, the district manager of the Wakefield-Edenwald LPC "was active in resolving disputes between contending segments of the community, in defining and evolving solutions to problems that plagued citizen–bureaucrat relationships, and in developing mechanisms whereby functionally related service chiefs could better coordinate their programs . . ." (Heginbotham 1977, 38–39). However, his success was a consequence of personal skills and the fact that the Wakefield-Edenwald LPC was one of the middle-class communities selected for inclusion in the ONG experiment—an area where community resources matched community problems.

There were also substantial difficulties in getting the city service agencies included in the program to institute the degree of command decentralization necessary for meaningful coordination through the DSC. From an organizational perspective, decentralization within large-scale bureaucratic organizations has a variety of meanings and can assume a variety of forms. It can mean "organization by purpose, process, clientele, or place" (Simon 1946, 58). Attempting to employ several of these bases for organizational decentralization, particularly if they are structured around mandates for decentralization by place, would raise organizational costs substantially. Agencies such as the Police Department, which already had a geographic organizational focus, were able to make significant strides in effecting command decentralization; other agencies, particularly those involved with human services, proved either unwilling or unable to decentralize their operations effectively. Moreover, some of the superagencies, created during the first Lindsay administration, were asked to designate district-level chiefs to represent often widely diverse and organizationally fragmented departments. In evaluating the relative success of command decentralization under the ONG program, Rogers concluded: "The distinction may be made, then, between traditional, old-line agencies with single, homogeneous functions that had a vertical command structure and field operations readily adaptable to decentralization and newer ones with multiple functions that had not yet been consolidated internally, let alone decentralized" (1990, 163).

From a political perspective, command decentralization was also a problem. Despite the fact that the ONG program was not an attempt to create community control over service providers, or even to institute direct community-based oversight, the mandates for command decentralization ran counter to over thirty years of geographically centralized and functionally decentralized standard operating procedures. Limitations notwithstanding, therefore, the ONG program represented a direct postreform assault on the institutionalized prerogatives of reform bureaucracies. Accordingly, the ONG program guidelines for command decentralization "only scratched the surface of institutionalized bureaucratic power; . . . they did not crack through the existing lines of functional specialization or begin to deal with the role of the districts in budget and personnel administration" (Mudd 1984, 87).

Early Postreform in New York: A Summary

In the New York of the 1960s, as in many other American cities, the postreform reaction to what was by then consolidated reform governance took many forms. It manifested itself generally in grass-roots, community-based mobilization against the policy priorities of reform governments, particularly in the city's minority neighborhoods. Grass-roots organizing ranged from self-help groups, through political activist associations, to community development corporations. Federal War on Poverty and Model Cities efforts were also early encouragements to community organizing in the city. Considered individually, each of these early postreform efforts was lost in the crowd of the nation's largest city. As a collective phenomenon, however, these efforts helped focus on community problems, define community interests vis-à-vis the larger city, mobilize community residents, and develop indigenous local leaders.

New York also experienced a city government push toward postreform. John Lindsay, who in many ways exemplified the classic reform candidate, was, as mayor, the catalyst for several city-sponsored community-empowerment experiments that served to clarify the feasibility of postreform alternatives to the reform status quo. Chapter four focused on two of Lindsay's efforts in this regard: One, community control of schools, had decidedly negative impacts on social and political interactions in New York. As a consequence, it made community control an untenable political decentralization option while encouraging by default a community-integrative approach. The other, administrative decentralization through the Office of Neighborhood Government, showed sufficient promise to provide a viable postreform option for future reference.

Lindsay's support for community empowerment was an effort to address the urban crisis and to develop a constituency for a fusion mayor. Regardless of its rationale, however, it encouraged the beginning of the end of reform's governing coalition, which, by the early 1970s, had already been stretched too thin. The regime's centrifugal political forces, coupled with the economic downturn of the period, produced the fiscal crisis of 1975. Chapter five examines that crisis and focuses on its resultant fundamental political transformation in New York by analyzing the fiscal and geographic components of the postreform regime that emerged in its wake.

CHAPTER FIVE

Institutionalizing Postreform: Fiscal Control and Decentralization

During the twelve years encompassing Mayor Wagner's final term and Mayor Lindsay's two terms, New York's reform regime was buffeted by increasingly intense centrifugal pressures. Under conditions of fiscal stability, the functional decentralization inherent in reform governance enhanced the regime's political responsiveness as governing coalition interests secured direct access to decision makers unencumbered by any need to accommodate competing concerns. However, in the early 1960s, new service demands began to force an increase in the nature and extent of the reform regime's obligations and consequently in the breadth of its governing coalition. The broader scope of regime activities, not unexpected when local officials vie for power within a changing political environment, began to further weaken reform's centripetal forces. When the continuing political pressures were coupled with economic slowdown in the early 1970s, New York's reform regime faced a crisis.

Wagner's abandonment of the regular Democratic party in 1961 forced him to develop first an electoral and then a governing coalition built around municipal employees. Indeed, Wagner's third term politically codified the influence of organized service providers, already a major factor in many city agencies, within city hall itself. Lindsay's outsider status prompted him to develop a political base responsive to the demands of increasingly organized community-based service recipients. Moreover, when his initial confrontations with municipal unions resulted in several costly strikes and widespread instability, Lindsay also fully embraced service providers' demands. As a consequence, Lindsay's governing coalition expanded to include not only reform's traditional interests but a host of new forces organized territorially around the city (David and Kantor 1979).

By 1973, therefore, the reform regime had evolved from its initial phase under LaGuardia, through its pluralist stage in the late 1940s and 1950s, to its increasingly fragmented statist phase of the late 1960s. By the early 1970s, fragmentation, economic slowdown, and postreform pressures meant ever-increasing problems for the regime. By the time Abraham Beame, a product of the Brooklyn political organization, was sworn in as New York's 104th mayor, the city was on the verge of crisis. Despite initial efforts to control expenditures, meaningful cuts could not be made because "the participants who had gained entrance to the political system during Lindsay's reign—the public-employee unions and minorities—were not expelled" by Beame (Kantor and David 1983, 269). As in previous periods in the city's history, a fiscal crisis, brought on by the confluence of regime fragmentation and economic pressures, was responsible for fundamental changes in New York governance.

Chapter five examines the regime changes brought on by the fiscal crisis of 1975 by analyzing the political dynamics involved in New York's postreform regime. The analysis suggests that the transformation from a reform to a postreform regime altered urban governance in New York in two fundamental ways. First, the coordinative machinery created to manage the crisis during the retrenchment period was institutionalized in city government by the postreform regime. This machinery, controlled by forces outside of formal city government, was less visible in the years following the fiscal crisis but nevertheless continued to have a major impact on city policy. Indeed, in the early 1990s, these fiscally centralizing forces reemerged as active participants in the city's budget debates. Second, political legitimacy, a function of reform's welfare state since the LaGuardia years, became more complicated in the post-1975 period. The charter reforms of 1975 institutionalized geographic decentralization in New York through the community board system, which, in the postreform city, would share the "burden" of political legitimation with a now more centrally controlled welfare state.

Fiscal Crisis and the "Ungovernable City"

As mentioned earlier, the fiscal crisis that destabilized New York's reform regime was the consequence of a variety of economic and political pressures.[1] Long-term dislocations in key aspects of the city's manufacturing base, the increasing suburbanization of the city's middle-class tax base, and the burden of national and regional recessions contributed to an 11 percent decline in real city income and a 14 percent drop in city employment between 1960 and 1975 (Drennan 1982). Coterminously, the disaggregation of the reform regime, produced by the centrifugal expansion in the size and cost of the governing coalition, reinforced and worsened the economic problems. The burden of recessions, ever-increasing claims on city budgets, fiscal gimmickry, and the leveling off of federal aid produced a short-term city debt of over $5 billion by 1974 and a loss of investor confidence in the city's creditworthiness (Morris 1980, 223).

Given the history presented in previous chapters, neither the fiscal situation nor the immediate reaction of elected officials was surprising. In 1973, the Advisory Commission on Intergovernmental Relations (ACIR) warned that a number of urban governments, including New York, faced structural imbalances between revenues and expenditures (cited in Tabb 1977, 324–26). In that same year, commissions reporting to the New York State Legislature and to the mayor affirmed the ACIR conclusions in separate studies of New York's finances.[2] In 1974, an advisory committee appointed by the city comptroller concluded that dramatic steps, including tax increases, personnel layoffs, and service cutbacks, were necessary to stave off an impending fiscal crisis.

In early 1975, the credit markets began closing to the city. A number of banks holding city bonds sold them, and the investors' services downgraded New York's credit ratings. The *New York Times* castigated Mayor Beame for proposing a budget that did not "grapple with these hard realities" (February 11, 1975, 38). As the day-to-day situation rapidly deteriorated, the perception spread that "politics as usual" would not be sufficient to cope with the problems. "When the city ran out of money on April 14, the banks were no longer there to lend it to them. The markets were closed, the city was broke" (Morris 1980, 231).

Between June and September 1975, fiscal authority was taken from New York City's elected government by state officials acting in concert with representatives of the financial community and placed within the purview of three state and/or quasi-public coordinating agencies: the Municipal Assistance Corporation (MAC), the Emergency Financial Control Board (EFCB), and the Office of the Special Deputy Comptroller for New York City.[3] Each of these state-created agencies represented checks on and, in the case of the EFCB, replacements for democratic accountability in the city. These agencies were designed to do what elected officials would or could not do—restrain government spending and increase government revenues at the expense of the city's middle- and lower-income groups.

Financial interests were well represented on MAC, which was described by one observer as a "classic private solution" to the city's fiscal troubles (Vitullo-Martin 1979, 4). Created in June 1975, MAC was essentially a debt-refinancing agent for the city. It was given a first lien on the city's share of the sales tax and the stock transfer tax in order to refinance New York's short-term debt. The Municipal Assistance Corporation Act of 1975 gave MAC the power to review city expense budgets and short-term borrowing plans (McKinney's 1975, chaps. 868 and 869). If MAC officials became concerned about fiscal practices, they could refuse to advance the city money from bond refinancing, thereby creating a new fiscal crisis. The MAC board was composed of nine members, eight of whom represented large business and financial concerns in the city (Newfield and DuBrul 1981, 160–62).

Created originally as a financial mechanism to restore investor confidence, MAC proved insufficient for the task. A dramatic political solution was necessary to restore investor confidence; it was found in September 1975 when the Financial Emergency Act of 1975 created the EFCB. Included among its statutory powers, the EFCB had the responsibility for approving a four-year city financial plan. In the context of overseeing development of this plan, the EFCB was empowered to evaluate and, if necessary, reject revenue estimates offered by the city; order aggregate expenditure reductions to ensure balanced city budgets; evaluate and, if necessary, reject city contracts, including those with municipal labor unions; administer a wage freeze on city employees; and approve borrowing by all agencies of city government.

The EFCB was designed to centralize fiscal policy decisions, and, as such, it became the primary retrenchment organ in the city. The EFCB was "an institution through which a coalition of forces seeking a contraction in the city's public sector operated in a changing political environment" (Bailey 1984, 128). The EFCB was composed of the governor, the state comptroller, the mayor, the city comptroller, and three private-sector individuals, all representatives from large business and financial interests in the city. "The business community was thus accorded a formal role in the most important decision-making body to handle the fiscal crisis," while Mayor Beame, with only one vote, "was literally left on the sidelines, with home rule temporarily suspended" (Bellush 1990, 314). Milton Friedman observed that "Mayor Beame is no longer in charge of New York. . . . At the moment New York does not have self government" (quoted in Alcaly and Bodian 1977, 33).

Reactions to the EFCB often focused on the role of the three private-sector members. Stanley Schuman, an executive vice-president of Allen and Company, who served on the board longer than any other private-sector member, noted:

> The role of the private members . . . is to take a detached and objective view of the issues before the board. . . . It has been an effective mechanism because the three private members, regardless of who they have been, have *spoken as a group* from the beginning. *We have the largest single voice, and we've been quite successful in being the conscience of the board.* (Quoted in Vitullo-Martin 1979, 5; emphasis added.)

Other observers were more critical of business and financial elite influence on the EFCB. Jack Newfield and Paul DuBrul argued that as a consequence of retrenchment, "New York City's sovereignty, home rule was lost, not to a pluralist coalition government . . . but to a group dominated by one economic interest, one economic class, with scarce comprehension of common life in the city beyond Manhattan" (1981, 163). Paul Kantor and Stephen David concluded: "Since the fiscal crisis the real locus of power in the budgetary process has shifted to financial and business elites who virtually set up and then came to dominate new government institutions established at the state and federal levels" (1983, 269). Richard Reeves observed that "a New Yorker who had been away for a few months might think there had been a coup d'état" (1977, 535).

In the 1870s, retrenchment managers, by replacing "gang rule" in the city with a restructured Tammany machine as the tool for fiscal coordination, set in motion the political forces that led to the eventual consolidation of Democratic party power in New York. In the 1930s, retrenchment managers, by centralizing government authority and responsibility in downtown city agencies, inaugurated the era of reform governance in New York. In the 1970s, retrenchment managers, by functionally centralizing fiscal authority in quasi-public boards composed of state officials and private-sector elites, heralded the beginning of a postreform era in the city.

Despite the similarities, however, the centralization of fiscal authority in 1975 was different from its historical counterparts. In all three periods, the authority of local officials was superseded by that of state officials and financiers. In 1975, however, retrenchment included both initial concessions to financial interests and long-term alterations in city governance, providing these interests with an institutional framework with which to influence fiscal policy long after the 1975 crisis was history.

Postreform Coordination of Fiscal Policy

As in previous retrenchment periods, the strategy for dealing with the 1975 fiscal crisis included state officials and local financiers assuming directive roles in city government. The ascendance of these actors had two consequences for New York politics, one proximate, the other far-reaching. In the short term, state officials and local financiers were able, with federal assistance, to manage the immediate crisis and prevent bankruptcy. From a longer-term perspective, city governance was altered fundamentally by new constraints on the capacity of local officials to determine budgets.

The long-term impacts of the 1975 fiscal crisis were evident in attitudinal, policy, and structural changes in city governance. Dick Netzer, addressing attitudinal changes, writes, "The 1975 crisis was a profound consciousness-raising experience with regard to perceptions about the vulnerability of the local economy. . . . After 1975, there was a radical change, and virtually every important decision was viewed as subject to constraints imposed by the vulnerability of the local economy" (1990, 53).

Although attitudinal changes are often precursors of policy revision, they have not proved sufficiently long-lasting in the past to ensure long-term fiscal stability.[4] New York State Senator Roy Goodman observed: "History has taught us a very bitter lesson, which is that we have not been able to rely on the *elected city government* to keep the budget in balance" (quoted in *New York Times,* May 21, 1978, sec. 4, 7; emphasis added). As the years pass, the memory of fiscal crisis dims, and governing coalitions expand in response to new interests and new claims on the local public treasury. This political expansion, coupled with a cyclical return to relative economic stability, eventually weakens the attitudinal restraints generated by the last fiscal crisis. As we have seen, such an evolution characterized the consolidation of machine power in the 1890s and reform governance in the 1950s.

A second long-term impact of the 1975 crisis resulted from policy adaptations. As a direct result of retrenchment management in the 1970s, the relationship between the city and its municipal workers changed. During the immediate retrenchment period, the city laid off more than sixty thousand employees; imposed a wage freeze on municipal employees; reduced annual fringe benefits contributions; and renegotiated existing contracts with teachers and transit workers (Hartman 1979; Levine, Rubin, and Wolohojian 1981, 25–26). More-over, municipal workers' pension funds were invested in city debt, tying the fate of workers' retirement to the city's future economic viability. "Their 'co-ownership' of the city created a conflict of interest between the demands for higher wages and the need to maintain fiscal stability" (Eichenthal 1990, 68). In another postcrisis change, the city's collective bargaining process was altered in two ways. First, under the new rules, arbitrators were to consider the city's fiscal situation as one of the criteria in determining its awards; second, all impasse awards were subject to judicial review.[5]

The city also reduced service delivery to citizens. During the 1975–78 period, the city curtailed garbage collection, cutting pickups in some neighborhoods in half; redeployed police from the "outlying boroughs" to Manhattan to attempt to protect the tourist trade; and closed firehouses, day-care centers, and health clinics. Mary McCormick summed up the policy effects succinctly: "An analysis of the impact of employment reductions on police, fire, sanitation, transit, and education services revealed that although service losses were not always proportional to employment cuts, either the level or the quality of these services fell in the 1975–80 period" (1984, 318).[6]

Coupled with the layoffs and service reductions were increases in the costs of remaining services. Income taxes for city residents went up an average of 25 percent during the crisis period. Free tuition at the City University of New York, a tradition since before the Civil War, was abandoned. The fare for the subway, the principle source of mobility for working-class and poor New Yorkers, was raised over 40 percent, partly in a symbolic attempt to impress state and federal officials and potential creditors with the seriousness of the city's intent.[7]

Obviously, the layoffs, service reductions, and revenue increases had negative impacts on the quality of life in New York. Streets became less safe and dirtier; parks were not maintained because of disproportionate cuts at the Department of Parks and Recreation; transit systems deteriorated more than they already had, with subways setting historic records for poor service; and resources for social services, insufficient before the onset of the crisis, were depleted further. Moreover, in policy areas such as education and substance abuse programs, the 1970s cutbacks continue to have negative repercussions nearly two decades after the crisis.

However, the changes in New York politics resulting from the fiscal crisis were more fundamental than revised attitudes or the policy effects of retrenchment. As Robert Bailey argues, "What has been largely misunderstood about the financial crisis is that its impact was not only, or even most importantly, in terms of actual policy. Rather, *its most lasting governmental impact was on the policy-making process*" (1984, 35; emphasis added). The fiscal crisis of 1975 resulted in permanent changes in the way city government managed its budget. Fiscal policy-making in New York was altered both by internal government reform and by institutionalizing the power of retrenchment managers within city government.

The 1975 charter revisions placed restrictions on mayoral budget authority. First, the charter provided for increased and extensive review of the mayor's preliminary budget proposals by the Board of Estimate and the city council. Second, the mayor was prohibited from voting on the budget when it came before the Board of Estimate and from vetoing budgetary reductions made by either the board or the city council. Third, the charter provided for a Legislative Office of Budget Review to assist the city council in assessing the executive budget.

However, the changes in budget policy were more fundamental than those involving internal governmental reform. In the wake of the 1975 crisis, financial interests assumed an institutional role in city governance as fiscal watchdogs.[8] As a result, fiscal policy in the postcrisis city incorporated the values and priorities of retrenchment management. Joining the bond-rating agencies (Standard and Poor's and Moody's Services), which evaluated city debt offerings and warned of possible fiscal problems, was a new structure of authority capable not only of issuing warnings but of directly constraining the behavior of elected officials. Writing more than twelve years after the fiscal crisis had been resolved, Gerald Benjamin took note of the revised system of authority: "The legacy of that crisis is still very much with us. The City now prepares a GAAP (Generally Accepted Accounting Principles) balanced budget and operates under the Integrated Financial System adopted in the 1970s under state supervision" (1990, 226).

In 1978, the state legislature, responding to federal pressures for structural reform as a condition for loan guarantees, extended the EFCB's life although it removed the "Emergency" from its title. The newly named Financial Control Board (FCB) was given a less directive but a more permanent role in city affairs than that exercised by the EFCB. Under the amended legislation, the FCB would exist until the year 2008, by which time all federally backed bonds would have been redeemed by the city. Moreover, during this thirty-year period, the FCB could assume a directive role in city affairs, similar to that exercised by the EFCB, under certain specified conditions: if the city incurred an operating deficit of $100 million or more; if the city failed to meet its debt-service mandates; or if the city lost access to the financial markets (Green and Moore 1988). In a 1978 analysis of the consequences of this legislative action, Lee Dembert wrote that "the Control Board, which until now has been an 'emergency' body with a limited duration, would be institutionalized, with power to overrule the Mayor, the City Council, and the Board of Estimate" (*New York Times,* May 14, 1978, sec. 21, 1).

Given the city's continuing tenuous fiscal situation, its need to reenter the municipal bond market, which was monitored by fiscally conservative bond-rating agencies, and its crisis-incurred obligations to the state and federal governments, the FCB, although a less active player than its predecessor, remained a major force in city politics in the late 1970s. Indeed, in describing New York politics in the immediate postcrisis period, a Twentieth Century Fund task force report noted that city finances are monitored by a number of oversight organizations including "watchdog agencies of the federal and state governments." The report went on to state that "one of these agencies, the FCB, has been given powers over the city's budget, borrowing and management decisions that before 1975 would have been unimaginable" (1980, 110).

In the 1980s, the FCB continued to influence the budgetary process in New York although with a significantly lower profile than it had in the late 1970s. As Charles Brecher and James Hartman contend, "despite the potential for quite different results borne of political conflicts, the FCB by mid-1982 had developed a fairly routinized set of procedures that limited its review of City plans to the reasonableness of estimates and the relative certainty of proposed gap-closing measures" (1984, 208). Two developments encouraged the FCB to adopt its less intrusive role. First, the city, as the financial center of the United States and the nation's only "world city," benefited greatly from the finance-driven recovery of the 1980s. Second, Edward Koch, the city's first postcrisis mayor, developed a political base quite different from the one that had supported the Wagner and Lindsay administrations—one that allowed him to challenge the spending priorities of previous mayors.

The first factor explaining the less directive FCB profile in the 1980s was the economic recovery in New York, which began during the final stages of the fiscal crisis. According to employment indicators, 1977 marked the end of an economic decline that had plagued the city for over a decade. Between 1969 and 1977, the city lost nearly 3 percent of its available jobs, many of these in local as opposed to export industries.[9] Beginning in 1977, however, the city began to experience a slow and steady increase in the number of available jobs. Between 1977 and 1981, there were less dramatic losses in manufacturing jobs than in the previous eight years, 4 percent increases in consumer service jobs (health and educational services), and an increase of over 4 percent in corporate service jobs (Drennan 1982, 16–23). Moreover, this economic recovery continued throughout most of the 1980s. In the period 1981 to 1988, the city added over three hundred thousand more jobs in all sectors of the economy (Netzer 1990, 29).

Not unexpectedly, growth in the private economy had positive impacts on city revenues. Between 1976 and 1983, city government experienced a decrease of almost 23 percent in revenues as measured in constant dollars; between 1983 and 1988, however, city coffers grew by nearly 16 percent in constant dollars (Netzer 1990, 52). Such growth in the city's available resources provided an environment within which the FCB might relax its more directive authority and monitor city finances from a greater distance.[10]

If the economic recovery provided a context for relaxation of direct controls, political decisions taken within that context were directly responsible for the diminished FCB role in the 1980s. Edward Koch, elected the 105th mayor of New York in 1977, developed a political base in the city's disaffected middle-class communities, enabling him to resist the demands of the service providers and service recipients who had provided political support for precrisis mayoral administrations. Indeed, throughout his tenure, Koch was remarkably popular among white ethnics in Brooklyn, Queens, the northern Bronx, and Staten Island, many of whom had been alienated from the Lindsay administration. At the same time, however, Koch was less well liked in minority communities and among organized city workers, the very constituencies that had supported previous mayors.

With impressive political skill, Koch used his resistance to the demands of previously politically powerful groups (or at least groups that were perceived in white ethnic communities as politically powerful) to his distinct advantage. The mayor kept costs down during the first two of his three terms by openly and often harshly confronting union and minority-group demands for increased expenditures. Moreover, Koch's aggressive, media-focused style afforded him the opportunity to use the confrontations with unions and blacks to shore up his support in the city's white ethnic communities. "Koch was quick to use his personality—his quick tongue, short temper and blunt manner—to develop a strong appeal to the white middle class and Latinos who vote. But those traits also made him enemies quickly, notably in the black population" (Bellush and Netzer 1990a, 15). Koch's overall political emphases were clearly evident in his successful 1981 election when he swept white ethnic communities, often with over 80 percent of the vote, but lost African-American communities like Harlem and Bedford-Stuyvesant to his Liberal opponent, State Assemblyman Frank Barbaro.

Initially, Koch continued the retrenchment policies that had been forced on the Beame administration. During his first term, he pushed for further reductions in the city's work force and supported a state policy to freeze welfare payments. Koch's early budgets reflected his commitment to fiscal austerity. The city's expense budget for fiscal year 1979, the first developed fully by the Koch administration, included a 3 percent reduction in city spending from Beame's final budget; Koch's fiscal year 1980 budget contained a further 3 percent reduction from his 1979 total; and, although his fiscal year 1981 budget included a 6 percent increase over the previous year, it was still less than 1 percent higher than Beame's final budget for fiscal year 1978 (Office of Management and the Budget Adopted Budgets, reported in Savitch 1990, 261). "Koch's rationale for his austere budgets was that he had no alternative" (Bellush 1990, 317). Given the fact that during the first years of the Koch administration the city was barely removed from the threat of insolvency, this contention has merit. At this historical juncture, immediately following fiscal crisis, attitudinal changes are most dramatic and the political capacity to resist spending most pronounced.

Moreover, in these early postcrisis years, Koch, although aggressively confrontational with unions and some black leaders, developed a more accommodative relationship with the EFCB than had Mayor Beame. Lee Dembart notes that Koch's supportive actions produced "relative calm at the Control Board." He goes on to contrast the two mayors' approaches to the board: "Former Mayor Abraham D. Beame used the board as an extra weapon with the labor unions, blaming the board for actions that he had to take. Mayor Koch, elected with a mandate to crack down on the unions, is tempermentally and politically less inclined to use the Control Board to strengthen his hand" (*New York Times,* May 21, 1978, sec. 4, 7).

In addition to not scapegoating the city's fiscal monitors, Koch's policy priorities were popular with the financial community. By emphasizing what Paul Peterson (1981) terms "developmental" policies over "allocational" or "redistributive" programs, Koch bolstered his support among FIRE groups in New York.[11] The mayor aggressively employed tax incentive programs, direct public investment, and friendly zoning policies to encourage real estate development and financial investment in Manhattan (Bellush 1990, 319–24). In precisely this context, Brecher and Horton note: "During the recovery period of 1978–82, municipal priorities were altered significantly. Developmental functions went from least-favored to most-favored status. . . . Redistributive functions were downgraded to the lowest priority; allocational functions continued to receive a slowly growing share of city service. . ." (1985, 270).

During Koch's first two terms, the economic recovery was so dramatic, the city's budgetary situation so improved, and the mayor's reputation as a fiscal conservative so well developed that by the mid-1980s the FCB's overt role in city governance was reduced once again. On June 30, 1986, the FCB relinquished its authority to reject city budget and financial plans, although it would continue in a primarily advisory role until 2008 (*New York Times,* June 30, 1986, B3). New York City was, in the words of a *New York Times* editorial, "free on probation" (July 2, 1986, A30). In 1978, the FCB had evolved from a direct player in the budget process to an active monitor of fiscal affairs; in 1986, the FCB adopted the even lower profile role of periodic commentator on the city's budget and financial plan.

The FCB's low profile continued throughout most of the 1980s. However, it returned to a decidedly more active role in the 1990s, and herein lies the best example of the coordinative capacity of the fiscally centralized postreform city. In 1989, David Dinkins became the city's first African-American mayor, with the active support of municipal unions and the city's minority populations. Dinkins's political base was reminiscent of that developed by precrisis mayors, and there was substantial pressure on the new mayor to address his constituencies' demands for "long overdue" attention. However, the Dinkins administration had barely been installed in office when it became evident that the growth produced by the economic recovery of the 1980s was being threatened by the financial downturn of the 1990s. By early 1991, trouble with the local financial sector, regional economic decline, and a national recession put great strains on the city's finances and on the capacity of the new mayor to respond to his constituencies.

The pressures generated by the combination of difficult economic conditions and constituency pressures were quite evident early in the administration's tenure. However, unlike prior regimes, the postreform city is structured to mitigate the tensions inherent in a situation of economic downturn and rising political demands at the expense of political interests. In the postreform city, fiscal stability is achieved by cutting allocational and redistributive programs, regardless of a particular mayor's political base. To accomplish these cuts in the face of a resistant administration, the FCB and MAC, abandoning their low-visibility profile of the 1980s, openly reentered the city's budgetary process in the 1990s.

In March 1991, an FCB staff report on the city's financial plan concluded that spending was increasing at too fast a rate in the areas of debt service, social service programs, and fringe benefits for municipal employees. Two of the three areas mentioned in the report, social services and fringe benefits, directly related to Mayor Dinkins's constituency base. The critical FCB report was characterized as "one more sign of the troubles Mr. Dinkins faces in striking a balance between his critics in the financial community and skeptics among his supporters in liberal and labor circles" (*New York Times,* March 8, 1991, A1).

In May 1991, Felix Rohatyn, the chair of MAC, offered to assist the city with the projected budget deficits by providing $1 billion over four years from funds generated through the refinancing of MAC bonds. In return, Rohatyn insisted that the administration accept an increased FCB role in the budget. Rohatyn's proposal initiated a six-month media battle between Dinkins, who was highly resistant to an increased FCB role, and the fiscal monitors.[12] In July 1991, in a not so subtle attempt to increase the pressure on city officials, the FCB expanded its own budget role by increasing the frequency of its scheduled meetings to review city finances.

In August 1991, succumbing to the pressure from the fiscal monitors, the administration made a number of adjustments to the financial plan based on FCB suggestions. Included among them were mayoral pledges to tie any nonbudgeted wage increases for municipal workers to cost-saving concessions by the unions and to abandon proposed tax increases. In the wake of the city's concessions, an FCB spokesperson announced, in a press release that left little doubt as to possible future scenarios, that at this time the FCB saw no "need to impose stringent controls on New York City spending" (*New York Times,* August 2, 1991, A1). Following the FCB's statement of self-imposed restraint, there were several more months of pressure on Dinkins from the fiscal monitors to include more labor-based cost savings within the financial plan. Finally, on December 13, 1991, the Dinkins administration agreed to consult with the FCB directly on revising the financial plan, ceding to the FCB an active role in city fiscal affairs.

The open reemergence of the FCB and MAC as active players in budget politics in the early 1990s was a clear indication of the new balance of fiscal power in New York's postreform regime. The fiscal monitors, institutionalized in city governance by state action in 1978, constrained the actions of New York's elected leaders through a carrot-and-stick approach. With the funds from the MAC refinancing as the carrot and the FCB's latent powers to intervene in city affairs as the stick, the Dinkins administration was sometimes enticed and sometimes threatened to move in the direction that the fiscal watchdogs desired. That the FCB "could not make Mr. Dinkins do anything that he would not have to do to avoid its intervention" was precisely the source of its power (*New York Times,* May 17, 1991, A1). Without assuming the directive control exercised by the EFCB in the mid-1970s, fiscal monitors used the structures created in the wake of crisis in the 1990s to work their will on city government. The Koch administration's cooperation with the fiscal watchdogs during a period of economic growth kept the influence of MAC and the FCB latent; the Dinkins administration's initial resistance during an economic downturn brought these agencies overtly back into the fray.

The fiscal monitors' reemergence as active players in city budgeting had definite implications for public policy. Their institutional role in the postreform city was to constrain the options available to elected officials by ensuring that the allocation of increasingly scarce resources was "fiscally responsible." Both MAC Chair Felix Rohatyn and FCB Executive Director Allan Procter pressed continually for cuts in labor and social program costs. As a result of the institutionalized conservatism of postreform fiscal coordination, New York's first postcrisis liberal mayor was unable to address the agenda of the political interests that helped elect him. In the postreform city, there is little danger of a return to "fiscal irresponsibility" because the problem of political fragmentation that eventually plagued both the machine and the reform city has been addressed. Because regime fragmentation is a consequence of political adaptation in an open system and because political adaptation is now so effectively constrained by New York's "closable" system, fiscal coordination is assured for the foreseeable future. To argue that the chosen solution violates normal democratic channels characterizes but, in many circles, does not challenge its adoption.

Institutionalizing the postreform regime, however, involved more than simply addressing the fiscal concerns of financial elites. The postreform regime also needed to establish political channels responsive to attentive nonelites and their decade-long demands for decentralization of and participation in city governance. As chapter one suggests, political constraints reemerge in the wake of retrenchment management, and new regimes require fresh legitimation mechanisms to deal with them. The remainder of chapter five examines the initial process of establishing postreform legitimacy in New York City through the creation of the community board system.

Postreform Legitimacy and Community Boards

Regime changes are evident first in retrenchment management and then in the emergence of new governing coalitions with new electoral bases. As the new governing coalitions develop, three changes occur in urban governance. First, the relationship of citizens and government is altered to reflect emerging regime values. Second, the geographic-functional balance in city politics changes to accommodate the new regime's political and policy interests. Third, based largely on the first two points, formal and informal notions of what constitutes reasonable demands on city government begin to reflect both regime values and governing coalition interests. Despite the sweeping changes following fiscal crises, however, past sources of political legitimacy cannot be abandoned completely without risking social instability. Accordingly, new urban regimes generate the widespread acceptance required for governance through a cumulative process that includes previous as well as regime-specific sources of legitimacy.

The machine's legitimacy was a function of electoral politics channeled through a community-based vote–service exchange system. Reform legitimacy, though also electorally based, focused on the administrative agencies of the welfare state, which increased the complexity of the legitimation process by expanding the scope and nature of government involvement in people's lives. Political legitimacy in the postreform city, reflecting that increased complexity, is based on three aspects of urban governance. First, as in previous regimes, electoral politics certifies winning coalitions in the postreform city. Second, the welfare city developed by reformers remains a source of political legitimacy in the postreform era although its scope has been limited by the fiscal constraints on city government instituted after the fiscal crisis. Third, and specific to the postreform regime, legitimacy is a function of systematic community-based involvement in city affairs.

The primary regime-specific, legitimizing strategy of the postreform regime was found in the community-empowerment movement. In New York, the charter reforms of 1975, which were enacted separately from but coterminously with retrenchment management, established a new community-based channel for political legitimacy in the city. By creating the modern community board system, the 1975 charter revisions increased the scope of resident involvement in policy-making; specified community responsibilities over land use, budgeting, and service-delivery issues; and, most importantly, institutionalized community-based politics in the city.

A History of New York's Community Boards

In the early 1950s, the City Planning Commission (CPC) prepared a revised map delineating sixty-six community districts throughout New York City. The CPC adopted this district breakdown as a strategy to improve the effectiveness of central-city planning rather than as a way to address community-based concerns. The districts, however, became the basis for early attempts at administrative decentralization. Upon assuming the office of Manhattan borough president, Robert Wagner set up twelve community planning boards in that borough based on the CPC's districting plan. In 1961, city charter revisions extended the community planning board concept from Manhattan to the entire city. The revised charter also expanded the planning board concept functionally in that the boards became more than simply adjuncts of the CPC. Each planning board was responsible to advise the borough president "in respect to any matter relating to the development or welfare of its district," and to "advise the city planning commission . . . in respect to any matter within the jurisdiction of the commission relating to its district" (New York City Charter 1963, sec. 84).

Each of these early planning boards comprised the city council representatives from the board's community district and borough. Because district lines were not coterminous with councilmanic district boundaries, several councillors representing different neighborhoods within each community planning district sat on the boards. In addition to these ex officio participants, five to nine other board members were appointed by the borough presidents and served at their pleasure, a procedure first employed with the local improvement boards in the early twentieth century. The charter provided no specific guidelines concerning the appointment or removal of planning board members for the borough presidents to follow (or to which they were accountable). Nor were there any specific guidelines to assist board members with their responsibilities.

Any reasonable analysis of the early planning board system leads to two inescapable conclusions. First, because of their lack of codified responsibility, the planning boards were consigned to the outer margins of the political process. Second, given their total reliance on the borough presidents, there was little potential for the appointed members to develop independent political influence in the city. As a consequence, the community planning boards served almost exclusively as channels for downward communication from city or borough officials to community residents. They were not intended and did not serve as grass-roots organizations in any meaningful sense. By keeping the planning boards' responsibilities ambiguous, by refusing to allocate any formal authority to them, and by making appointed board members fully accountable to the borough presidents (who were themselves unaccountable under the system), the 1961 charter revisions produced a form of decentralization in New York with few political or administrative implications.

In 1968, Mayor Lindsay, as part of the larger package of decentralization reforms (see chapter four), proposed local law 39. This law addressed what, by that point, were fully developed postreform demands for decentralization by delineating more specifically the community planning boards' role in land-use and service-delivery questions (Local Laws for the City of New York, 1969). Much like the 1961 charter revisions, local law 39 mandated the community planning boards to develop plans for the district's welfare and advise public officials on community concerns. However, this legislation went further than the 1961 charter revisions by specifying more clearly planning board responsibilities. Under local law 39, each community planning board was mandated to

> cooperate with other boards on matters of common concern; keep a record of its activities and transactions . . . and provide the borough president with copies of all records; render an annual report to the mayor and the borough president; keep the public informed on matters relating to the welfare or development of its district; make recommendations at or before public hearings on matters relating to the district, including capital projects proposed by the City Planning Commission or sites selected by the Site Selection Board; and employ such assistants as it may require with funds appropriated or contributed for the purpose.

Moreover, local law 39 qualified the borough presidents' authority over the recruitment and appointment of planning board members. The legislation provided for up to fifty members on each planning board and included three guidelines for the appointment, removal, and behavior of board members. First, the borough presidents were to make board appointments only after consultation with the relevant city council members, who remained ex officio members of the boards. Second, board members were removable only "for cause" and not at the whim of the borough presidents. Third, board members were advised that certain actions, such as extended or numerous absences, would serve as grounds for removal (Local Laws for the City of New York, 1969).

Although community planning board operations were more detailed under local law 39 than they had been under the 1961 charter revisions, board responsibilities remained only vaguely defined. And, despite efforts in the 1968 law to constrain borough presidents by providing that board members were removable only for cause, the statutory protections afforded planning board members were minimal. Indeed, one assessment of the community planning boards' operations under local law 39 concluded that although "the boards had increased citizen participation through their involvement in public hearings . . . they had exercised only minor influence on governmental responsiveness; and they had little impact on city policy" (State Charter Revision Commission [SCRC] 1973). The report went on to conclude that the greatest deficiency in the community planning board system was the lack of specificity regarding board responsibilities.

In summary, New York's community planning boards originated in the borough of Manhattan and were based on district lines prepared by the CPC; They were then extended to the entire city by the charter revisions of 1961; and they were further elaborated and refined by local law 39 in 1968. Although each step in the evolution represented either a geographic or functional extension of planning board responsibilities, the fact remains that these boards, in and of themselves, were not meaningful agents of decentralization. However, coupled with the other city-sponsored decentralization efforts during this period, particularly the aforementioned Office of Neighborhood Government and community school boards, the early community planning board system was to serve as an institutional framework for the decentralization of New York City in the 1970s.

Institutional Decentralization: The 1975 Charter Revisions

By the early 1970s, more than a decade had passed since the last major revision of New York City's charter. Although not a particularly long time chronologically, the 1960s saw dramatic changes occur in American cities (chronicled in chapters three and four). Indeed, since the 1961 charter revisions, there had been significant demographic, socioeconomic, and political changes in New York, and many of these were reflected in a growing dissatisfaction with existing norms and institutions of private and public life in the city.

Such dissatisfaction with political institutions was evident in various citizen opinion surveys. In a 1972 poll conducted by Peter D. Hart Associates, for example, only 8 percent of those responding believed that conditions in their neighborhoods had improved during the previous five years, whereas nearly 50 percent of the respondents thought that their communities had declined during that period. Moreover, in a Gallup poll conducted that same year, nearly 75 percent of the respondents questioned favored changing city government, and over 80 percent of the change-oriented respondents recommended decentralization as their reform of choice.

In May 1972, in response to the pressures for decentralization and participation, the New York State Legislature created a State Charter Revision Commission (SCRC) for New York City.[13] The legislature mandated the SCRC to:

> (i) encourage genuine citizen participation in local city government; (ii) ensure that local city government is responsive to the needs of its citizens; (iii) achieve for cities active local self-government in accordance with the declared purpose of the people of the state expressed in the constitution; and (iv) effectuate state purposes in so far as city governments are called upon to implement state programs for the health, safety and welfare of the citizens of the state and are recipients of substantial state assistance. (McKinney's 1972, chap. 634, 1224–25).

Joseph Viteritti characterized the creation of the SCRC as "the culmination of years of planning, debate, and experimentation designed to effect a structure for neighborhood government in New York City" (1989, 27).

The SCRC's introductory report characterized the geographically centralizing tendencies of New York politics quite succinctly: "Beginning with the consolidation of the five boroughs into a single city in 1898, the sum result of the charter revision process has been to centralize power at the topmost levels of City government" (SCRC 1973, 6). During the early rounds of public hearings, the SCRC uncovered two recurring postreform themes in the testimony presented: citizen dissatisfaction with government unresponsiveness and calls for decentralization and wider participation in decision making. Concerning the former, an SCRC report noted that there was "a pervasive feeling that regardless of who fills the City's elective and appointive offices, New Yorkers cannot get done what they want done in their own neighborhoods." The SCRC went on to report that "a sense of remoteness and apathy was found in much of the testimony." On the latter theme of areal decentralization and citizen participation, the SCRC concluded that people "wanted in; they wanted a greater say in how the City operates especially in their own communities" (SCRC 1973, 11–14).

Some of the witnesses expressed their views forcefully; two examples suffice. One witness testified that "people should not have to spend hours pleading their cause to a *faraway* City Council or Board of Estimate, both of whom themselves are part of a *centralized big City juggernaut* that moves slowly, blindly, unfeeling. . . . Decentralize the City government." Another argued that "when government gets too big, too bulky, too unwieldy, it can't respond in time to do much good. Like the dying dinosaur, whose body thrashed about long after its pea-sized brain ceased functioning, our huge city is slowly dying, but the brains in City Hall have still not received the message" (SCRC 1973, 12–13; emphasis added).

Based on its legislative mandate and the extensive public hearings it conducted, the SCRC's introductory report concluded:

> The Commission believes that the people of New York City should have a stronger, more direct say in the operations of government, particularly in their own communities. We believe that more power and responsibility should be shared by the City with its residents. We believe that more decisions on local governmental activities should be made locally, preferably by the people most directly affected by those decisions. In accordance with these beliefs, we plan to give the people of New York City the opportunity to decentralize their government. (SCRC 1973, 14)

The SCRC's plan for decentralizing city government, though influenced by the ONG and community school board experiments, focused on the existing community planning board system. The charter revisions of 1975 formalized geographic decentralization in New York City by creating a new community board system with enhanced power in city government. The charter revisions resulted in the creation of fifty-nine community boards, each with a maximum of fifty members selected by the borough presidents, with one-half of the members nominated by local city councilors. The new charter allocated to these boards advisory power over land-use issues, expense- and capital-budget priorities, and service-delivery matters within their community jurisdictions (*New York City Charter and Administrative Code [NYC Charter]* 1976, chaps. 69 and 70). The charter provided that the boards receive expense-budget funding for such operating expenses as rent, office supplies, clerical assistance, and the salaries of a full-time district manager and board staff who serve at the pleasure of the board.

Because the boards receive line-item budget allocations, they are considered to have "independent agency status in the municipal arrangement" (Greenblatt and Rogowsky 1980, 20). Such a status assists community board efforts to the extent that it puts them on the same level as the city agencies with which they interact. It also serves to constrain local autonomy, however, by subjecting board hiring practices to Department of Personnel review.[14]

Many of the responsibilities allocated to the boards by the revised charter were, like prior grants of power to the community planning boards, rather general. For example, each board is to: "consider the needs of the district which it serves" (*NYC Charter* 1976, sec. 2800-d, 1) and "cooperate, consult, assist, and advise any public officer, agency, local administrators of agencies, legislative body, or the borough president with respect to any matter relating to the welfare of its district and its residents" (*NYC Charter* 1976, sec. 2800-d, 2). In a number of ways, however, the 1975 charter revisions are qualitatively distinct from past efforts at decentralization in New York City. First, the 1975 reforms specified, in significantly more detail than had been done previously, the scope and nature of community board authority and responsibility. Second, borrowing from aspects of several of the city's previous decentralization experiments, the 1975 revisions created a community-based system incorporating a degree of both political and administrative authority over a range of public policies within the same community organizations. Third, the 1975 reforms made operational, that is, standardized the procedures for, the authority that was allocated to the boards.

The increased emphasis on and specificity about community-based authority included in the 1975 revisions are evident in the three major areas of charter-mandated board responsibility: land-use review, local budget priorities, and service monitoring. Community board influence over land-use planning was codified in the charter-mandated Uniform Land-Use Review Procedure (ULURP), which increased the influence of and standardized the process for community input into the process of land-use review. The charter revisions also provided the boards with an opportunity to suggest board-initiated proposals for inclusion in the city's expense and capital budgets, each of which was to be broken down by community districts. In addition, borrowing from the administrative decentralization included in Mayor Lindsay's ONG, the new charter standardized the communities' service-monitoring role through a system of district service cabinets. These cabinets, composed of designated city agency representatives and the boards' district managers, formalized agency relationships with community boards. Moreover, the charter revisions mandated coterminality of community and service districts, a reform intended to systematize all ongoing relationships between central-city officials and community representatives.

The 1975 charter provided for interboard communication and countywide coordination through a system of borough boards and borough service cabinets. Each borough board was composed of the borough president, the city councillors from the borough, and the chairs of the various community boards. The borough boards had several responsibilities, including managing ULURP for proposals affecting more than one community district, submitting borough-based proposals for inclusion in the expense and capital budgets, and mediating disputes among community boards from different districts. The borough service cabinets, chaired by the borough presidents, were composed of the community boards' district managers and designated borough representatives of the city agencies. The borough cabinets were charged with coordinating and monitoring boroughwide service delivery.

Redistricting New York City

During the process of developing the modern community board system, the SCRC had to address the question of community district size. Early in the considerations, the SCRC examined the option of creating relatively small community districts, with populations of roughly fifty thousand people. With districts of that size, the city would have over 150 community boards, with Brooklyn alone containing some fifty board districts. Although such small districts affirmed the postreform value of geographic decentralization, there were several concerns about such a plan. First, because the districts were so small relative to the city and even to borough populations, there was fear that their residents' interests might simply be "lost in the crowd." Second, because each board's operating expenses, including rent, office supplies, and salaries, were to be paid with annual citywide budget allocations, the smaller the district, the greater the cost of the overall board system. Third, the smaller the community district boundaries, the more complicated and expensive was charter-mandated coterminality of community and service district lines. Accordingly, the SCRC opted instead to recommend larger district boundaries, which, while providing less immediate spatial representation, would result in a potentially more influential, less expensive, and less complicated community board system.

The 1975 charter revisions mandated that no later than January 1, 1977, the Department of City Planning was to prepare, and the Board of Estimate was to adopt, a map of community districts which would:

> (1) So far as feasible, lie within the boundaries of a single borough and coincide with historic, geographic and identifiable communities from which

the city has developed; (2) be suitable for the efficient and effective delivery of services by municipal agencies to be made coterminous with the community districts . . . ; (3) be compact and contiguous and be within a population range of one hundred thousand to two hundred fifty thousand persons. (*NYC Charter* 1976, chap. 69)

To meet the criteria outlined above, the SCRC recommended the creation of from forty to fifty community districts, each with a minimum of one hundred thousand people. Despite the recommendation, however, the city's Board of Estimate eventually decided on fifty-nine community districts. On one level, it might appear that the Board of Estimate's action in creating more numerous and hence smaller community districts than those recommended by the SCRC indicated a commitment to postreform decentralization among city officials more positive than that of SCRC members. Several observers contend, however, that it was actually the Beame administration's disinterest in and indeed hostility to the decentralizing mandates in the charter revisions that resulted in the proliferation of community districts. According to these analysts, the increase in the number of districts was simply the result of administration concessions to interest groups throughout the city looking for new channels of access. As Jewell Bickford contends, "There is general agreement today that the Beame administration did a very poor job in failing to resist the pressures of narrow interest groups and thereby produced the current design of 59 districts" (1980, 40).

The increase in the total number of community districts from that recommended by the SCRC had three notable effects on the community board system as enacted. First, as noted above, the smaller size of community districts made it less likely that any one district could command city- or even boroughwide attention. Second, as a consequence of the relatively small district size, several historical communities throughout the city were split by the drawing of community district lines. Third, existing police and sanitation district lines were often needlessly ignored, which complicated the task and increased the fiscal and administrative costs of achieving coterminality. The political reasons for settling on fifty-nine districts aside, the number did represent something of a compromise between arguments emphasizing a postreform economy of scale and those focusing on the value of territorial decentralization.

The actual division of the city into the fifty-nine community districts generated intense political battles in a number of the city's neighborhoods, including Chinatown, Gramercy Park, and Bay Terrace, as residents attempted to maximize their ethnic and/or block representation on the boards. Redistricting conflicts were particularly heated in Brooklyn, where, for example, two community districts had to be created in the Crown Heights section of the borough to satisfy the mutually exclusive demands of the area's polarized African-American and Hasidic communities. There were also heated redistricting battles in other more middle-class communities in Brooklyn, such as Midwood and

Bensonhurst. As Robert Greenblatt and Edward Rogowsky astutely noted at the time, "The appearance of these skirmishes in middle-income communities . . . suggests that district boundaries and the resulting service delivery lines have taken on an importance in these neighborhoods that was not expected in the earlier debate over decentralization and its relevance to lower income areas" (1980, 24).

Representation and Community Boards

Aside from the size and placement of district boundaries, another pressing issue facing the SCRC concerned the manner of selecting community board members. The issue of representation is obviously crucial to democratic government in general and to postreform governance in particular. Indeed, the lack of community-based representation in city policy-making during the reform era was a primary motivation behind the postreform reaction. Despite its ideological salience, however, the concept of representation is far from operationally clear. Hanna Pitkin (1967) identifies three distinct types of representation: formal, descriptive, and interest. Formal representation concerns the procedural arrangements for selecting representatives; descriptive representation involves the issue of whether the demographic and socioeconomic makeup of representers matches that of the represented; and interest representation focuses on which specific groups are being served by the system, that is, who the political winners are (Viteritti 1979, 10–18).

The SCRC was clearly divided on the issue of representation. Some on the commission favored the direct election of community board members by district residents, arguing that in the absence of such democratic procedures, the boards would never develop political legitimacy within their districts. Others, however, favored appointed boards with members selected by elected city officials, such as borough presidents and/or local city councillors. The former group defended its position as the one most closely tied to the postreform demands for community control and resident participation, whereas the proponents of appointed boards emphasized the shortcomings and questioned the political feasibility of community-based elections.

Those in favor of direct elections of board members offered several arguments in support of their position. First, they emphasized the importance of formal representation as a way for the boards to address postreform pressures for participation and to achieve political legitimacy. In that context, the proponents claimed that the SCRC mandate to "encourage genuine participation in local city government [and to] ensure that local city government is responsive to the needs of its citizens" was best achieved through democratic elections. "Traditional democratic values and standard political science dogma suggests that citizen bodies involved in significant decision making should be elected" (SCRC 1973, 18).

Second, reflecting an emphasis on interest representation, the proponents argued that elected boards would be less likely to be dominated by any one official or interest in city or borough government. From this perspective, for the board system to be participative and reflective of local interests and to provide a meaningful channel for community concerns, board members should be accountable to community residents and not to some "external" appointing power. Moreover, under an elective system, board members would be forced to seek local support for their decisions among area residents. The need to generate community support would encourage outreach efforts, which in turn would increase the visibility of the boards, heighten resident interest in board affairs, and add to the probability that board members and residents would be aware of each other's positions on community issues. In short, elected boards had the potential to serve as the focal points for community organization, as clearinghouses for community-based proposals, and as the local centers of postreform politics in the city.

Third, addressing the issue of descriptive representation, proponents of elections argued that democratic selection was the only way to ensure that board members would be representative of area residents, even as neighborhoods underwent change. They feared that appointment of members would result in community boards that were reflective more of the political needs of appointing officials than of the districts the boards were supposed to represent. Moreover, the proponents suggested that if the boards were perceived as unrepresentative, they would not be viewed as legitimate by community residents and consequently would not be taken seriously by representatives of city agencies. In that event, local activists would simply develop alternative community-based organizations and the boards would become increasingly irrelevant.

The proponents of appointed boards countered with several arguments. They contended that community-based elections, as institutional manifestations of formal representation, did not ensure participation, responsiveness, accountability, or legitimacy. The proponents of appointed boards offered several examples of community elections with very low participation rates. Community school board elections, which produced an initial 14 percent participation rate in 1970 during the height of the school decentralization controversy, saw barely 10 percent of eligible voters participate in later contests. Furthermore, a citywide average of 2.5 percent of eligible voters participated in community corporation elections, despite a "comprehensive set of guidelines and regulations . . . issued by the City's Council Against Poverty" (SCRC 1973, 20). The opponents of elections argued that, rather than promoting interest representation and political legitimacy, such dramatically poor turnout rates would condemn community boards to a marginal role in city politics.

Counteracting the descriptive representation argument, proponents of appointed boards also suggested that on the community level, such democratic mechanisms do not ensure representative boards. They pointed to the great success of well-organized interest groups such as the United Federation of

Teachers in the school board elections as an example of how local elections can result in the accumulation of power by one group or in favor of one interest. Moreover, according to an SCRC staff report, although the problem did not appear to be widespread, "some conflict of interest situations have arisen with respect to associations of [community school board] members with organizations doing business with school districts . . ." (1974, 65). As a result, advocates of appointed boards argued that the move toward community empowerment would be hindered by a system that encouraged the dominance of interests organized primarily around the institutions of reform governance and seeking to use community elections as a means of reaffirming their functional relationships with city officials.

The opponents of elected boards also defended the appointment process on interest representation grounds. They argued that the appointment process could ensure greater representation of geographic, ethnic, and other interest groups if the appointing officers were carefully monitored. They also offered a defense of appointments that, in the context of postreform politics, was rather ironic. As opposed to elected representatives, the argument suggested, appointed board members have some independence from immediate political pressures in the community, which permits them "to make tough—unpopular decisions for their districts since they are not subject to the pressure of having to run for reelection." As a result, appointed boards will encourage "talented individuals to participate who would not wish to become embroiled in an election campaign for public office" (SCRC 1973, 24).

In deciding the crucial issue of representation, the SCRC opted for a process of appointing community board members, and the voters of New York City approved. The commission operated in an environment conditioned by the recent memory of intense conflicts over school decentralization. In seeking to develop a feasible postreform alternative both to the reform status quo and to community control, each of which were no longer politically acceptable, the SCRC proposed a hybrid system for board members' selection designed to decentralize city government without fragmenting city politics. According to the revised charter, community boards would consist of "(1) not more than fifty persons appointed by the borough president, one-half of whom shall be appointed from nominees of the district council members and the council members at large from the borough and (2) as non-voting members, council members at large and council members elected from any area which includes a part or all of the community district" (*NYC Charter* 1976, sec. 2800, a).

In addition, unlike the authors of the 1961 charter revisions or local law 39, the SCRC attempted to specify the responsibilities of board appointers and appointees. Aside from the requirement that borough presidents select one-half of their appointees from nominations made by city council members, the revised charter placed other restrictions on board selection: "Not more than twenty-five percent of appointments shall be city employees. No person shall be appointed to or remain as a member of the board who does not have residence, business, professional, or other significant interest in the district. And the Borough President shall assure adequate representation from the different geographic sections and neighborhoods within the community district" (*NYC Charter* 1976, sec. 2800, a). The revised charter also provided that community board members were to serve for staggered two-year terms, were not to be reimbursed for their time and efforts, and were to be removed for cause by either the borough president or a majority vote of the community board (*NYC Charter* 1976, sec. 2800, b and c).

Although the board system was a clear indication of the ascendance of postreform politics, its formal structure pointed to the understandable hesitation in New York City about postreform ideals. Indeed, commenting on the appointive system selected by the SCRC, one observer noted: "In framing its proposals, the Charter Commission was primarily interested in 'responsible government' not 'participatory democracy'" (Rich 1982, 11).

Research on the borough presidents' extensive role in the board appointment process is largely impressionistic.[15] In an early study of the appointment process, Lebenstein was "generally impressed with the quality of appointments in Queens and Staten Island," but less so with those in Brooklyn and the Bronx (1980, 18). Greenblatt and Rogowsky contend that in Brooklyn, however, Borough President Howard Golden has played a "leading role as an advocate for the community board system" and has advised the community boards of "their autonomous authority to remove members for inactivity and lack of attendance" (1980, 20).

The argument was made that appointed boards would reflect more accurately the spatial, economic, ethnic, and interest group diversity of a community district than would elected boards, which could, in effect, be captured by one or a few well-organized special interests. An examination of the community board system indicates that the appointive board system has not yet produced descriptively representative boards across community districts but that there seems to be some movement in that direction. An early supporter of the board system, while admitting that board membership in the late 1970s was heavily weighted toward professionals and even prodevelopment types, saw some indication of change: "As the number and range of applicants has increased, the borough presidents, and the City Council members whose advice they are required to take in making appointments, have had a wider choice from which to select" (Fowler 1980, 9).

Other studies also uncovered unrepresentatively high proportions of professional and managerial types on the boards. In Brooklyn, "the professional and managerial group constitutes a majority on two of Brooklyn's eighteen boards, and is a significant plurality on at least seven others." Moreover, "more than 26 percent of all board members in Brooklyn are employed by the city, state, or federal governments" (Greenblatt and Rogowsky 1980, 22). Another study notes: "The poor are often dependent upon the willingness and commitment of the middle-class groups who control most boards" (Wolf 1980, 54).

Demographic changes in city neighborhoods often complicate the notion of representation further and generate factionalism on community boards. As a general rule, organizational conflict develops between established and new members. When such conflict includes racial and economic components, the resulting tensions are frequently intense. Community District 14 in Brooklyn is a classic example of such a situation. By 1990, following a decade of steady increase, blacks represented 40 percent of the Flatbush district's population but only 22 percent of the community board membership (up from 6 percent in the 1980s). Despite the pledges of Brooklyn Borough President Howard Golden and the two city councillors from the district, Noach Dear and Susan Alter, to increase the board's representative character, protests by black activists continued unabated in the early 1990s (*New York Times,* February 10, 1992, B1). Although the intensity of the intraboard conflict in Community District 14 may have been unusual, the nature of the representation problem it exemplified was not.

The literature differs as to the influence of political parties on board appointments. One observer reports charges that in Brooklyn and the Bronx local political club members dominate the community boards (Lebenstein 1980, 18). However, another study, referring to Brooklyn's boards, contends that "The issue of clubhouse domination through the appointment of board members and influence upon board decisions has, by and large, not been evident" (Greenblatt and Rogowsky 1980, 24). Still another study reports that over 70 percent of the district managers chosen by board members were previously involved in their local party clubhouse. However, the authors place their findings in the context of city politics: "But it is obviously impossible in this city to entirely escape the forces of politics, and so the boards' recruitment patterns so far seem to reflect the realities of city life much more than did reformers' illusory notions of 'nonpartisanship'" (Adler and Bellush 1980, 50). When Staten Island selected a Republican borough president in 1988, there were many personnel changes on that borough's community boards, which some argued reflected more party than community politics.

Because the studies agree that community board members and managers were not descriptively representative of district residents, particularly in low-income areas, the question of resident information about and approval for community board actions emerges as important. One early study reports that 36 percent of a random pool of community residents had heard of the board system but only 6 percent could accurately identify the board that served their area and only 3 percent could describe how the board operated (Rich 1982, 20). These percentages varied widely across the city, with Manhattan residents more aware of the board system than residents of other boroughs. The study concluded that "information about New York's community boards is confined to a minority of the city's citizens" (Rich 1982, 22).

On the issue of support for the board among knowledgeable residents, the report found high levels of approval for board activities and accomplishments. Only 5 percent of respondents felt that the boards had lessened the quality of life in their communities, whereas nearly 50 percent believed that the boards had produced positive effects (Rich 1982, 22–24). These positive perceptions were particularly high among African-American and Latino respondents, although there is more recent evidence indicating that those support levels for the integrative community board system among minorities have dropped considerably since the late 1970s.

Based on studies of the demographic characteristics of board members and the level of knowledge and information about the boards among community residents, it is obvious that the boards have a long way to go to achieve a legitimizing status within their community districts. Several observers have suggested that the boards should increase substantially their outreach efforts in the community districts so that more residents will be aware of their efforts. Other analysts contend that civic groups must monitor more carefully appointments to the boards in order to ensure representativeness, particularly in lower-income areas.

New York's Postreform Regime: A Summary

The 1975 fiscal crisis signaled the collapse of the governing coalition underlying New York's reform regime. During the retrenchment period immediately following the crisis, state officials and financiers created quasi-public agencies with the power to supersede the authority of local government. Through these agencies, they implemented personnel reductions, service cutbacks, and tax increases designed to return the city to fiscal stability with minimal cost to their interests.

In the wake of the 1975 fiscal crisis and the retrenchment it precipitated, a postreform regime emerged in New York. The new regime, like its predecessors, incorporated formal rules and informal norms addressing the concerns of both financial elites and attentive nonelites. It attended to the interests of financial elites by institutionalizing the influence of the quasi-public agencies created during the retrenchment period. As a result, the postreform regime includes a coordinative fiscal capacity useful for overcoming political demands on government. Second, the new regime also addressed attentive nonelite demands by institutionalizing community power in New York. The new governing coalition included a community board system designed to formalize and standardize community involvement in land-use, budgetary, and service issues.

During the economic downturn of the early 1990s, the new regime's coordinative capacity became quite evident, as the city's fiscal monitors pressured the Dinkins administration to adopt budget policies acceptable to them. As a consequence, New York's first traditionally liberal postcrisis mayor was forced to confront constituents in his own political base in order to avoid the direct involvement of the fiscal monitors in city budgeting. On the other hand, the impact of community empowerment has been less dramatic and less visible. Nevertheless, by codifying community board responsibilities, the 1975 charter created the potential for community-based influence on city policy-making. To assess the nature and extent of that influence requires an evaluation of community board effectiveness in dealing with charter-mandated policy responsibilities. Such an evaluation is presented in the next chapter.

CHAPTER SIX

Evaluating Community Board
Effectiveness

As indicated in chapter five, the 1975 charter revisions created a community board system that coupled political decentralization on land-use and budget issues with administrative decentralization on service matters. In chapter six we address the question of what community power has meant to city governance by examining community board effectiveness. The analysis is divided into three periods. The first focuses on the years immediately following charter adoption, 1977 to 1981, a period of adjustment for the boards and the agencies dealing with them. The second period, 1982 to 1989, is defined by a maturing board system as well as economic recovery. The third follows the adoption of the charter reforms of 1989, which had some important effects on board operations.

Evaluating Land-Use Responsibilities

There is no more basic issue confronting city government than the use of its scarcest resource—land. By definition, cities are densely populated, heterogeneous collections of people (Wirth 1938). Consequently, the demand for land is great, the variety of land uses is as diverse as an urban population, and control of land use is a major source of political power. "Land is capital for those who own it or manage it, a context for the day-to-day lives of the citizens who live in the city, and a source of political benefits and revenues for the officials who govern the city" (Elkin 1987, 90).

City governments exercise substantial control over land use. "Although there are constitutional limits to its authority, the discretion available to a local government in determining land use remains the greatest arena for the exercise of local autonomy" (Peterson 1981, 25). During the machine era, land-use policy in New York was defined by overt intervention in the market for explicitly political ends: Tammany used its control of land to reward contributors. During the reform age, land-use review, though professionalized, continued to serve the political interests of the regime's supporters.

Under reform, formal authority over land-use planning in New York was vested in five agencies: the Board of Estimate, the City Planning Commission, the Board of Standards and Appeals, the Site Selection Board, and the Borough Improvement Boards. The Board of Estimate acted as the "upper house" of the city legislature. It comprised eight ex officio members: the mayor, the comptroller, the president of the city council, and the five borough presidents.[1] "The Board of Estimate has been viewed as the center of gravity in the City's political process, and this applies with equal relevance to planning and budgeting processes as well" (State Charter Revision Commission [SCRC] 1973a, 36). In its most recent incarnation and until its demise in 1990, each of the citywide officials had two votes and the borough presidents one vote on matters before the board. It served as the "court of last resort" for those not content with the land-use decisions of other city agencies.

The City Planning Commission (CPC) comprised six members, appointed by the mayor for eight-year terms and removable only for cause, and a chair, who served at the pleasure of the mayor. The CPC, established by the reform charter of 1938, was responsible for developing and reviewing proposals to modify a master plan for the city, reviewing modifications to the city map, developing zoning regulations, and drafting capital budgets and five-year capital improvement plans. The CPC's mandate illustrated its reform origins: "It is therefore proposed to create a responsible independent commission concerned with the welfare of the whole city . . ." (cited in Silverman 1989, 188). By 1975, the Department of City Planning, the administrative arm of the CPC, had 350 full-time staff positions and a budget of over $5 million.

The Board of Standards and Appeals, composed of five mayoral appointees with six-year terms, who were removable only for cause, heard appeals for zoning variances. The Site Selection Board, charged with choosing sites for capital projects, was made up of five ex officio members, the directors of city planning and the budget, the administrator of municipal service, the comptroller, and the borough president from the site-specific borough. Lastly, the Borough Improvement Boards, composed of the borough's president and city council members, advised the CPC and the Board of Estimate on borough land-use concerns.

Under both machine politicians and reform professionals, the accommodations between market forces and public policy that characterize land-use planning in American cities excluded community input. The city did experiment with the local improvement districts at the turn of the century and the community planning board system sixty years later, but, as we noted in chapter five, neither of these involved meaningful community input. During the machine and reform eras, land-use policy in New York was the domain of central-city actors. The community board system, however, changed this by widening the scope of interests around land-use decisions. "Perhaps the most striking innovation of the new Charter is the inclusion of most of the wide variety of land-use decisions in a single formal process requiring community involvement and participation before final decisions are made" (SCRC 1977, 10).

The Formal Mandate and Land-Use Review

The 1975 charter revisions empowered the community boards to "exercise the initial review of applications and proposals of public agencies and private entities for the use, development or improvement of land located in the community district, including the conduct of a public hearing and the preparation and submission to the city planning commission of a written recommendation" (*New York City Charter and Administrative Code [NYC Charter]* 1976, sec. 2800-d, 15). The right of community review, made operational through the Uniform Land-Use Review Procedure (ULURP) (*NYC Charter* 1976, sec. 197-c), was coupled with the boards' authority to initiate plans for "the development, growth, and improvement" of land within their community districts (*NYC Charter* 1976, sec. 197-a). These charter provisions gave the boards a direct role in land-use planning in New York City. Indeed, an SCRC staff report suggested that advisory power over land-use planning takes on a more substantive meaning in the "real world" of city politics: "Because local rulings would probably be upheld in the majority of cases, developers would be forced to negotiate with the board about their projects, thereby insuring increased responsiveness to community interests and needs" (SCRC 1973b, 102).

Under ULURP, land-use proposals were certified initially by the CPC. Following the precertification process, the community boards had sixty days to evaluate land-use proposals for their community districts and to advise either the CPC or, if the issue involved a zoning variance, the Board of Standards and Appeals (BSA) of their recommendations. Among the proposals that had to be submitted to the boards under ULURP were changes, approvals, contracts, consents, permits, and authorizations respecting the city map, designations of zoning districts, special zoning permits, site selection for capital projects, site selection for landfills, and urban renewal decisions. If the CPC rejected the boards' recommendation, such action had to be explained in writing with the explanation returned to the local board and sent to the Board of Estimate for final disposition (*NYC Charter* 1976, sec. 197-c). The Board of Estimate had the authority to accept, modify, or reject the CPC's decision. If the BSA rejected the communities' advice, the boards had thirty days to appeal the decision to the Board of Estimate (*NYC Charter* 1976, sec. 668, c).

In 1977, the year ULURP went into effect, it was complemented by a mayoral executive order creating the City Environmental Quality Review (CEQR) process. Under CEQR, any proposal for a discretionary land use must include a "project data statement" forwarded to the CPC and the city's Department of Environmental Protection. In cases where these co-lead agencies determine that a proposal has potentially significant environmental impacts, an environmental impact statement must be prepared specifying these impacts and offering strategies to mitigate them. Only after the environmental impact statement is certified, following public hearings, can the ULURP process begin.

The Boards and Land Use: The Early Period

Observers of the early board system saw land use as an area of board effectiveness. Glenn Fowler (1980) argued that land-use authority was "the most dramatic change experienced by the community boards." Moreover, reflecting the view that by the 1970s community activists had learned to use whatever political levers they were provided, Fowler went on to note that, although the boards were allocated only advisory power, "in practice their power has been considerable" (1980, 8).

Fowler's view is supported by a Center for Responsive Government report, which suggested that land-use review "may offer the boards their most direct opportunity to shape the futures of their districts because of the relatively immediate and highly visible economic and social consequences of land-use decisions." The report also points out that in an early opinion survey about the boards, board members, community activists, and citizens "rated the community boards' work in land-use review quite highly" (Rich 1982, 65). Indeed, because the boards' land-use activities could unite the community in visible and effective interactions with city officials, they also helped legitimize the boards during this early period.

David Lebenstein (1980) was more reserved about the extent of boards' land-use influence. While acknowledging that the boards submitted ULURP recommendations in a timely and professional fashion, he pointed out that many board members had previous experience with land-use issues because of their involvement with the planning boards. Moreover, he noted that board members received technical assistance from the borough offices of the Department of City Planning in handling these issues. However, despite these advantages, Lebenstein concluded that "the boards still function in a 'reactive' fashion" and that they need to be encouraged "to take the initiative more often on planning and development issues" (1980, 11–12).

To determine how effective the early community boards were under ULURP, we need some idea of how their recommendations were treated by city officials. Although the data are sketchy, estimates of board success in the early years, that is, the number of times city agencies followed board recommendations on proposed projects, are quite high. The Department of City Planning estimated that it affirmed over 90 percent of board decisions under ULURP between 1977 and early 1983, while the BSA claimed an 82 percent approval rating during the same period (Mudd 1984, 195). Carter Wiseman reported that the Department of City Planning "goes along with roughly 80 percent of board recommendations" (1981, 62). In the most positive assessment, Robert Wagner, Jr., then chair of the CPC, estimated that the commission went along with the boards "in 98 percent of the cases before us" (quoted in Fowler 1980, 8).

Given the sketchy data, it is difficult to judge whether the boards' high success rates indicated that community power had begun to emerge or that most land-use proposals were not controversial. In the latter case, the few losses might be more telling than the many successes. Whatever the case overall, there is evidence of specific board influence on land-use planning during this period. In 1979, Community Board 17 in Brooklyn successfully challenged a Community Development Agency decision that the Canarsie–East Flatbush district be classified a "neighborhood development area." Although such a classification would have brought additional federal funds to the neighborhood, board members argued that such a designation would hurt the district's reputation and its overall chances for economic revitalization. In the late 1970s, Community Board 7 in Queens helped establish a community development corporation and a community stabilization organization in Flushing to guide that neighborhood's growth. During the same period, Community Board 7 in Brooklyn helped create a development strategy for its Sunset Park neighborhood and Community Board 7 in Manhattan was able to help leverage an urban renewal grant for its district.

Generally positive evaluations notwithstanding, the boards established an early reputation for effectiveness on land-use issues that masked the differences among them. An Interface Development Project report found that

> factors which enable some boards to work effectively—well established community organizations, continuity of leadership, professionals who make their skills and expertise available to the board, attentive elected officials, easy access to high-level policymakers—are not available to many boards. The 20–30 boards in poverty and lower-middle-class areas lack most of these ingredients. (Interface Development Project 1980, 4)

In summary, during the early period, board performance on land-use issues was both promising and uneven. Without exception, the research points to the ULURP process as containing the potential for the effective demonstration of community influence. Indeed, reform-style critics bemoaned the new land-use review system precisely because they perceived it as potentially injurious to citywide interests. The general consensus in the literature and among the varied participants was that the boards' land-use advice was taken seriously by the CPC, the BSA, and the Board of Estimate.

The Boards and Land Use: The Maturation Period

During the 1980s, the combination of economic growth and an increase in policy initiatives mandating locally unwanted land uses (LULUs) placed distinct and substantial pressures on land-use planning in New York. In terms of growth, the city experienced a population increase of more than 280,000 people between 1980 and 1988 (Bahl and Duncombe 1991, 3–5). Much of the economic growth was in the financial and corporate service sectors in Manhattan. As the slow growth of the early 1980s became the financial boom of the mid-1980s, real estate development in Manhattan proceeded at a record pace. The saturation of that borough's commercial and residential markets produced spillover development pressures in the other boroughs. The spatial pressures accompanying growth are intense because development produces substantial gains for some and high costs, including dislocation, for others.

The other side of the urban coin in the 1980s was the increase in policy initiatives including LULUs. For example, city officials were running out of waste-disposal options, and proposals for solid waste transfer stations, rubbish incinerators, and sewage treatment plants met understandable resistance in targeted communities. In the social policy area, proposals for prisons, homeless shelters, treatment centers for substance abusers, and group homes for the developmentally disabled generated intense opposition among residents in impacted communities.

The pressures for economic development and LULUs are usually geographically distinct. As Peter Marcuse notes, with the exception of gentrification, "poor areas do not generally have major development proposals submitted to them, because developers are not interested in areas where there is no effective demand" (1987, 16). Poor areas do, however, experience more than their share of government-sponsored LULUs.

The Boards and Economic Development Proposals

To review land-use proposals effectively, the boards had to develop expertise in this area. Developing a system of standing committees has been a traditional organizational approach to creating in-house expertise. Because their members focus on one policy area over time, standing committees are able to provide their parent organizations with the information necessary to assess complex issues. By the mid-1980s, prompted by the Community Assistance Unit and the Department of City Planning, most community boards had established standing committees focused on land-use review. The boards generally divided responsibilities functionally among several committees, each charged with a specific land-use concern, such as open spaces, zoning regulations, or commercial development. Moreover, some boards combined the functional division of committee labors with a postreform emphasis: by creating neighborhood-based committees, they brought a more refined spatial perspective to land-use issues.

In cases where community boards and developers disagreed about proposals, one of four outcomes was evident. In the first, the community board recommended rejection of the proposal, and the central-city officials with ULURP responsibilities concurred. According to representatives at the Department of City Planning, acceptance of board decisions throughout the 1980s occurred, as it had in the early years, in nearly 90 percent of the cases (New York City Charter Revision Commission [NYC CRC] 1988, 4–5). In a study of board land-use review actions during the maturation period, Fainstein and Fainstein concluded that: "even though the community board's decision is not binding, it is very influential with both the CPC and elected officials representing the district" (1986, 23).

The second outcome saw a board's negative recommendation overturned by either the CPC the BSA, the Board of Estimate, or some combination of city agencies. In these cases, although the development proceeded, there were often modifications mandated by the CPC or the Board of Estimate that addressed some of the community's concerns. Internal board divisions over the proposal, as evidenced, for example, by a split board vote, made reversal at a higher level more likely.

A third outcome saw project modifications negotiated between the board representatives and the developer. In these cases, a board provides a majority vote for approval, thereby sparing a developer time and uncertainty at the CPC or the Board of Estimate, in return for board-requested changes in the original proposal. For example, based on environmental impact assessments, boards have asked developers to scale back a project's size or include more amenities, (e.g., increased parking facilities at a commercial site) within the plans.

The fourth outcome took the notion of direct board–developer negotiations a step further and had the developer agree to provide amenities, which might or might not be related to the original proposal, in exchange for a favorable board vote. For example, boards have insisted that developers spruce up local parks or rehabilitate local subway stations in exchange for positive recommendations on projects only indirectly related to the amenities sought. As the boards became increasingly knowledgeable and resourceful about development proposals, this type of negotiated settlement became more common.

The boards' increasing use of the fourth strategy prompted criticism. Sylvia Deutsch, chair of the CPC, expressed concern that the practice "may have the effect of distorting the land-use review process" (1988, 10). Steven Spinola, president of the Real Estate Board of New York, argued: "Though there is no indication that anything incorrect is occurring [in the negotiations between boards and developers], board members should be held to the same ethics requirements as other elected officials to avoid possible conflicts of interest" (1988, 9). In 1987, the Koch administration proposed limiting negotiations to those amenities directly involving the environmental impact statement filed with the proposal. "The Board of Estimate will only require an applicant to provide an amenity as a condition of land-use approval when the proposed amenity addresses a need *directly created by the proposed contract*" (Office of the Mayor 1987; emphasis added). Such a change, although it was not enacted, was intended to constrain the boards' range of options in seeking benefits from developers.

The Boards and Locally Unwanted Land Uses

In terms of the responses to policy initiatives that included LULUs, board effectiveness was decidedly uneven. There is little question that projects with LULUs were concentrated in lower-income, generally minority communities. A large part of the explanation for this inequity rests in larger socioeconomic and political patterns; however, some part may also be traced to the actions of the local community boards.

Some community boards in lower-income areas remained mired in reactive decision making. These boards continued to approach land-use review in an ad hoc fashion, reacting to proposals for community changes without a clearly defined notion of what they wanted for their communities. Although by the mid-1980s nearly every board had adopted at least some formal system of standing committees for dealing with land-use issues, some boards failed to translate these systems into meaningful input.

The problem is more class-based than organizational. Board success in dealing with technical land-use issues is often related directly to interaction with outside professionals. Unquestionably, boards with access to stable community leadership and indigenous sources of expertise (i.e., residents with backgrounds in law, architecture, urban planning, or some other skill relevant to land-use issues) have a greater potential to influence their communities' development than boards lacking such expertise.

A major source of necessary expertise for some lower-income boards existed outside of their immediate communities in the offices of city agencies, private-sector developers, or advocacy planners. However, two factors militated against the use of these sources: (1) With the exception of advocacy planners, there would undoubtedly be suspicion among board members in low-income communities about the motives of either city officials or private developers. Indeed, in the absence of such suspicion, the board system itself would be redundant. (2) Research indicates that activists from lower-income areas tend to emphasize more parochial approaches to city politics and have less confidence in city officials than do their middle-income counterparts (Cingranelli 1983; Fainstein and Martin 1978). Consequently, for organizational, socioeconomic, and political reasons, lower-income communities remained at a comparative disadvantage in exercising land-use review responsibilities during the 1980s.

Overall then, during the maturation period, the boards evidenced growing, if uneven, capabilities to handle land-use review. Moreover, there remained several areas of general disappointment with community board land-use review. The 1975 charter encouraged the boards to "prepare comprehensive and special purpose plans for the growth, improvement, and development of the community district" (*NYC Charter* 1976, sec. 2800, d, 9). Despite this clear invitation to develop a proactive planning response, only a minority of the boards actually produced formal, written plans in the 1980s. The 1975 charter also envisioned an activist role for community boards in developing specific community land-use proposals. Again, only a minority of boards took advantage of this potentially substantial source of influence over community development.

During this period, board members complained about several problems that they claimed hindered their ability to exercise land-use review. First, the practice of not including board representatives at the ULURP precertification phase meant that on occasion the boards were presented with a fait accompli by a developer and the CPC. Second, the city was charged with avoiding ULURP reviews by "privatizing" some social services (e.g., facilities to care for the homeless) and by using the Department of General Services for internal transfers of building use. In each instance mentioned, the contention is that the city is violating at least the spirit of land-use review procedures under the 1975 charter.

Land Use and the 1989 Charter Revisions

The 1989 charter revisions were precipitated by the courts. In 1986, Federal District Judge Edward Neaher ruled that, given the boroughs' population differences, the practice of allocating one vote to each borough president on the Board of Estimate violated the one-person, one-vote principle.[2] The court ordered the city to move with "all deliberate speed" to rectify the board's unconstitutional voting procedures (*Morris* v. *Board* 1986). In 1987, the United States Court of Appeals upheld the ruling; in 1989, the Supreme Court unanimously affirmed the decision.

The 1989 charter revisions were neither prompted by nor directly related to the community board system. However, as the two charter commissions dealt with the fundamental changes in city government mandated by the federal courts, they could not help but have an impact on the boards, particularly in the area of land use.[3] Moreover, the commissions went further than required by the federal courts and addressed some of the difficulties they uncovered with the community boards' land-use review procedures.

After examining a host of proposals to restructure the Board of Estimate, including weighted-voting and jurisdictional limitations, the Charter Revision Commission, created in December 1988, decided that abolition of the board would most directly address the constitutional question.[4] Because of the Board of Estimate's central role in ULURP, this decision had substantial impacts on the community boards' land-use review responsibilities.

The revised charter, adopted by the voters on November 7, 1989, altered land-use planning in New York in five distinct ways:

1. It redesigned the city's ULURP system by replacing the Board of Estimate with the city council as the agency of last resort on land-use decisions.
2. It increased the size and the powers of the city council, impacting that body's new land-use responsibilities.
3. It broadened the scope of representation on the CPC.
4. It included a "fair-share" plan designed to equalize the allotment of LULUs throughout the city.
5. It increased the boards' financial and informational resources in an effort to promote equity across districts and encourage board-initiated, proactive planning.

Many of the charter's land-use revisions took time to implement: the changes in CPC membership did not go into effect until July 1990, the Board of Estimate was not officially defunct until September 1990, and the expanded city council would not meet until January 1992. Although any overall assessment of the new system is premature, several preliminary comments are in order.

First, while maintaining both the community boards' and the CPC's land-use review responsibilities, the new charter altered the appeal process under ULURP. Following review by the boards and the CPC, all zoning changes, housing and urban renewal plans, general economic development plans, and plans for the disposition of most city-owned residential property are automatically reviewed by the city council. Other CPC decisions under ULURP are subject to council review upon objection of the affected community board and borough president or upon a majority vote of the council.

The new ULURP appeal process has been termed the "triple no" by some observers because it allows a project that has been rejected at the community level but has passed CPC review to be appealed to the council by either the board and the borough president or by a majority vote of the council. It creates an agency of last resort on ULURP appeals, which, because of the inherently local perspective of its members, might be friendlier to community demands than was the Board of Estimate. Indeed, some critics warned that this approach weakened the CPC and created an appeal process in which parochial interests would overwhelm citywide concerns.[5] Others pointed out that the appeal process promoted increased confrontation over land-use issues because it encouraged negative votes on the part of the boards. For example, Ruth Messinger, Manhattan borough president, advised the boards to vote "no" on ULURP proposals, rather than "yes with reservations," since "no" votes would preserve their right of appeal (*New York Times,* September 23, 1990, 3).

Second, the new charter increased the number of councilmanic districts and augmented the powers of the city council. Going from thirty-five to fifty-one council districts meant that the average district size went from over 200,000 to under 140,000 people, a 30 percent decrease. The Schwarz Commission concluded that a larger council increased the opportunities for minority representation while enhancing members' responsiveness to their constituencies (NYC CRC 1990, 11–12). Moreover, the charter encouraged the professionalization of the council. It affirmed a strong council leadership system with checks to promote equity, increased the council's oversight role over mayoral agencies, provided for increased council control over its internal budget, and enhanced the council's ability to recruit professional staff. In the area of land use, the 1989 charter mandated the creation of a land-use review committee with representation from every borough to review ULURP appeals. By increasing the number of city councillors and consequently decreasing the size of councilmanic districts, the new charter emphasized the city council's representativeness, a postreform notion, at the expense of its efficiency of operation, a reform value.[6] Joseph

Viteritti, wary of the logrolling strategies so prominent in legislative politics, warned that the combination of the council's increased representativeness and its newly enhanced authority meant that on land-use issues "a system of reciprocal parochialism is likely to rule the day" (1990, 425).

Third, the charter revisions reconstituted the CPC. The CPC, created initially by the 1938 reform charter and further refined by the complementary 1961 reform revisions, was a quasi-independent entity with only the chair directly accountable to the mayor. The 1975 postreform charter mandated that each borough be represented among the mayoral appointees on the CPC. The 1989 revisions went further by broadening the CPC's representation. The mayor now appoints seven of thirteen members, including the chair, and the borough presidents and the city council president appoint six. With the exception of the chair, all appointments require the advice and consent of the city council.

Fourth, the 1989 charter included a "fair-share" plan for locating unwanted city facilities, which was designed to distribute LULUs more equitably throughout the city. Under this charter mandate, "the City Planning Commission would be required to develop criteria for locating city facilities emphasizing fair distribution of such facilities among communities, taking into account the social and economic effects of such facilities on the areas surrounding the sites" (NYC CRC 1989, Appendix A, 31). The charter requires that the mayor produce an annual citywide "statement of needs" and a borough-by-borough listing of all existing and proposed city facilities designed to meet these needs. The borough presidents then have ninety days to propose specific sites for facilities targeted for their boroughs. For a city agency to substitute a site for the one proposed by the borough president requires an augmented majority of nine votes on the CPC. A CPC vote for substitution can be appealed to the council by the impacted community board and the borough president.

The fair-share plan attempts to mitigate socioeconomic inequities through procedural reform. By assessing facility placement across the boroughs, the plan forces officials to confront publicly the issue of distributive equity in the siting of LULUs. By empowering borough presidents to select specific sites, it places responsibility on officials connected directly with community boards. Finally, by mandating a nine-vote CPC majority to approve a substitute site, the plan requires the appointee of at least one borough president to vote against another for a substitute site to pass.

One possible scenario the under fair-share plan is a form of "borough courtesy" on the CPC, where the appointees of the borough presidents honor each other's desires concerning site placement. This would ensure that the borough presidents have the last word on site selection. Under this scenario, the borough presidents have both substantial authority and substantial political problems. The outcome of the fair-share plan would become a function of several factors, including a borough president's notion of equity, his or her base of intraborough political support, and community-based alternative sources of political influence in city and state governments. The fair-share plan opens the site selection process but, given the socioeconomic and political differences among districts, cannot ensure equitable distribution of LULUs.

Lastly, the 1989 revisions also included specific changes to help the boards carry out land-use review. First, addressing a common complaint among members, the revised charter mandates that the boards be notified of all relevant ULURP proposals at the precertification stage. By including the boards in the earliest stages of the ULURP process, the revisions give the boards the opportunity to effect modifications in proposals prior to their formalization by the CPC. The charter also provides that board members be invited to all agency meetings involving environmental impact statements for proposals in their districts. Critics point out that these changes will increase the total time required for proposal review.

Responding to the complaint that intra-agency transfers of facilities violated the spirit of ULURP, the charter revisions mandate that the city send the boards annual reports detailing plans for the use of city facilities within their community districts for the following two years. Under the charter, the boards have the right to make recommendations concerning these plans to the CPC. This reform is intended to increase board influence over internal city transfers of property use within community districts. Moreover, the 1989 charter requires the city to provide the boards with all requests for proposals and letters of intent concerning the disposition of city land within their districts. This reform provides the boards time to study and possibly to influence decisions in this area.

In an attempt to encourage proactive community planning, the charter requires the CPC to review all board-initiated community development proposals. Moreover, it mandates that the city complete environmental impact assessments for all such board-initiated proposals. Furthermore, by excluding rental costs from the boards' base budgets and authorizing the boards to hire professional staff and consultants, the new charter attempts to help augment and equalize board land-use review procedures across community districts.

The Boards and Land Use: A Summary

Community board authority under ULURP has had important effects on land-use policy in New York. Under reform governance, land-use planning was the tightly guarded domain of central-city forces. By opening land-use decision making to public scrutiny, the board system has made it more difficult for pro-growth coalitions to alter city neighborhoods without extensive and public consideration of proposed changes. By extending the range of legitimate conflict over land-use issues, the board system has socialized land-use planning in the city.

Since the implementation of the reforms, many boards have developed professional land-use review procedures, and several boards are renowned for their influence on development projects. The 1975 charter revisions were not intended to guarantee that the boards would control local development—only that they would have the opportunity to influence, through open forums and first-level decision making, land-use planning in their communities. Reports indicate that many boards are taking advantage of this opportunity.

By continuing the trends begun by the 1975 charter revisions, the 1989 changes reemphasized a postreform perspective. By giving each borough president one appointment on the CPC, the 1989 revisions encouraged increased geographic diversity within the commission. By making a larger and more powerful city council the agency of last resort on land-use questions, the charter increased the influence of local interests in this area. Lastly, by encouraging community-based proactive planning, the new charter reinforced the 1975 rejection of a citywide master plan.

Despite the community-empowerment focus of recent charter revisions, problems remain. Board effectiveness is still hostage to socioeconomic variables. The 1989 revisions increasing discretionary funds for hiring outside consultants and implementing fair-share planning for siting locally unwanted facilities may help, but socioeconomic inequities do not readily lend themselves to structural redress.

Another problem involves city efforts to circumvent ULURP. Some board members charge that the city still sites LULUs by acting through not-for-profit organizations not subject to ULURP. In 1992, a bill was introduced into the New York State Legislature making not-for-profit groups operating municipal facilities and receiving at least 10 percent of their funding from government sources, subject to ULURP. Although the bill was defeated in the 1992 session, the high profile of the issue is further evidence of the institutional nature of community power in New York's postreform regime and the fact that central-city forces remain on the political defensive on land-use issues.

Evaluating Budget Responsibilities

Like land-use planning, budgeting is a fundamental, complex, and inherently political task. "The way in which the budget is decided maps the distribution of power among governing officials within the City, as well as the relationship between the City and its residents" (Schick 1974, 1). Because municipal budgeting requires officials to decide the spatial allocation of funds and programs, it was a process that reform governments kept rigidly centralized. To the reformers, budgeting was a task best undertaken by professionals in city government's executive branch.[7] In contrast, an integral component of the postreform reaction was the notion that community residents have a unique vantage point from which to speak to local budget concerns. From this perspective, community residents, because they experience day-to-day life in their neighborhoods, are important information sources on local budget needs. Reflecting this postreform idea, the community board system in New York included a mandate for geographically based budgeting.

Geographic budgeting requires an accounting system that assesses expenditures spatially. Under reform, the Bureau of the Budget (BOB), the comptroller, and city commissioners had primary responsibility for assessing expenses. They categorized expenditures by broad functional categories such as "personnel" and "other than personnel expenses." As a staff report for the SCRC concluded, however, "the city's present accounting systems cannot report expenditures by geographic area. . . . [N]o one including the Mayor, Comptroller, and Sanitation Commissioner can tell how much was spent on refuse collection last year in Bushwick or Borough Park" (SCRC 1973c, I–1).

The Formal Mandate and the City Budgets

The 1975 charter provided the boards with budgetary input by creating procedures for geographic assessment of city budgets and by giving the boards a formal role in determining budgetary priorities within their communities. The provisions of the revised charter dealing with geographic budgeting are scattered throughout the document. With an eye to providing the budgetary information necessary for board decision making, the 1975 charter mandated city service-delivery agencies to generate estimates of their expenses on a district-by-district basis (*NYC Charter* 1976, sec. 112, d). Moreover, copies of departmental estimates for capital budgets for the ensuing fiscal year as well as the three succeeding fiscal years were to be forwarded to the community boards (*NYC Charter* 1976, sec. 214-a), and the boards were encouraged to send representatives to all public hearings on the expense and the capital budgets (*NYC Charter* 1976, sec. 216-a).

Under the new charter, the boards were to have a role in the city's expense budget, which deals with the costs of the day-to-day operations of city government, including salaries and fringe benefits, short-lived equipment, and general supplies. The revised charter requires that "each agency that delivers local services within community districts shall consult with the respective community boards in the preparation of its estimates" (*NYC Charter* 1976, sec. 112, a). With respect to the community boards' responsibilities in the city's expense-budget process, the charter revisions empower the boards to "consult with agencies on the program needs of the community district to be funded from the expense budget, review departmental estimates, hold public hearings on such needs and estimates, and prepare expense budget priorities for the next fiscal year" (*NYC Charter* 1976, sec. 2800, d, 12). The charter also mandated that as soon as "the local reorganization of the City's service-delivery agencies permits," the Executive Budget Message will include "a statement of proposed direct expenses in each service district for each unit of appropriation and a statement of the basis for the allocation of direct expenses to local service districts of each such agency" (*NYC Charter* 1976, sec. 117-b, 8).

The boards were also given capital-budget responsibilities. The city's capital budget involves the construction or acquisition of property and equipment designed to produce a public "betterment or improvement" (*NYC Charter* 1976, sec. 211). It may include expenditures for site acquisition, design, construction, and furnishings and equipment. Since most capital-budget projects take several years to complete, the charter required the city to prepare a three-year capital improvement plan including the two fiscal years following the year the capital budget is adopted.

Charter-mandated community involvement in the capital budget formalized a process initiated earlier by the CPC. In 1973, the CPC had requested that the community planning boards submit priority proposals for inclusion in its draft capital budget. The 1975 charter revisions institutionalized that arrangement for the community boards. With respect to the city's capital budget, the boards were to "consult with agencies on the capital needs of the district, review departmental estimates, hold public hearings on such needs and estimates and prepare capital budget priorities for the next fiscal year and the three succeeding fiscal years" (*NYC Charter* 1976, sec. 2800, d, 10).

According to the Office of Management and the Budget, "The New York City Charter amendments of 1975 require the City to establish and maintain a system for reporting budget and actual expenditures of agencies providing services on a local level" (New York City Office of Management and the Budget [OMB] 1984, 127). Such a mandate requires that the community boards have district-level information concerning both capital- and expense-budget allocations in order to make informed decisions about their district needs and their local budget priorities. The district-level information required was to be provided in a variety of annual and biannual reports allowing the boards to follow the development of the preliminary, the executive, and the adopted budgets for each fiscal year.

New York's system of geographically based budgeting has evolved since the charter revisions of 1975. Under the current system, community board representatives and agency personnel are involved in a series of district and borough meetings designed to provide participants with information and feedback about each other's positions. In June, board representatives and agency local service chiefs meet at district-level consultations where they discuss district needs and their respective expense- and capital-budget priorities. These early district-level interactions often serve as preliminary negotiation sessions where community and agency desires are balanced with budgetary feasibilities. In early July, based at least in part on the interactions undertaken at the district-level meetings, the community boards submit their district needs statements to the Department of City Planning.

For the remainder of the summer and into early fall, the boards hold public hearings on their budget requests and their district needs statements. During these hearings, community activist groups, individuals impacted by specific issues under consideration, or other interested citizens can receive information about and offer reactions to the boards' district plans for the fiscal year. During the summer, the boards also prepare their agendas for the borough-level consultations, which commence in mid-September. At these meetings, chaired by the borough president, each board within the borough sends representatives to meet with commissioners or deputy commissioners to discuss budget priorities and the districts' needs from a boroughwide perspective.

Following more public hearings and votes of the full membership, each board may submit up to forty capital-budget and fifteen expense-budget proposals to OMB in November. OMB staff consider these proposals, giving special attention to the boards' top ten priority requests. OMB's input is reflected in the mayor's preliminary budget, which is made public in mid-January, serves as the focus of community and citywide public hearings during January and February, and evolves into the executive budget. By early June, the city council approves some version of the executive budget, which at adoption becomes operative for the fiscal year starting that July.

The Boards and Budgeting: The Early Period

Research indicates that the early experiences with community-based budgeting were mixed. After examining the budget process during its first three years of operation, David Lebenstein concluded that the "the overall quality of community board budget proposals varies greatly from excellent to very poor" (1980, 12). It is fair to say that, initially, board involvement with the budget was, at least, problematic. Several boards did not even submit board-initiated proposals to OMB, and those boards that did frequently made procedural mistakes that hampered their efforts to secure resources (OMB 1979). Moreover, social critics noted that among the boards that correctly submitted budget proposals there was a tendency to favor hard as opposed to soft services, which did little to assist those in need of expanded social service (Interface Development Project 1980, 1–2).

Much of the early confusion about community-based budgeting is understandable. The municipal budget process is complex, and board involvement with the process, particularly on the expense-budget side, was a recent innovation when these initial studies were done. Moreover, a city in fiscal crisis, where state intervention had made home rule more nostalgia than reality, is hardly the optimal locale to implement geographic decentralization of the budget. Neither is it particularly puzzling that successful board proposals tended to emphasize hard as opposed to soft services. By the late 1970s, the deterioration of the quality of life in New York City occasioned by years of deferred infrastructure maintenance was obvious to even casual observers. By the mid-1970s, "the net replacement of the city's basic infrastructure components was being carried out on cycles that ranged from approximately 250 to 300 years," which was well beyond the anticipated life of most components of the built environment (Grossman 1982, 127). The resulting deterioration did not escape the attention of community board members, particularly in light of the Koch administration's emphasis on this problem in the years immediately following the fiscal crisis.

As with land-use decisions, it is difficult to measure precisely whether the boards had influence on the budget process in the early years. Several studies attempted to do so by calculating the boards' success in having their proposals included in the city's expense, capital, and community development budgets. Summarizing the findings from studies of fiscal years 1979 through 1981, John Mudd reports that "with some minor variation, the funding approval rate has remained in the 40 to 50 percent range for capital items and the 30 to 40 percent range for expense budget priorities" (1984, 199).

An OMB study found that the strongest predictor of board success on the budgets was the number of years the proposal had been in the pipeline, followed by whether the proposal had an agency cosponsor. Moreover, for the expense budget, the socioeconomic status of the district represented by the board was positively related to board success; that is, the poorer the district, the less successful it was in obtaining approval for its locally initiated proposals. Echoing OMB's findings, a Center for Responsive Government study concluded that there was "a positive correlation between the socioeconomic status of a district and the total number of requests made . . . and the number of requests accepted into the budget" (Rich 1982, 86).

The Boards and Budgeting: The Maturation Period

During the boards' maturation period, changes in environmental and organizational variables had substantial impacts on boards' budgetary behavior. By the mid-1980s, there was a dramatic improvement in the city's fiscal situation. Although some questions remain concerning the breadth of the city's recovery in those years, the aggregate data indicated signs of economic revival. New York's expense budget produced surpluses for five consecutive years, and the city's debt was once again considered a good risk in the municipal bond market. Indeed, as indicated in chapter five, the city's positive economic climate, coupled with the fiscally conservative policies of Mayor Koch, had the effect of easing the most pervasive oversight functions brought on by the fiscal crisis. As economic growth continued and spending constraints loosened, agency budgets began to include increased resources in search of problems. The larger environment then presented organized interests, including the boards, with an enhanced opportunity to secure resources.

Community board organizational effectiveness also increased in these years. Since fiscal year 1982, each of the city's fifty-nine boards has submitted budgetary proposals to OMB, with the overwhelming majority of boards submitting their full complement of prioritized proposals. Indeed, officials at OMB's Office of Community Board Relations indicate that not only are most boards submitting proposals but the quality of the proposals has also improved.

There are four general responses to board-initiated proposals to either the capital or expense budgets.[8] First, a proposal can be included in the respective budget as either a line-item or a lump-sum appropriation. A line-item appropriation is more direct because it specifies funding for a proposal, whereas a lump-sum approach allows greater agency autonomy in the use of funds. In either case, this type of acceptance can be considered a first-time success for a board-initiated proposal. Second, a board-initiated request for continued funding can also be included in city budgets. This is a less impressive success than the first because requests for continued funding incorporate sunk costs from prior approvals and are often accepted. Third, a board proposal can be rejected because of insufficient information or procedural errors. This occurred frequently in the early period when the boards, unfamiliar with the process, were prone to making errors. Fourth, a proposal can be rejected for cause.

Table 6.1 illustrates the disposition of board-initiated capital-budget requests between fiscal years 1982 and 1985.[9] It indicates that the percentage of board-initiated proposals (BIPs) included in the capital budget as line-item, lump-sum, or continued funding rose to roughly 50 percent by fiscal year 1983 and remained there for the next two years. However, it is important to note that between fiscal years 1982 and 1985, the percentage of first-time BIPs, that is, proposals not involving continued funding, included within the city's capital budget either as a line-item or a lump-sum appropriation increased over 50 percent, while the percentage of proposals rejected for cause decreased over 60 percent. Recent experience appears to be affirming Mudd's contention that the budget process "guaranteed the boards an unusual amount of information and access to influence the city's capital and expense budgets, if all the provisions were used correctly" (1984, 197).

Overall increases in board budgetary success notwithstanding, there were differences evident among the boards in their capacity to secure local budgetary priorities. Based on research findings from the boards' early years, we examined two possible explanations for differences in board budgetary success: one focused on interorganizational variables; the other emphasized socioeconomic factors.

Community boards are involved in a host of interorganizational relationships within and outside their communities. The public administration literature has long recognized that interorganizational relationships affect organizational behavior (Thompson 1967; Katz and Kahn 1978). Pfeffer and Salancik note that "because organizations import resources from their own environments, they depend on their environments. Survival comes when the organization adjusts to, and copes with, its environment, not only when it makes efficient internal adjustments" (1978, 19).

Community boards can emphasize one of two strategies when tending to their interorganizational environments. First, they may seek to institutionalize themselves within their communities by developing horizontal alliances with other community-based associations. Second, they may opt for a more integrative approach and seek vertical relationships with city agencies. In the former case, the boards pursue a parochial interorganizational strategy; in the latter, a cosmopolitan strategy.[10]

Table 6.1

The Disposition of Board-Initiated Capital-Budget Proposals
(in percent)

Outcome	Period			
	FY 1982	FY 1983	FY 1984	FY 1985
Line-item appropriation	20	20	20	11
Lump-sum appropriation	2	5	7	22
Continued funding	14	26	18	17
Rejected for procedural errors	5	12	25	28
Rejected for cause	59	37	30	22
Total	100	100	100	100
Total successes	36	51	45	50
First-time success	22	25	27	33
N	568	555	562	589

Note: The data are based on each board's top ten priority proposals for each fiscal year.

A second explanation for board differences in securing budget priorities focuses on district socioeconomic factors. From this perspective, three hypotheses, involving intracity service allocation, can be employed to analyze board success in having their proposals included in the capital budget. The underclass hypothesis suggests that intracity resource allocation reflects historic discrimination against poor and/or minority areas (*Hawkins* v. *Town of Shaw* 1971; Bolotin and Cingranelli 1983); the curvilinear hypothesis posits that, because of voting strength, resource allocation favors middle-class communities at the expense of other income groups (Jones 1978); and an unpatterned inequality hypothesis suggests random allocation of resources across spatial units within a city (Mladenka 1980; Lineberry 1977).

Table 6.2 indicates that board-initiated budget proposals submitted with a city agency cosponsor have a significantly better chance of being accepted than proposals submitted by the board alone or with a community-group cosponsor. Overall, proposals cosponsored by city line agencies were nearly three times as likely to be included in the city's capital budget as proposals submitted alone and over four times as likely to be accepted as proposals cosponsored by community groups. The strong relationship between agency cosponsorship and eventual inclusion of a proposal in the city's capital budget held in each of the four fiscal years examined. A parochial method of proposal submission was the least effective in helping districts to secure their local budget priorities.

Table 6.2

Board-Initiated Proposals and Capital-Budget Success

Interorganizational Factors			
Manner of submission	No. submitted	No. accepted	Success rate
Community-group cosponsor	239	34	14
Board alone	769	169	22
City agency cosponsor	350	214	61

Socioeconomic Factors			
Household income	No. submitted	No. accepted	Success rate
Low	366	84	23
Middle	731	234	32
Upper-middle	261	99	38
Total	1,358	417	31

Table 6.2 also indicates that community boards from middle- and upper-income districts are more likely to be successful in having their proposals included in the capital budget than are their counterparts from low-income community districts. Indeed, table 6.2 shows a linear relationship between community wealth levels and acceptance rates. As the underclass hypothesis suggests and as a Center for Responsive Government study (Rick 1982) affirmed, lower-income communities are less successful than the other community types in achieving their budgetary priorities. Multiple regression analysis was used to examine the relationships in Table 6.2 in more detail. A ratio of successful to total BIPs was calculated for each community board and served as the dependent variable in the equation.[11] To assess the impact of socioeconomic variables on the success ratio, we tested whether the district percentage of minority residents and median household income were related to board success. To address interorganizational factors, we developed a cosmopolitanism index for each board and tested it against the success ratio.[12]

Table 6.3 confirms that both interorganizational and socioeconomic factors help predict a board's budget success. Indeed, bivariate analyses indicate strong, statistically significant support both for the underclass hypothesis and for the notion that cosmopolitan boards are more successful in securing budget priorities. However, the large drop in the impact of the socioeconomic variables under

Table 6.3

The Cosmopolitanism Index, District Socioeconomic Factors, and Board Budgetary Success

	Board success ratios			
	Bivariate analysis		Multiple regression	
	Pearson's r	Slope	Beta	Slope
Cosmopolitanism index	0.51	0.21	0.45	0.19
Percentage minority	−0.43	0.04	*	*
Household income	0.45	0	0.24	0

R = 0.64
N = 59

* Dropped from equation.

Table 6.4

Socioeconomic Factors and Capital-Budget Success: Controlling for Manner of Submission

	BIP Submitted		
Household income	With community-group cosponsor	By board alone	With city agency cosponsor
Low	22	54	24
Middle	16	59	25
Upper-middle	16	55	28

multiple regression indicates that much, though not all, of the predictive capacity of these variables is attributable to the tendency of boards from lower-income districts to adopt parochial interorganizational strategies.[13]

Table 6.4 confirms that boards from low-income districts submit more of their capital-budget proposals with community-group cosponsors and fewer with city line agencies than boards from either middle-income or upper-middle-income areas. This parochial tendency among community boards from low-income districts, however, is not substantial enough to explain completely the lower acceptance rates they experience for proposals submitted to the capital budget. In short, although socioeconomic factors matter, they are much less crucial for explaining budgetary success during the maturation period than board interorganizational strategies.

Four characteristics summarize the evolution of board budget responsibilities during the period of maturation. First, overall board success rates have remained remarkably constant since the early years. The boards were successful in having roughly one-half of their proposals included in the capital budget in any given fiscal year. Second, overall constancy notwithstanding, the boards became more active in submitting and more successful in obtaining first-level local budget priorities during the maturation period. Third, city budget officials appear to employ decision rules that reward boards for vertical but not horizontal integration. In other words, since the inception of the board system, board budgetary success is enhanced by cooperation with city agencies and not by interactions with community organizations. For board leaders the lesson is clear: integration with the diverse interests in their communities may be one part of the mandate given to the boards by the 1975 charter revisions, but it is not a formula for budgetary success. Fourth, community-based budgeting favors the proposals of middle-class boards, which have a greater percentage of their proposals funded than lower-income boards.

Budgeting and the 1989 Charter Revisions

The 1989 charter revisions had profound impacts on the city's overall budget process. Abolishing the Board of Estimate meant that one of the primary checks on New York's mayor was gone. The charter sought to reestablish budgetary balance in a newly empowered city council. The community boards were disadvantaged by the revisions to the extent that the borough presidents' votes on the Board of Estimate might have reflected their interests; they were advantaged to the extent that the city council, operating through a process of district logrolling, might address those interests more directly. The new charter also included expanded responsibilities for the Department of Environmental Protection (DEP) and the city agencies involved in capital-budget projects. Under the new rules, the DEP holds the public hearings on a proposed contract, and agency procurement heads accept or reject bids, subject to mayoral review (*Staten Island Advance*, August 27, 1990, A1).

There were only a few charter provisions relating directly to the boards' budgetary authority. One established borough budget offices to assist the boards; a second made district and borough budget consultations a charter mandate, not just an executive order; and a third required formal and "meaningful explanations" for rejecting board-initiated budget proposals. To the extent that these provisions codified the geographic budgeting that developed as a result of the 1975 revisions and increased the information and access available to board members, they helped institutionalize board influence over the budget process. To the extent that the creation of borough budget offices assists boards from low-income districts to develop and realize their local priorities, the 1989 revisions might help equalize the spatial distribution of city resources.

The 1989 charter did include a strategic planning initiative that, although not directly related to the boards' budgetary authority, has potential impacts on that authority. Under the initiative, the Department of City Planning must designate a deputy executive director in charge of strategic planning for the city. Strategic planning involves assessments of the city's long-term policy environment and goals. It includes developing options for reorganization and feedback designed to enhance successful policy implementation. Robert Bailey (1989) suggests that strategic planning relates directly to capital budgeting and has the potential to overcome urban factionalism without mandating direction "from a few to the many." Bailey argues that because New York's strategic plan would be advisory and provide useful information to all interested parties, it affords "skeptical neighborhood groups a basis for more serious policy debate" on capital planning issues (1989, 174).

The Boards and the Budget: A Summary

Budgeting is a complex responsibility that requires technical information and political accommodation. For New York's geographically based budgeting to work effectively, it is essential that all the actors be informed about the process and about each others' issue positions. This command of information is particularly important to the boards, because, as the newest players in the game, they must prove themselves capable of representing their districts' needs while accommodating larger questions of fiscal and political feasibility.

The district and borough consultations among board members, local officials, and city agency representatives are quite useful in developing relationships among relevant actors. In an early study, Serre Murphy and Ira Wechter noted the benefits of these meetings for the boards: "The benefits derived from those sessions were clearly shown in the agencies' request budgets: agencies that were assigned to consult with the boards recommended a significantly higher number of their proposals for funding than did those agencies that did not consult" (1980, 47). By using these consultations to develop mutually respectful relationships with agency representatives, the boards can avoid unnecessary community–agency conflicts, which would hamper community budgetary goals.

The Office of Community Board Relations (OCBR) at OMB has been a notably useful source of technical assistance on budgetary matters for the boards. OCBR has worked to ease board involvement in the process by providing budget manuals and staff support to assist board members. Such efforts on the part of not only OCBR but also the Department of City Planning and the Community Board Assistance Unit are particularly crucial for boards from lower-income, minority communities, which are lagging behind middle-class districts in securing local budget priorities. Budgeting, perhaps more than the other board responsibilities, requires technical assistance provided by sources outside of the immediate community. As an early Interface Development Project study concluded:

In budget situations where community boards are competing for an increasingly shrinking pool of funds, the weakness of some boards may be creating a tremendous risk for poor communities. Consequently, the current board structure, which does not officially recognize any differences among New York City's communities, may in fact be responsible for widening the gap between poor and middle-class communities in terms of services and resources. (1980, 5)

Evaluating Service Responsibilities

As representatives of the level of general government closest to the people, city officials are intimately involved in service-delivery issues. Whereas federal and state policies often appear remote and distant, the allocation of local services is immediate and highly divisible in its impact: "Virtually all of the city's rawest nerves touch the delivery of urban services" (Lineberry and Sharkansky 1978, 261).

Service allocation during Tammany's reign was often informal, reflecting the machine's quid pro quo politics. Under reform, service delivery was considered essentially an apolitical exercise. Reformers believed that city agencies, comprising professional civil servants, were best suited to make the macro- and microlevel decisions involved in urban service delivery. Reformers argued that the agencies' downtown locations enabled them to view service needs from a citywide perspective while their professionalism provided them with the necessary expertise to develop efficient and equitable "decision rules" for spatial service allocation around the city. As chapter three made clear, the agency autonomy implied in these basic reform values (functional decentralization) was augmented by the political power of service providers, who sought to insulate themselves from political interference.

Reform's self-contained notion of service delivery was replaced by the 1975 charter revisions, which, borrowing from the ONG experiment under Mayor Lindsay, mandated the administrative decentralization of city services. The charter-mandated system included district service cabinets chaired by the boards' district managers, coterminality of agency and community district lines, and management decentralization within city agencies.

The Formal Mandate and Service Coordination

As the SCRC was meeting, there were unmistakable indications that many New Yorkers were growing increasingly dissatisfied with the quality of public services in the city. Moreover, it was becoming clear that dealing with the fiscal crisis would necessitate dramatic cutbacks in existing service levels. To address the issue of service delivery, the charter revisions established a formal role for community boards in coordinating service delivery within their community districts. Pursuant to the revised charter, the boards were required to "evaluate the quality and quantity of services provided by agencies within the community district; and within budgetary appropriations for such purposes disseminate information about city services and programs, process complaints, requests, and inquiries of residents of the community district" (*NYC Charter* 1976, sec. 2800-d).

The 1975 charter reforms operationalized the boards' service role by creating a system of district service cabinets (DSCs). These cabinets comprised the community boards' chairs and district managers, the service agencies' community district representatives, local city councillors, and representatives of the Department of City Planning. The boards' district managers serve as DSC chairs. According to the charter, the DSCs were to:

> (1) coordinate service functions and programs of the agencies that deliver services in the community district; (2) consider interagency problems and impediments to the effective and economic delivery of services in the district; (3) plan and recommend joint programs to meet the needs and priorities of community districts and their residents; and (4) consult with residents of the community district and their representatives about local service problems and activities. (*NYC Charter* 1976, sec. 2705)

Although there were obvious similarities between the DSC system created by the charter revisions of 1975 and that which operated under the ONG experiment, there were also important differences between the two approaches (Mudd 1984). First, under the 1975 charter mandates, the chair of the DSC, the board's district manager, was directly accountable to the board and not, as the ONG district managers had been, to the mayor's office. Second, the emphasis on management decentralization within city service-delivery agencies was greater under the charter revisions than it had been under ONG. Third, the mandate for community and service district coterminality made systematic agency–community relationships more likely under the charter revisions than it had been under ONG.

To facilitate the work of the DSCs, the SCRC sought to end the hodgepodge of community and service-agency lines in the city. To that end, the revised charter mandated that three years after acceptance of the community district map, several agencies should rearrange their operating divisions so that their district service boundaries were coterminous with those of the community districts. Agencies required to redraw their district service boundaries included patrol services of the police department; local parks and recreation; street cleaning and refuse collection of the sanitation department; and several divisions of the Human Resources Administration (HRA), including community services, community development, youth services, child development, and special services for children (*NYC Charter* 1976, sec. 2704-a, 1). Moreover, several other agencies were to move toward coterminality with aggregates of community districts, including Housing Preservation and Development's housing code enforcement, neighborhood preservation, and related housing rehabilitation services; the Department of Highway's programs for street maintenance and repair and sewer maintenance and repair; and the Department of Health's services other than municipal hospitals (*NYC Charter* 1976, sec. 2704-a, 2).

The revised charter also required that service-delivery agencies decentralize their administrative operations so that the district service chiefs who represented the agencies on the DSCs would have sufficient authority to influence agency policy in the district. The charter mandates each designated agency to:

> assign to each such local service district at least one official with management responsibilities involving the exercise of independent judgment in the scheduling allocation and assignment of personnel and equipment and the evaluation of performance or the management and planning of programs. Each such official shall have operating or line authority over agency programs, personnel and facilities within the local service district. (*NYC Charter* 1976, sec. 2704-d)

To administratively decentralize city service delivery, then, the SCRC employed four separate but interrelated strategies. First, the commission mandated the necessary geographic decentralization through sections 2702 and 2703 of the charter, which required that the city prepare, review, and adopt a community district map. Second, it addressed the issue of community and service district coherence by mandating coterminality of community and agency district lines (*NYC Charter* 1976, sec. 2704-a). Third, the SCRC addressed management decentralization, at least formally, by requiring the head of each designated agency to assign to local service districts officials with "operating or line authority over agency programs, personnel and facilities within the local service district" (*NYC Charter* 1976, sec. 2704-d). Fourth, the charter vested control over the DSCs in the boards' district manager (*NYC Charter* 1976, sec. 2800-f).

The Boards and Services: The Early Period

With few exceptions, coterminality of community and agency lines went reasonably well. Housing Preservation and Development's neighborhood preservation service continues to employ districts that cut across community district lines, and the Police Department received one three-year extension from the charter-imposed deadline in the boroughs of Brooklyn, Manhattan, and Staten Island and a second one-year waiver in midtown Manhattan and parts of Staten Island before it achieved coterminality. The exceptions notwithstanding, all other designated agencies and operating divisions developed coterminous districts with the community boards on or close to the charter-mandated schedule.

Much of the credit for achieving coterminality more or less on schedule goes to the Koch administration's Community Board Assistance Unit (CBAU), which actively pushed the designated agencies toward the January 1, 1980, goal. The Beame administration had shown little real interest in the charter reforms and had not accomplished much in the way of even planning for coterminality when Koch took office in 1978. Jewell Bickford argues that the CBAU was as successful as it was because it enjoyed the complete support of the mayor, was staffed with competent professionals, and avoided partisan conflicts by emphasizing its technical assistance role (Bickford 1980, 36–37).

The success in achieving coterminality aside, early reports on the effectiveness of the DSCs as service coordinators were largely negative. David Lebenstein concluded in 1980 that service delivery represented "the weakest link in the community board chain" (1980, 12). In a survey of board members and other city officials, the Center for Responsive Government found "a good deal of dissatisfaction" with the DSCs (Rich 1982, 69). Madeleine Adler and Jewel Bellush noted that many district managers tried to circumvent the DSCs because they found them to be ineffective in influencing service delivery within their communities (1980, 49–52).

Observers of the DSCs' early years cite three basic problems with the system. First and foremost, the degree of management decentralization within the service-delivery agencies was not sufficient to allow district service chiefs to be responsive to local input (Axelrod 1980, 330–32). One district manager stated, "The greatest failure in implementing [the charter amendments] was the complete failure to implement command or management decentralization within the agencies" (quoted in Mudd 1984, 207). Adler and Bellush spoke directly to this point when they concluded:

> In the three years since the new charter was passed, there have not been any institutional or structural changes within the bureaucracy of the city. The Charter Commission's expectation that community-based boards, assisted by a professional, locally appointed manager, could serve as leverage on the city's administrative agencies in helping to pull some authority down to street-level operations has not been realized. (1980, 52)

The authors go on to note that Mayor Beame had no interest in the community board system and Mayor Koch had neither the fiscal resources nor the political incentive to push for management decentralization.

A second problem involved poor communication between the boards and the agencies as well as a lack of information about agency operations available to the boards. Not surprisingly, service agency representatives viewed the DSCs with some suspicion, and the relationship between district managers and district service chiefs was often more competitive than cooperative. A third related problem was that because the district managers were appointed by the boards and not by the mayor, as they were under the ONG program, they were viewed by agency representatives more as community advocates than as service coordinators.

Disappointments aside, early analyses of the DSCs were not universally negative. In 1981, the CBAU was renamed the Community Assistance Unit (CAU). A 1981 CAU study indicated that although the DSCs were poor coordinators of public services within their districts, they did function reasonably well in an ombudsman role as complaint processors. During that year, the DSCs handled an average of 1,252 complaints from community residents. Moreover, by the early 1980s, over 30 percent of the DSCs had developed formal processes for tracking complaints through the various agencies and over 50 percent notified complainants of agency actions. The CAU reported that 73 percent of complaints referred to the DSCs were resolved (Community Assistance Unit 1982).

Moreover, some boards developed innovative approaches to their service responsibilities. Community Board 14 in Brooklyn worked with the Department of Sanitation to redesign the collection and street-cleaning services for its Flatbush–Midwood district. Community Board 5 in Queens instituted monthly "one-stop service days," during which providers of various social services assemble to answer residents' questions and facilitate assistance. Community Board 2 in the Bronx developed a plan to deal with illegal dumping in its South Bronx neighborhood. Moreover, several agencies attempted to implement management decentralization. Parks and Recreation and the Sanitation Department, for example, revised district supervisors' job descriptions and organized training programs at the Urban Academy. Cases like these, however, were more the exception than the rule.

Community effectiveness within DSCs was also a function of the capabilities of the district managers. Madeleine Adler and Jewel Bellush offered the following portrait of the early district managers: They tended to be young (under thirty-five), male (67 percent), married (69 percent), and well educated (86 percent were college graduates), and had social science or public administration training (1980, 49–50). The early district managers tended to view their positions as "launching pads" for managerial careers, and their turnover rate in the late 1970s was roughly 40 percent. Indeed, Lebenstein, in noting that turnovers were a major problem, reported that "at least one-third of the original DMs have left (three years later) and the more competent DMs generally get swooped up by entities (both public and private) that can pay them a lot more" (1980, 13).

Many of the early managers complained that the 1975 charter revisions left their responsibilities ill-defined and that the boards placed too many restrictions on their activities. Most acknowledged that they were more effective when dealing with informal contacts in administrative agencies than when working within the DSC structure. As Adler and Bellush point out, "their [district managers'] skill in developing and utilizing contacts and forging links between different bodies is central to their success" (1980, 52). Moreover, some managers felt that they lacked the necessary training to be truly effective.

The Boards and Services: The Maturation Period

The boards' service-monitoring capabilities increased during the 1980s, although the potential of the DSCs as service coordinators remained largely unrealized. Community–service district coterminality helped the district managers monitor service delivery by clarifying agency lines of responsibility and by simplifying the process of transmitting specific complaints to agency personnel. By the mid-1980s, many district managers were serving a community ombudsman role quite effectively.

A number of boards sought to expand their ombudsman role. Several adopted one-stop service days, allowing their district managers to move beyond the processing of specific complaints. Indeed, service days encouraged the kind of interagency cooperation that the DSCs were intended to develop. Other boards began publishing ratings of agency effectiveness in delivering services within their districts.[14] According to Barbara Gunn, director of the Mayor's Office of Operations under Mayor Koch, these board activities served as checks on the mayor's annual management reports, which include ratings on service agency outputs for a given fiscal year.[15] The district managers of still other boards, relying on their informal relationships with agency personnel, were able to overcome bureaucratic red tape and secure rapid responses to service emergencies in their districts (*New York Times,* November 9, 1986, sec. 1, 56).

Moreover, during the 1980s, several city agencies experimented with methods of improving their interactions with the community boards. HRA, for example, continued a program initiated in the late 1970s by maintaining human service cabinets in five community districts. An Interface Development Project report indicates that these cabinets, chaired by the community boards' district managers, made some progress in coordinating services to children and dealing with the effects of housing abandonment in their communities (1981, 24–25). In general, however, these experiments have not moved beyond the bounds of particular communities.

Specific innovations notwithstanding, the DSCs proved more adept at processing individual resident complaints than at coordinating service delivery within the communities. As one former district manager noted, "Service delivery is complaints, rather than coordinated planning" (quoted in Mudd 1984, 212). In fact, of the three grants of authority given to communities by the charter reforms of 1975, service coordination continued during the maturation period as the weakest link in the community board system.

Two factors, one internal to the boards and the other a function of bureaucracy, produced this limited service role for the DSCs. First, service coordination within a community district of between one hundred thousand and two hundred thousand persons is a complex and time-consuming job, particularly in light of the number of specific service complaints board district managers must handle. Moreover, district managers, as appointees of the community boards, bring little or no central-city backing to their roles. They are expected to coordinate the agency activities of service-delivery professionals as outsiders without a city-wide political or administrative base.[16]

Indeed, district managers' working conditions left much to be desired during the maturation period. Their responsibilities remained vaguely defined, and several were victimized by internal political battles on the community boards they served. The funding levels for their offices had not increased sufficiently by 1983 to counter turnovers, and several district managers reported in 1988 that these problems remained unresolved. Such in-house political conflicts and budgetary restraints made a difficult situation all the more problematic.

Diane Morales, director of community services for Manhattan, points out that these problems are especially intense in poorer communities, where information concerning agency operations is often minimal.[17] Moreover, in these communities, service problems are often critical, and the need for redress is often immediate. As Lebenstein noted, because poorer communities "are dealing with survival, drugs, housing, life-and-death issues . . . [t]hey don't have the time for the process" (quoted in the *New York Times*, November 9, 1986, sec. 1, 56).

A second overriding problem with the boards' service role is that the degree of management decentralization within the service-delivery agencies remains insufficient to ensure agency responsiveness to community concerns. In fact, several observers question whether there are even "open channels of communication" between district representatives and policy-makers in a number of agencies. Jane Planken, director of community boards for Queens in the 1980s, noted that after some early progress, particularly in the Department of Sanitation and in Parks and Recreation, there was a noticeable deterioration in the effort toward management decentralization among agencies. She attributed much of the problem to the lack of city incentives for decentralization.[18]

There are several organizational reasons why management decentralization has not taken place. Initially, the demands of agency retrenchment brought on by the fiscal crisis diverted managers from the task of administrative decentralization. Indeed, the fiscal crisis produced a need for agency fiscal centralization to deal with budget cutbacks. Following the retrenchment period, city administrations have been hesitant about engaging in the political battles that would be necessary to redirect agency management to a more decentralized emphasis. Edward Rogowsky, then director of community boards for Brooklyn, noting an absence of administration "passion" on this issue, contended that "without a concentrated mayoral effort, meaningful management decentralization will not occur."[19]

Ironically, another difficulty in achieving management decentralization is that New York's reform-style bureaucracies have never developed sufficient levels of internal coordination to permit geographic decentralization. The centrifugal pressures found in analyses of the effects of specialization on reform governance as a whole also influence internal agency operations. In a policy sense, reform-style bureaucracies are internally fragmented by the same type of intraorganizational pressures that plague reform governance generally. Indeed, such fragmentation represents a major constraint on agency influence generally. However, it also means that reshaping internal organizational modes of operation is very difficult. In short, to decentralize geographically, agencies must first centralize functionally, and that is antithetical to reform-style agencies.

The problems with management decentralization, however, are more fundamental than the lack of political will or the absence of internal coordination. Indeed, nearly fifty years ago, Herbert Simon pointed out the difficulties of even operationally defining organizational decentralization. Simon argued that, in many ways, decentralizing by purpose, process, clientele, and place were internally inconsistent and even contradictory strategies. Because of the diverse emphases of these four organizational dynamics, each of which is present in urban bureaucracy, a reasonable analysis of centralization or decentralization "would reveal a more complex picture of the decision-making process than any enumeration of the geographical locations of organizational units at the different levels" (Simon 1946, 58). Indeed, it may be that implementing management decentralization either leads to unacceptable violations of the principle of unity of command or requires enormously complex and expensive organizational designs.

Services and the 1989 Charter Revisions

Although service delivery was not an impetus for change, the 1989 charter revisions included four provisions to increase community and borough leverage on service matters. First, the charter refocused administration attention on the city's decentralized service system by mandating that the mayor publish an annual community district breakdown of city services and a biennial report on the overall functioning of the system. If nothing else, such mandates force city administrations to periodically and publicly assess the service system from a geographic perspective.

Second, the new charter gave the borough presidents increased responsibilities for services by requiring them to publish an annual district-by-district service report for their boroughs. Moreover, the charter mandated that if meetings between borough presidents and borough agency representatives do not resolve disagreements on particular service issues, "the borough president would have the power to require reallocations within the borough which do not increase or decrease personnel or resources within any community board . . . by more than five percent" (NYC CRC 1990, 25). This authority might provide the borough presidents, and perhaps through them the boards' district managers, with a useful negotiating tool in their interactions with agency representatives.

Third, the charter created two external sources of oversight on service issues. It mandated that, within two years, a task force, with center-city, borough, and community representation, suggest improvements for service decentralization. In addition, the charter empowered the city council president to monitor the system on a day-to-day basis. Given that office's diminished role following the demise of the Board of Estimate, council presidents might seek to develop community political bases through their service oversight function and consequently increase district and borough influence on service matters.

Fourth, in an effort to bring more equity to the decentralized service system, the charter created "an office of language services" to monitor agencies and assist boards in districts where English is not the primary language. In the face of the larger socioeconomic factors promoting inequity, this effort seems more symbolically than substantively noteworthy.

The Boards and Services: A Summary

For the reasons explored above, the 1975 charter's mandate for a formal, community-based service coordination role through DSCs has not been realized. Instead, the DSCs have evolved into mechanisms that practice an extended, yet often informal, ombudsman role within their communities. From a postreform perspective, the DSCs' extended ombudsmen role, given the original charter promise, is only a partially satisfying development.

Nevertheless, DSC meetings force periodic interactions between representatives of service providers and service recipients. Rejected by reformers as external interference in professional decision making, such interactions provide continual and informative feedback to all parties. DSC meetings give service providers information on service recipients' perceptions of the quality of their operations. In an increasingly heterogeneous city, they provide a forum for the airing of neighborhood-specific cultural issues, which may elude professionals designing service-delivery rules. Conversely, DSC meetings provide agency representatives with opportunities to inform community activists about the legal, organizational, and budgetary constraints under which they operate and to help them distinguish feasible from fanciful demands.

Indeed, increased coterminality might improve the system. The boards compete with city councillors and community school boards in dealing with community service questions. Joseph Viteritti suggests that "coterminality between community districts, school districts and council districts is essential in order to achieve effective community government and assure that the [city] council fulfills the important role assigned to it under the new charter" (1991, 38).

CHAPTER SEVEN

Postreform and Community Activists

Having examined community board efforts in the areas of land-use planning, budget priorities, and service monitoring from a macroperspective in chapter six, we now turn to an exploration of the attitudes and behavior of individual board members. As noted previously, by the time community empowerment was incorporated into the formal processes of city government in the 1970s, the power of central-city interests coupled with the overall constraints of urban fiscal stress had acted to moderate the nature and the extent of formal decentralization in American cities. Considered within the larger context of the early postreform demands for participatory democracy and community control, the community board system in New York, with its appointed membership and its advisory powers, represents a moderate and integrative form of decentralization.

This chapter focuses on community board members in light of postreform politics. In a theoretical sense, it examines the impact of efforts to address attentive nonelite demands on individual attentive nonelites. In an operational sense, the chapter addresses several questions about the attitudes and behaviors of community board members working within New York's postreform regime. Does the community-control model, which originally characterized the postreform movement of the 1960s and early 1970s, remain relevant to board members in the late 1980s and early 1990s? If so, what factors best explain the continued salience of such an approach to urban politics? What are the effects, if any, of current attitudes toward community empowerment on the operation of an integrative model of decentralization like New York's community board system?

Community Board Members

To address these questions, I contacted a sample of community board members. Between April 1985 and February 1987, I distributed questionnaires to more than 1,800 board members, 628 of whom sent back usable responses. The respondents represented 35 percent of the members contacted and over 20 percent of the nearly 3,000 community board members across the city.

Sixty-eight percent of the respondents in the sample were men. Seventy percent were between thirty-five and sixty years of age, with 14 percent over the age of sixty. Sixty-two percent of the respondents sampled were white, and 35 percent were African-American. More than 50 percent had resided within their community district for longer than ten years.

The board members sampled were relatively well educated. Nearly 50 percent of the sample had earned baccalaureate degrees and 17 percent had master's degrees. Of the 291 respondents with baccalaureate degrees, 42 percent had majored in the social sciences in college, 15 percent had focused on the humanities, and 14 percent had earned business degrees. Of the over one hundred postgraduate degrees earned by the board members in the sample, 36 percent were in law, 21 percent were in the social sciences, 13 percent were in education, and 12 percent were in business.

The board members in the sample had a wide diversity of occupations. Twenty percent described themselves as businesspeople, 16 percent as government workers, 13 percent as professionals, and 12 percent as employees of nonprofit organizations. Most of the respondents were middle-class. Sixteen percent earned less than $20,000 per year; over 60 percent had annual incomes between $20,000 and $40,000; and slightly less than 25 percent earned more than $40,000 per year.[1] The respondents sampled were active participants in community affairs. Aside from their community board positions, more than 70 percent were also members of either neighborhood civic associations or community activist organizations; 30 percent were active in local party affairs; and 20 percent belonged to area development corporations. Prior to their appointment to the community board, more than 50 percent of the respondents had been active in local civic or activist groups, 25 percent had been political party activists, and slightly more than 10 percent had been involved in local development corporations. Fewer than 10 percent of the sample had previous experience with New York's community school boards.

Attitudes toward Community Empowerment

The examination of board members' perceptions about community empowerment in New York was conducted during the boards' maturation period and was focused on members' attitudes toward the nature of the responsibilities allocated to the boards. On the first level, the research sought information about whether board members were satisfied with the community integration system in New York or whether they would prefer a greater emphasis on community control. On a second level, the study focused on selected socioeconomic and political characteristics of the sample to determine whether they helped account for the expected differences in attitudes toward the community board system. On a third level, the research explored whether different attitudes toward the board system resulted in distinctive behavior patterns among board members.

To assess board members' attitudes about community power, a scale was developed to distinguish board members who were generally satisfied with New

York's system of integrative decentralization from those who believed that it did not incorporate sufficient community-based authority to protect local interests. Board members were asked whether they favored community advisory or decision-making power over nine policy matters relating to urban communities; their responses determined their placement on a community-empowerment scale.[2] Respondents satisfied with the advisory power allocated to community boards were considered supporters of the community integration system in New York City; those who sought greater amounts of community-based decision power were considered community-control advocates who were less than satisfied with the board system in New York. In addition, to tap any differences across the three areas of responsibility allocated to the boards by the 1975 charter revisions, the community-empowerment scale was subdivided into three smaller scales, each composed of three items focused on either land-use issues, budgetary responsibilities, or service-monitoring concerns.[3]

Table 7.1 indicates that respondents' reactions to the board system were clearly divided. Although 44 percent of the sample indicated some degree of support for community integration in general, only 15 percent professed strong support for the current community board system.[4] To the majority of its supporters, then, New York's integrative board system appears to be a satisfactory, if not a particularly impressive, attempt to share policy-making responsibilities with local interests.

Conversely, over 55 percent of the board members sampled disapproved of the current integrative system in New York and expressed at least moderate support for community control, with 20 percent of the respondents strongly disapproving of the board system. For them, the community integration model does not satisfactorily address the original postreform demands for local empowerment. Indeed, several respondents in this second group indicated that they considered New York's community board system as only "a first step" in what they hoped would be an ongoing process of devolving political power to communities. For a substantial number of community board members, then, the dissatisfaction with city governance, which first destabilized and then helped reformulate politics in the city, has been addressed only partially by integrative decentralization. For this group, the emergence of a truly postreform regime means that community representatives should control and not just influence many of the land-use, budgeting, and service matters involved in day-to-day community life.

Table 7.1 indicates that land-use issues generated the most pronounced community-control reactions among the board members sampled. Some 67 percent of the respondents desired an increased amount of community authority in this area, with nearly 40 percent of the sample strongly opposed to the current integrative land-use review process in New York. Indeed, of the three areas of board responsibility, the community role in land-use review enjoyed the least amount of strong approval among the respondents, with fewer than 20 percent expressing strong support for the current system. It is noteworthy that among

Table 7.1

Community-Empowerment Attitudes: Support for Integrative Decentralization (in percent)

	Support		Opposition	
	Strong	Moderate	Moderate	Strong
Overall score	15.3	29.0	35.7	20.0
Land-use issues	18.6	14.6	27.3	39.5
Budget priorities	36.5	23.4	15.5	24.5
Service delivery	25.2	13.7	25.4	35.6

N = 614

board members who expressed strong opinions on the land-use issue, more than twice as many strongly opposed the current system as strongly supported it.

Such lingering attachments to community control over land-use issues were not totally unexpected. As noted in chapters three and four, the community-control movement was in large part a reaction to land-use concerns as residents of diverse neighborhoods felt threatened by reform government's land-use policies. Local activism in minority neighborhoods was often a reaction to the urban renewal and highway projects that threatened to destroy these areas; community consciousness among white ethnics was frequently a reaction to land-use proposals designed to promote racial integration.

Moreover, land-use decisions are often singular in their impact on urban communities. As chapter six points out, estimates of community board success in achieving desired outcomes under ULURP range from 80 to 95 percent. However, overall success notwithstanding, a series of positive community experiences in dealing with land-use proposals, where the board either successfully blocks or forces changes in unpopular projects, can be easily counterbalanced by one or two less effective ULURP interactions. Failures to stop or at least force revisions in unpopular land-use projects stand as literally concrete reminders of community board limitations under the current integrative system in New York.

The strong community-control reaction to land-use issues among the respondents, then, has roots that are both historical and immediate. Whatever the underlying causes, however, it is clear that land use remains a particularly noteworthy source of tension between city and community interests in New York. Even board members who are generally satisfied with the current system in other areas have serious doubts about the nature and extent of community influence over land-use issues.

Alternatively, Table 7.1 indicates that budget matters are the least likely of the boards' three responsibilities to prompt strong community-control reactions among board members. Nearly 60 percent of the board members in the sample expressed at least moderate support for the boards' role in the current budgetary process, with more than 36 percent expressing strong support for geographically based budgeting in New York. Of the three areas of board responsibility, community involvement in budgeting provoked the fewest expressions of strong disapproval among the respondents. Implicit in this greater willingness by many board members to accept community integration approaches to fiscal issues is an acknowledgment of the inherent interdependence involved in the municipal budget process. It is also important to note that this research was conducted when memories of the budgetary effects of the city's most recent fiscal crisis were still relatively fresh in the minds of politically attentive New Yorkers. Such memories may well have prompted a hesitancy among the board members sampled to control local budget allocations.

Moreover, budget failures do not usually have the dramatic impact of community land-use setbacks that budget successes often do. Chapter six indicates that, although the boards vary in their capacities to obtain community capital-budget priorities, few if any boards are completely shut out of the process. Accordingly, every board can point to at least some success, and, in dealing with capital-budget priorities, some visible success, in the budget area. In community districts throughout the city, board budget priority successes are often as evident as land-use review failures, and this may help explain the widespread acceptance of integrative budget practices by board members in New York.

Lastly, the data indicate that over 60 percent of the board members sampled were at least moderately dissatisfied with the integrative approach to service delivery and favored more local control in this area. Indeed, nearly as many respondents expressed strong opposition to the current integrative community service-delivery function as did to the community land-use review procedure. However, it is also worth noting that, despite the general dissatisfaction, over 25 percent of the board members sampled expressed strong support for the current integrative service system, which is a good deal more than expressed strong support for land-use review. The findings may well reflect frustration as much with services in New York as with the integrative system for monitoring them.

In summary, a majority of the board members sampled are at least moderately dissatisfied with the boards' authority. This dissatisfaction is particularly pronounced in relation to land-use issues. Nevertheless, despite the majority support for community control, a large number of respondents are satisfied with New York's integrative community board system, particularly when the question concerns budgetary matters.

Accounting for Different Attitudes: Hypotheses

This section of chapter seven addresses the issue of whether there are socioeconomic or political variables that help account for the attitudinal differences between supporters of the community board system and those who desire more community control. In operational terms, it examines whether the distinctions among board members on the community-empowerment scale are a function of racial, ideological, and/or political variables.

Previous research suggests that perceptions of urban life and evaluations of urban politics are often strongly affected by race. In the context of postreform values, Fainstein and Fainstein (1976) found that although widespread support exists for community control across city neighborhoods and policy areas, such support tends to be stronger among African-American community elites. Echoing the racial distinction on community empowerment, Ross and Stedman note that the philosophy of community control maintains a "very strong psychological attraction," especially in "the rapidly growing black and Latino areas of the largest cities" (1985, 304–5). Chapter three of this book chronicles the importance of the black power movement as an independent contributing factor to the early development of postreform politics in American cities.

Other studies emphasize the differences between African-American and white political mobilization in American cities. In analyzing the issue of ethnic-group transference of political power in New York, John Hull Mollenkopf notes that the process has been more difficult and less politically satisfying for African-Americans and Latinos in part because of the 1975 fiscal crisis and in part because "race has introduced a qualitiatively different element into the politics of group succession" (1991, 336). Hamilton sees important differences between African-American political participation in New York and that of other groups. He argues that the political focus on protest- and demand-side politics resulted in an underemphasis on African-American electoral mobilization in the city (Hamilton 1990). Nelson (1992) contends that even black electoral success in cities has not been characterized by the kind of organizational institutionalization of group influence that accompanied the electoral ascendance of other groups.

Still other research focuses on racial differences concerning specific urban policy areas. Several studies report that residents of predominantly minority communities express greater dissatisfaction than their counterparts in white neighborhoods with the quality of city services in those communities (Cingranelli 1983; Brown and Coulter 1983). Moreover, chapter six notes that community boards from predominantly minority districts tend to be more parochial, that is, community-focused, than boards from mostly white districts in their approach to securing capital-budget priorities.

In general, then, the literature suggests that African-Americans, reacting to the institutionalized white racism as well as the overt discrimination they have experienced in American cities, have developed distinctive attitudes about and approaches to urban politics. Furthermore, given the negative impact of the larger social order on urban minorities, the research suggests that these attitudes and approaches among African-Americans led to an increasingly inward and community-focused political perspective. Accordingly, we expect that African-American board members will be more suspicious of and hostile to the community integration approach to urban decentralization and will therefore indicate stronger support for community control as a decentralization alternative than will their white counterparts.

A second factor that might be helpful in explaining differences on the community-empowerment scale is political ideology. Although there was a conservative ideological dimension to community empowerment even in the early years, evident in the defensive reactions against racial integration in white ethnic neighborhoods, the intellectual and emotional origins of the postreform movement lie on the liberal left. Saul Alinsky, one of the earliest proponents of community organizing, rejected ideological labels. However, his self-description as a radical organizer places him firmly on the populist left of American politics. "The radical is deeply interested in social planning but just as deeply suspicious of, and antagonistic to, any idea of plans that work from the top down. Democracy to him is working from the bottom up" (Alinsky 1969, 17).

In a study of New York, Fainstein and Martin found that "minority respondents are more likely to support community control because they are more likely to be ideological leftists" (1978, 456).[5] Robert Fisher suggests that the participatory political attitudes articulated in the 1960s and the community organizing that characterized such attitudes in American cities were at their roots manifestations of "radical organizing efforts responding to the contradictions of life in the 'affluent society'" (1984, 91). Marilyn Gittell contends that community organizing in the 1960s provided a "break with the past" because it raised a "serious challenge to the political system" (1980, 30). These analyses, emphasizing the ideological component of community politics, suggest that ideologically liberal board members will maintain an attachment to postreform ideals and tend to favor community control, whereas moderate and conservative respondents will be relatively satisfied with the integrative status quo in New York.[6]

Finally, recognizing the importance of the organizational process in both forming and reflecting individual attitudes, the study examined immediate structural aspects of the board system to determine if they helped explain the differences in member perceptions of community empowerment. Chapter five notes that board members are appointed by borough presidents, with one-half of the appointments coming from nominations supplied by local city council representatives. The appointment process, then, would appear as more a constant than a variable. However, formal requirements aside, board members have taken a number of diverse routes to their initial community board appointments. Some have approached the borough president's office, others have consulted with their local city council representatives, and still others have gone directly to the boards and sought community support for their appointments. It is reasonable to expect that board members who sought their initial appointments by securing community-based support are, by definition, more locally focused and consequently more likely to support community control than members who adopted more cosmopolitan approaches.

Table 7.2

Community-Empowerment Attitudes by Race, Manner of Appointment, and Ideology (beta weights)

	Community-empowerment attitudes			
	Overall	Land use	Budget	Services
Race	0.38	0.33	0.25	0.32
Appointment	0.10	0.04	0.09	0.11
Ideology	0.03	0.03	0.03	0.06

$N = 592$

Note: The beta weights are based on analysis of variance (ANOVA). Because there was no theoretical ordering of the variables (factors), each was entered controlling for all the others.

Accounting for Different Attitudes: Findings

Table 7.2 presents the strength of the relationships between attitudes toward community empowerment and the three variables reviewed above.[7] It clarifies several points. First, race is a highly relevant variable when assessing the different attitudes of board members toward community empowerment. Second, the manner in which board members sought their initial appointments is only weakly tied to community-empowerment attitudes. Third, political ideology has little independent effect on respondents' community-empowerment attitudes.

Table 7.3 elaborates on the relationships presented in Table 7.2. It presents the average community-empowerment scale scores across different categories of respondents in the sample.[8] The average scores range from 0 through 1, with the higher scores indicating greater support for community control. Accordingly, whereas the average scale score for all respondents on land-use issues (0.63) indicates relatively strong support for a community-control alternative to the current system in this policy area, the 0.41 average on budgetary practices points to more acceptance of New York's community integration approach in this area.

The data in both tables indicate that African-American board members are more likely than their white counterparts to favor increased community power overall and in each of the three areas of board responsibility. In an earlier study of attitudes toward community empowerment, Fainstein and Martin found that "interracial differences in support for community control are important but seem to be decreasing" (1978, 452). The data in Tables 7.2 and 7.3, however, indicate

Table 7.3

Community-Empowerment Attitudes by Race, Manner of Appointment, and Ideology (average scale scores)

	Community-empowerment attitudes			
	Overall	Land use	Budget	Services
	.54	.63	.42	.57
Race				
White	.45	.54	.35	.47
African-American	.69	.79	.55	.74
Appointment				
Cosmopolitan	.50	.61	.37	.51
Parochial	.56	.64	.45	.60
Ideology				
Conservative	.55	.63	.43	.60
Moderate	.54	.61	.43	.57
Liberal	.54	.64	.41	.55

Note: A scale score of 0 would indicate complete acceptance of the current system; a score of 1 would mean total rejection of that system.

that race remained one of the most important distinguishing factors when examining support for community control in the 1980s.

These divergent findings may be a function of the time frame surrounding each study. Fainstein and Martin's study examined community elites' attitudes in the early 1970s, as the Lindsay administration, which many white ethnics perceived as overly friendly to minority demands, was coming to an end. In fact, it is difficult to think of a period in New York's recent history when white ethnics were more alienated from city government than during the Lindsay years. Such alienation, translated into increased community-control attitudes among white ethnics, may well explain Fainstein and Martin's findings of a convergence in attitudes concerning community control. On the other hand, the data in Tables 7.2 and 7.3 were collected in the mid-1980s, following nearly ten years of "neoconservative populism" under Mayor Koch, which may have lessened the political alienation among the city's white ethnics while renewing or reaffirming existing distrust for city government among African-Americans.

It is entirely possible that the election of David Dinkins as the city's first African-American mayor in 1989 will eventually result in less pronounced community-control attitudes among minority board members in the 1990s, a concomitant increase in such attitudes among white ethnics, and consequently more of the racial convergence of the type uncovered by Fainstein and Martin in the 1970s. However, as was pointed out in chapter five, the Dinkins administration took office during a period of economic downturn in New York. As a consequence, the symbolic and substantive impact of Dinkins's election on African-American board members may have been lessened as the forces of fiscal centralization, incorporated into the postreform regime, successfully pressured the new mayor to adopt policies adversely affecting his own constituency base.

The differences in community-empowerment scores across the categories of manner of appointment, although not particularly strong, are generally in the expected direction. Board members who pursued more community-focused strategies in their initial efforts to gain appointment to their local community boards tend to be slightly more parochial in their attitudes toward community empowerment, particularly in relation to service-delivery issues. Indeed, it is reasonable to conclude that New York's integrative procedures for board appointment may be responsible in some small way for tempering the attitudes of the community activists selected to serve on the boards. The integrative system for board appointment obviously does not exclude advocates of community control from being selected, but it does encourage the appointment of community activists with more interactive perspectives. If other more directly postreform member-selection mechanisms had been mandated by the 1975 charter, the extent of support for community-control options may well have been more pronounced among board members.

Lastly, the data make it clear that political ideology is unrelated to attitudes toward community empowerment. The beta weights in Table 7.2 indicate that no relationship exists, and the average community-empowerment scale scores in Table 7.3 for conservatives, moderates, and liberals hover around the overall average for each of the three policy areas and for community empowerment in general.[9] It is clear that knowing a board member's general political ideology indicates nothing about his or her more specific attitudes toward community empowerment.

The Politics of Race and Class

Race and class are obviously interrelated demographic facts in American cities; African-Americans and Latinos represent disproportionately high percentages of low-income populations in urban areas. There is evidence of increasing economic diversity within the black community, however, as expanding private- and public-sector employment opportunities (often promoted by affirmative action) have provided upward mobility for some African-Americans over the past twenty years (Bailey and Waldinger 1991). According to a 1992 Census Bureau report, the continuing loss of blue-collar jobs in the city coupled with the rise of two-income households "have widened the gulf between haves and have-nots in the black population" (*New York Times,* September 25, 1992, A12). As a consequence, the question emerges of how (or whether) economic diversity within the

African-American community affects social and political attitudes.

There are analysts who argue that the political behavior of the black middle class is more likely to reflect economic rather than racial antecedents. Indeed, William Julius Wilson (1978) makes the point that labor force segmentation in American society has left behind a large low-income cohort in the inner cities whose social and political behavior reflect values that the African-American middle class no longer shares. Frank Levy (1987) affirms that there are increasing income disparities within the African-American population, particularly among young males. Such bifurcated class relationships may well lead to systemic attachments among the economic "winners" while increasing alienation and anger among the economic "losers."

Moreover, the political realities of the post-1975 crisis years in New York may have especially alienated the city's low-income African-American population. Despite the fact that Koch's appeal to white ethnics was often as psychological and cultural as it was political, his early economic conservatism may have generated support among the city's African-American middle class while increasingly alienating low-income African-Americans. Indeed, despite his administration's political emphasis on and strength within white communities, Koch maintained a sizable support base in minority communities, even when he was opposed by an African-American candidate (Mollenkopf 1991). Although it is unclear whether the support for Koch was based on class, it has been suggested that it was likely to be "found within the blue-collar, immigrant 'middle' of the black community" (Mollenkopf 1991, 346).

Accordingly, within the limits of the data, we examined the effects of economic variables on the relationship between race and the community-empowerment scale.[10] We expected that lower-income board members, particularly those from the African-American community, would tend to be more alienated from what they perceived as unresponsive city government and consequently would be more likely to support community-control alternatives than their middle-class counterparts.

Table 7.4 portrays the effects of economic controls on the relationship between race and board members' attitudes toward community empowerment. As expected, given previous findings, significantly larger proportions of African-American as opposed to white respondents support community control across the board. Indeed, African-Americans in the sample support community control by roughly a two-to-one ratio over their white counterparts. Table 7.4 indicates, however, that income level does have some effect on attitudes, particularly among African-Americans. On the overall community-empowerment scale as well as on each of the three issue-specific scales, low-income African-Americans are more likely than their middle-class racial counterparts to support a community-control perspective.

In summary, there are differences within the African-American community in the extent of support for community control that are attributable to economic

Table 7.4

Community-Empowerment Attitudes by Race, Controlling for Income
(percentage favoring community control)

	Overall		Land use		Budget		Services	
	White	African-Amer.	White	African-Amer.	White	African-Amer.	White	African-Amer.
Income								
Low	25	60	28	66	17	47	29	60
Middle	16	43	28	58	18	31	23	47

Note: Low income, $20,000 or less annually; middle income, more than $20,000 annually.

variables. Intragroup differences notwithstanding, however, middle-class African-Americans express attitudes toward community empowerment that are much closer to those held by their lower-income racial counterparts than to those of their middle-income economic counterparts. The conclusion that racial background, tempered only slightly by economic class, is a crucial factor distinguishing board members' perceptions of New York's community integration system seems inescapable.

Specific Community-Empowerment Attitudes

By displaying reactions to each of the nine items composing the community-empowerment scale, Table 7.5 offers an in-depth picture of board members' attitudes. It shows the percentage of community-control responses (members who favored community decision-making authority) for each of the items in the scale. In addition, Table 7.5 provides the percentage of item-by-item community-control responses within racial categories, the most relevant variable for distinguishing between supporters and opponents of integrative decentralization in New York.

Responses to the first three (land-use-related) items in Table 7.5 make it clear that large majorities of the board members sampled support community decision-making authority over the granting of zoning variances and the siting of group homes. Both issues have substantial implications for communities. Just as a municipal zoning plan proactively defines a community's physical character, the authority to grant zoning variances can reactively redefine that physical character. Such variances have been employed frequently in New York since the city first developed and subsequently revised its overall zoning plan. Indeed, Jewel Bellush notes that New York's zoning law "has been amended so many times that the additional modifications are longer than the original zoning resolution"

Table 7.5

The Community-Empowerment Scale: An Item-by-Item Breakdown
(percentage favoring community control)

Proposal topics	Overall	Race White	African-American
Zoning and variances	69	60	84
Group-home sites	66	55	85
Private development	53	44	70
Expense-budget allocations	38	30	49
Capital-budget allocations	46	37	60
Economic development allocations	45	36	58
Sanitation services	62	52	77
Housing services	50	41	64
Police services	60	48	80

(1990, 321). Moreover, the power to locate group homes, considered locally unwanted land uses (LULUs) by many residents, can have a negative impact on a community's residential desirability.

It is notable that the issues generating the most widely pronounced community-control reactions among the respondents are those that place community boards in direct interaction with city officials. Indeed, the members expressed greater satisfaction with the city's current land-use procedures and consequently opted for community control least frequently when the issue involved proposals by private developers for use of community land. Apparently, board members are more comfortable with integrative decentralization when negotiating over specific private-sector proposals than when dealing with city officials over public plans for community land.[11]

This reaction is, in part, explainable by the distinct nature of private and public land-use proposals. Although private-sector development proposals may include negative environmental and quality-of-life externalities, which require careful board attention and review, they also involve, by definition, investment in the community. On the other hand, government land-use proposals are often designed to address citywide needs, with locally unwanted facilities perceived as threats to community property values and even resident safety. Indeed, at times, even city proposals to improve land use meet resistance because of local fears that the improvement will encourage misuse of community facilities by "outsiders." For example, negative community reactions have sometimes accompanied city efforts to refurbish small neighborhood parks (*New York Times,* October 12, 1992, 6).

Given the findings presented earlier in the chapter, it is not surprising that African-American board members are much more supportive of community control over each of the three land-use items than are their white counterparts. Indeed, frustration among African-American respondents with the city's practice of placing LULUs in low-income, minority districts is clearly reflected in the responses. No other two items in the community-empowerment scale elicit such widespread community-control responses among African-Americans sampled than those focused on siting group homes and the related issue of zoning variances. Moreover, even private-sector development proposals prompt community-control reactions among a large majority of African-American respondents. In part, this may reflect differences in the nature of private-sector development proposals in middle-class as opposed to lower-income neighborhoods.

The racially diverse item-by-item reactions are to be expected. As the analysis in chapter six made clear, community board effectiveness with the technical questions involved in land-use review is related to board capacity to deal effectively with central-city or private-sector experts on these matters. These questions are often considered within a context defined by legal and professional jargon, which can be employed to first overwhelm and then eventually silence nonexpert participants in land-use discussions. As a result, those boards with indigenous sources of expertise (i.e., large numbers of active, upper-middle-class professionals) have greater opportunities to use their land-use authority effectively than boards with less such expertise. At the time of this study, then, the boards representing low-income districts were at a disadvantage in exercising land-use responsibilities. The resulting frustration with integrative land-use mechanisms may well account for the greater community-control temperament of African-American respondents across all three land-use items in the scale.

It remains to be seen what effects, if any, the 1989 charter revisions will have on attitudes toward the boards' land-use responsibilities. Chapter six notes that these revisions attempt to address the inequities in land-use review capacity by providing boards from lower-income districts with Department of City Planning assistance in assessing specific land-use proposals. In that fashion, the charter revisions were an effort to spread planning expertise more evenly throughout the city. If these revisions accomplish their goal, or at least are perceived as being a good-faith attempt to accomplish their goal, they may help moderate some of the discontent that many board members feel toward New York's integrative land-use review procedures. However, the fact that board members are more supportive of community control over land-use issues involving city policy than over those focusing on private developers may mitigate the positive impact of the 1989 revisions. Given the apparent widespread distrust of city government, charter-mandated programs for official city assistance, of the kind included in the 1989 revisions, may not be perceived by board members as an answer to their problems with the present system.

Table 7.5 also reaffirms and elaborates on previous findings about geographic budgeting in New York. The three items focusing on budget matters are the least likely of the nine on the scale to provoke community-control reactions among respondents. In part, this is a function of the interdependent nature of budget decisions as well as the complexity of establishing community control in this area. There are two community-control alternatives to integrative budgeting. One would allocate revenue-raising authority to the community boards, making them responsible for budgeting over some range of public programs within their districts; the other would involve the allocation of city revenues to the community boards in the form of block grants. For the block-grant system to incorporate community control, the boards would have to have wide discretion over the expenditure of city money within their districts. Indeed, board discretion over the use of funds would have to resemble that given to state and local governments by the federal revenue-sharing programs of the 1970s.

There are a number of problems with the first alternative. Providing the boards with full budgetary authority, including taxing power, even if only over a limited range of policy areas, means literally creating another tier of general-level government in the city. As a consequence, community budgetary control would have required a more developed and expensive community board system than city or state officials were prepared to create or perhaps able to finance. Moreover, it would almost certainly have required the election of community board members, since the boards would be defined as local governments.

The block-grant alternative is less complex than full community budgetary control and was cited favorably by several of the respondents who favored community control of budgeting priorities. Nevertheless, it too includes great difficulties. Coordinating services is a problem when communities are free to fund a mix of available services. This becomes particularly problematic if local choice extends to inter- as well as intraservice mixes. Moreover, accountability issues emerge as funds raised by one level of government are expended by another.

Recognition of the extent of these difficulties may well have prompted board member resignation to the current budgetary system. Moreover, by their maturation period, a number of community boards were dealing quite effectively with their integrative budgetary responsibilities. Table 7.5 indicates the relative satisfaction board members have across all three items related to the city's current geographically decentralized budgetary process. A large majority of the respondents sampled support the current expense-budget system, while a lesser but nonetheless decisive majority express satisfaction with the capital-budget process. This particular finding was surprising in that several borough officials, board district managers, and previous analysts of the board system had expressed the view that geographically based capital budgeting in New York was more readily subject to community board influence than was expense budgeting (Mudd 1984; Pecorella 1986).

The overall disparities between the attitudes of white and African-American board members sampled toward the city's integrative budget are reflected in all three budget items in the scale. While overwhelming majorities of white respondents support the current integrative system on each of the three budgetary items, a majority of African-American board members advocate community control for two of the items and essentially divide evenly on the expense-budget process. As was the case with land-use issues, these results are not surprising. Chapter six presented the differences between boards from white districts and boards from minority communities in their budgetary success rates. Part of the explanation for the distinctions was found in the strategies selected by the boards for submitting their budgetary proposals; part, however, was not. Whatever the full explanation, less satisfying experiences with board-initiated budgetary proposals may well account for the greater dissatisfaction with the boards' budgetary authority expressed by African-Americans in the sample.

The 1989 charter attempted to address inequities in the city's community-based budgeting system. The revisions mandated borough-based budget assistance to the boards and detailed, written explanations from city agencies as to why local priorities were excluded from the expense or capital budgets. Such changes, coupled with the development of a geographically decentralized strategic plan, may help equalize the amount of both substantive and strategic information available to board members across the city and therefore modify some of the attitudinal differences on the budget process. Because African-American respondents were less emphatic in their support for community control of budgeting than they were on the other areas of board responsibility, the 1989 revisions, if they are implemented seriously and prove to be effective, may help generate widespread support for integrative budgeting among all board members in the future.

The distinctions among respondents concerning the three service-delivery items in the scale reflect past research, including the analysis in chapter six, which has shown greater dissatisfaction with local service delivery among African-American than among white residents. In fact, the widest racial separation on all nine items (32 percent) relates to different assessments of the current community integrative approach to police services. Overall, the members sampled distinguished between and among the service areas listed. The substantial majorities for community control of sanitation and police services did not exist when the issue involved housing services, where the respondents split evenly.

The current integrative system for monitoring the delivery of sanitation services was the only one of the three service items to provoke majority opposition among African-American and white board members. The majority community-control reaction in this area may in part be the result of the numerous complaints heard by board members and district managers from small shopkeepers across the city, in both white and African-American neighborhoods, about overly zealous Sanitation Department ticketing policies. Store owners complain that they are held accountable for litter found in front of their stores even though they may have swept, as per city regulations, earlier in the day. This issue arose again and again in interviews with community board members, district managers, and borough officials when the boards' service-monitoring responsibilities were the subject of discussion. In many ways, it represents a classic postreform issue in that its initial visibility and perhaps its eventual resolution are functions of the institutional channels created by decentralization in the 1970s.

Board members' assessments of community integrative policing reflect immediate service-delivery issues and basic differences between the African-American and white experience in cities. Community control of the police was favored by an overwhelming majority of African-Americans in the sample but by fewer than one-half of the white board members. Two distinct perspectives toward police services are submerged in these findings.

Community control of the police was a rallying cry of the black power movement of the 1960s. For many African-American board members, the problems with the current integrative system for monitoring police services relate to basic and long-standing tensions between the police and the African-American community. African-American perceptions that white police officers are both less than zealous in enforcing the law in African-American communities and less than respectful when dealing with community residents reflect these larger racial tensions in the city. Although the Police Department has made some efforts to ease the tension through community-relations training courses and the recruitment of minority officers, the problems appear to be growing worse. Indeed, in 1992, despite the fact that two of the three most recent police commissioners were African-American, New York had one of the lowest percentages of African-American officers of any major city in the country.

These racial tensions, which over the past three decades have simmered just beneath the surface of New York politics, sometimes manifest themselves in open and ugly fashions. Several incidents in which African-Americans, usually but not always young men, were killed in confrontations with white police officers have served to unleash racial hostilities. In 1992, much of the racial tension in the city became painfully obvious in the nature and intensity of the debate over Mayor Dinkins's proposals for an all-civilian, mayorally appointed police review board. Consequently, the overwhelming desire for community control of the police among African-American board members, though it may reflect in part concrete service problems in the community, also represents a fundamental social and political cleavage in New York City politics.

For white board members, on the other hand, the problems with monitoring the police are almost exclusively service-oriented and nowhere near as fundamental as the those defining police relationships with the African-American community. For white board members, concerns with police services tend to involve demands for increased police presence to ensure greater safety and extensions of the community policing concept. The former is an understandable reaction to the widespread fear of crime, although, by definition, it will never be fully satisfied; the latter reflects a desire among many white, middle-class residents to have a sufficient police presence to deal with quality-of-life problems in their neighborhoods.

Although the tensions between the police and the African-American community are so profound that they are not readily dealt with by structural change, the
perceptions of problems in other service areas related to the community boards
may not be nearly as deep. The 1989 charter revisions included two reforms that
may impact on minority board members' perceptions of the current system. One
increased the borough presidents' responsibilities for and authority over service
issues; the other created "an office of language services" in the mayor's office to
monitor agencies and assist boards in districts where English is not the primary
language. The first may increase the impact of all community boards by allowing
their members to call on a county as opposed to a city arbiter on service questions; the second should assist Latino communities in interacting with service
agencies. Although such reforms may be more symbolic than substantive, they
may help promote more positive feelings about the board system in general.

Attitudes and Political Behavior

The final section of this chapter focuses on the effects of board member attitudes
on their behavior as community representatives. The central question of interest
is: Do different perspectives on community empowerment result in different
behavior patterns among community board members?

The research concerning the impact of different community-empowerment
attitudes was guided by the notion that board members who expressed great
dissatisfaction with the current integrative system and strong community-control
attitudes would tend to employ a more community-focused strategy to carry out
their responsibilities than would their counterparts who supported the integrative
approach. The concept of a community-focused strategy was made operational
by examining the sources of advice board members employ when making decisions. In short, we expected that community-control advocates would rely more
extensively on community-based sources of advice than would proponents of
integrative decentralization, who would be more prone to interact with citywide
or external actors.

Table 7.6 presents selected respondents' answers to questions about their
sources of advice on land-use and budget issues.[12] The board members examined
are those who expressed either strong feelings of support for or strong feelings of
opposition to the current board system in New York; moderates were not included in this analysis. The findings clarify several issues concerning board
member reliance on community-based as opposed to external sources of advice.

First, it is quite clear that community board members rely extensively on each
other when making both land-use and budget-priority decisions. Indeed, for all
intents and purposes, there is universal agreement among community-control
advocates that fellow board members represent a useful source of advice on
land-use issues. (The responses were quite similar when board members were
asked about community board chairs, district managers, and committee chairs as
sources of advice.) Given their common community-focused perspectives, such

Table 7.6

Community-Empowerment Attitudes and Sources of Information
(percentage with frequent contacts)

	Attitude toward the board system	
Sources of land-use advice	Strongly supportive	Strongly opposed
Other members	89.6	97.9
Community activists	53.9	82.0
City council member	33.9	69.3
Department of City Planning	87.8	80.2
Community Assistance Unit	64.3	28.8
Sources of budget advice	Strongly supportive	Strongly opposed
Other members	89.3	92.1
Community activists	43.8	80.9
City council member	34.5	63.8
Office of Management and the Budget	69.5	39.1
Community Board Assistance Unit	65.9	37.1
City service agencies	68.6	45.7

Note: N for land use: 113 supportive, 243 opposed; N for budget: 223 supportive, 151 opposed.

responses are not surprising. They do indicate, however, that dissatisfied board members are alienated from the board system rather than from their fellow participants within that system.

Second, there is a clear division between the two sets of board members on the value of the advice emanating from community activists. Overwhelming majorities of community-control advocates rely on these activists for advice on both land-use issues and budget priorities. Conversely, only a slim majority of the system's supporters on land-use concerns and less than 44 percent on budget priorities seek such advice.

Third, city council representatives are contacted much more frequently by the opponents than by the supporters of the current system. It appears that during the maturation period, city councillors were seen as local allies by community-control advocates rather than as part of city government. It remains to be seen how the 1989 charter revisions affect that perception. On the one hand, the decreased size of councilmanic districts might promote an even greater identification of city councillors as community-based representatives. On the other hand, the increased responsibilities of the city council as a whole may force council members to at times ignore community wishes in the interest of a "greater good." In that event, political realities could negatively impact the positive perception of city councillors among community-control advocates.

Table 7.6 also contains information about the use of external sources of advice by board members. First, both supporters and opponents of the current system rely on the Department of City Planning when making land-use decisions. In part, this reflects the department's direct involvement in the ULURP process, which makes it a critical player regardless of attitudes toward community empowerment. But the extensive interactions between the department and board members may also reflect positive perceptions of the City Planning's borough-based community assistance offices.

Other city agencies were not as well received by the board members sampled. There were evident differences in members' reactions to the city's Community Assistance Unit (CAU), the Office of Community Board Relations (OCBR) within the city's Office of Management and the Budget, and service-delivery agencies. Strong supporters of the board system were much more likely to interact with CAU, particularly on land-use questions, and with OCBR and service-agency representatives on budgetary issues than were advocates of community control. It is worth noting that, as chapter six made clear, such community-focused strategies have implications for achieving budget priorities.

Board Members and Community Empowerment:
A Summary

The analysis of board members' community-empowerment attitudes clarifies several issues. First, the data indicate clearly that community-integrative decentralization receives decidedly mixed reviews from members of New York's community boards. While a majority of the respondents in the sample were moderately dissatisfied with board authority overall, a substantial number were pleased with the integrative system in New York.

Second, respondents distinguished among board responsibilities in their evaluations. Board members were more likely to favor community control over land-use and service issues than over budget priorities. Moreover, respondents drew distinctions within specific categories of responsibility. They were more supportive of the interactive land-use system in their negotiations with private developers than in their dealings with city officials. On service issues, board members were more likely to support the integrative process for monitoring the Department of Housing, Preservation, and Development than they were when dealing with the Police and Sanitation departments.

Third, members' attitudes toward community empowerment influence their decision-making behavior. Board members who support the city's community integration approach are more likely to seek advice from central-city political actors, whereas community-control advocates are more likely to rely on local activists as sources of advice when making decisions on land-use and service matters.

Finally, the findings clearly indicate different attitudes based on race. One explanation for the great dissatisfaction with the current board system and the extensive support for community control among African-American respondents focuses on sociopolitical issues. From this perspective, the history of racism, economic deprivation, and unfulfilled political promises have produced alienation from city government among African-American activists. Moreover, the postcrisis emergence of a city administration based politically in New York's middle-class, white neighborhoods strained city relationships with the African-American community and may well have generated a rebirth of community-control sentiment.

A more regime-specific interpretation of the data, however, emphasizes that city policy during the community boards' maturation period has been guided by oversight organs with primary responsibility to the city's creditors. From this perspective, recent mayoral policies have had less to do with a particular mayor's political base and more to do with the socioeconomic constraints under which the postreform city was forced to operate. The Dinkins administration's experiences with reactivated fiscal monitors during the economic slowdown of the 1990s points to the long-term relevance of this interpretation. These regime-specific constraints generated an overriding emphasis on retrenchment and "developmental policies" at the expense of "allocational" and particularly "redistributive" concerns. Such constraints acted to minimize mechanisms of accountability, such as community boards, and resulted in particularly negative impacts on low-income, service-demanding areas. In the process, such policies may have produced or at least reaffirmed among lower-income, minority activists a distrust for the integrative system as a whole.

CHAPTER EIGHT

Summary and Conclusions

Three distinct political regimes have governed New York City over the past 120 years. They had common historical roots in that each emerged in the wake of a fiscal crisis that destabilized prior political arrangements; each included a unique set of formal and informal political interactions among the components of its governing coalition; each developed its own particular source of political legitimacy; and each was defined by a distinctive balance between central-city and community power.

As a result of the fiscal crisis of the early 1870s, the era of gang rule in New York gave way to a long period of machine rule under Tammany Hall. Machine rule assisted the business elites of the day by imposing a hierarchically ordered system on the city, which, by coordinating government decision making, aided the industrialization process. Coterminously, the Tammany machine's geographically decentralized base and its quid pro quo style of politics made the urban community the focus of attentive nonelite political interactions. Tammany Hall consolidated its power in the early twentieth century under the leadership of Charles Murphy. In the wake of the 1930s fiscal crisis, however, a weakened and fragmented machine, bereft of creative leadership and politically overextended, was defeated by a coalition of urban reformers backing the fusion candidacy of Fiorello LaGuardia.

Reformers geographically centralized the focus of city government while functionally decentralizing administrative responsibility among relatively autonomous city agencies. The reform regime accommodated financial interests with professional government and progrowth development policies while addressing attentive nonelite concerns though the administrative agencies of the welfare city. By 1945, reformers had so transformed the formal and informal interactions defining normal city politics that, despite the election of three consecutive Democratic mayors in the post-LaGuardia years, reform values continued to dominate city governance. Reform reached its apex in New York with the 1961 reelection of Mayor Robert Wagner, who, by running against the leadership of his own party, formally certified reform's consolidation. However, as a result of intraregime conflict and the consequent incorporation of increasingly diverse interests within its governing coalition, the highly fragmented reform regime was unable to cope with the intense fiscal pressures of the mid-1970s.

Since the collapse of the reform regime, the city has been governed by a postreform coalition that has recentralized fiscal authority in quasi-public boards and has geographically decentralized land-use planning, local budget priorities, and service-monitoring responsibility in a system of community boards. On one level, the postreform regime was structured to address the fiscal pressures resulting from the increasing costs of reform's welfare state; on another level, it was a response to grass-roots political pressures for increased community-based involvement in policy-making. Indeed, from an attentive nonelite perspective, postreform governance involved the reemergence of the community in New York as a basis of political legitimacy.

The moderate form of community power institutionalized in New York City's community board system reflected postreform's evolution from an emphasis on community control to one on community integration with central-city government. The classic integrative system adopted in New York allocates to community representatives an advisory role in policy-making. Integrative decentralization was facilitated in New York City by the community leadership base, which emerged from a variety of grass-roots and federally sponsored local organizations; the intensity of the conflict over school decentralization, which delegitimized the community-control option; and the relative success of the ONG experiment, which helped promote the feasibility of administrative decentralization.

The charter revisions of 1975 created the modern community board system in New York. The revisions redefined the nature and increased the extent of community involvement in policy-making; specified community responsibilities over land-use, budgeting, and service-delivery issues; and, most importantly, institutionalized community politics in the city. As a consequence of the charter-based imposition of postreform values on city politics, political legitimacy in New York currently rests on three foundations: electoral politics, which decides intraregime political conflicts and certifies specific policy options; a scaled-back, though still substantial, welfare city; and systematic community-based involvement in city affairs.

The 1975 charter revisions were not intended to guarantee that the community boards would control land-use planning in their districts—only that they would have the opportunity to influence the physical character of their communities. The evidence indicates that many boards are taking advantage of the opportunity to have an impact on land-use policy, but in a reactive, not proactive, fashion. Most boards have created standing committees to review land-use proposals, which provide them with a degree of consistency and internal expertise on these matters. Indeed, many of the boards have proved quite adept at negotiating changes in or obtaining community amenities as the price for the private-sector development projects proposed for their districts. Other boards, however, particularly those from lower-income districts, are less effective when dealing with land-use planning matters. This disparity is in part a function of board capacity and the distinct nature of the proposals dealt with by different types of communities. However, it is largely a result of socioeconomic factors and can be only partially addressed by structural reforms in the board system.

The 1975 charter revisions were also designed to give the boards influence over budget priorities in their communities. Such influence requires that the boards have information, the opportunity to make their desires known, and some impact on the process. The system of geographically based budgeting mandated by the charter ensures that the necessary information for board action is available and that the formal procedures for submitting board-initiated budget priorities, including the district and borough consultations with agency personnel, provide the boards with the opportunity to make their desires known. As for impact, the boards obtain roughly one-half of their top ten priority capital-budget proposals each fiscal year. City budget officials tend to reward boards for cooperation with city agencies and not for their interaction with other community organizations. As with land-use issues, board impact on the budget process has been variable across districts, with boards from middle-class districts having a greater percentage of their proposals funded than those from lower-income communities.

The 1975 charter's original conception of community-based service coordination through district service cabinets (DSCs) has not been realized. The greatest impediment to district service coordination has been the lack of meaningful management decentralization within the essentially reform-style city service-delivery agencies. Nevertheless, the boards have developed an important service function. District managers process large, in some boards extraordinary, numbers of service-related complaints from community residents and use a variety of formal and informal channels, including DSC meetings, to raise such complaints with city agencies. As a result, the DSCs serve an extended, and often informal, ombudsman role within their communities.

Given the early postreform emphasis on participation and local control, it was instructive to see how community activists in the 1980s responded to New York City's moderate form of integrative decentralization. Accordingly, we questioned a diverse sample of community board members in the city. Board members gave the integrative decentralization of New York's community board system mixed reviews. A majority of those sampled expressed dissatisfaction with the advisory nature of current board authority by indicating at least moderate support for the original postreform notion of community control. Support for increased community power was particularly strong in relation to land-use matters and among the African-American board members questioned. Dissatisfaction notwithstanding, a substantial minority of respondents was at least moderately pleased with community board authority overall, and a clear majority of the sample was supportive of geographically based budgeting in New York.

Board members' attitudes toward New York's community integration system affected their behavior as community representatives. Those members pleased with the advisory power incorporated within the board system have adopted cosmopolitan decision-making strategies; they rely more on central-city political actors for information and advice on land-use and budget issues than their dissatisfied counterparts. Conversely, community-control advocates were more likely to employ parochial decision-making strategies, focused on community activists, for advice on these issues.

The postreform regime coped with its first major budgetary pressures during the economic downturn of the early 1990s, when the fiscal monitors, institutionalized as part of the regime's governing coalition, forced cutbacks in programs directed toward the mayor's political base. Whether such fiscal coordination is possible down the road, however, is an open question. As the 1975 crisis recedes into history, the pressure for political conflicts to be resolved through group incorporation into the regime's governing coalition will grow. However, for the first time in the city's modern history, coordinative fiscal power can be exercised directly during a period of normal urban politics by financial interests utterly outside the reach of democratic control. Nevertheless, given the nature of urban politics, the issue of continued postreform fiscal coordination in New York rests on three variables: the political capabilities of future mayors who may wish to resist the fiscal monitors, the level of interest the fiscal monitors themselves maintain in city politics over time, and the severity of attentive nonelite pressures on government. In the postreform city, the rules governing fiscal policy interactions have changed; however, the players remain essentially the same.

In terms of attentive nonelites, community empowerment has been institutionalized in New York to an extent that should surprise the critics but disappoint the true believers. Through the community board system, the postreform regime has not only changed legitimation rules in the city, it has also expanded the number and diversified the interests of the players. However, as with the issue of fiscal coordination, the future evolution of community board influence in city politics is also an open question. To a great extent, any assessment is dependent on the definition of the term *community power*. Community-control advocates, including many board members, are disappointed by the advisory nature of the decision-making power allocated to communities under the current system. From their perspective, the board system does not go far enough in empowering community-based interests. Given the continuing importance of citywide, progrowth forces and the codification of reform values within highly professionalized and relatively autonomous city agencies, the type of community control envisioned by these activists will in all likelihood not be realized in New York City in the foreseeable future. Consequently, community-control advocates will continue to see the boards as organs of central-city co-optation and will continue to mobilize residents in alternative community organizations.

From the perspective of more moderate advocates of community power, on the other hand, integrative decentralization fulfills the promise of postreform politics. If the board system has not produced community control, neither has it left the reform status quo undisturbed. As we have seen, the boards are merely advisory bodies, but they have opened land-use review in New York to public scrutiny; they can neither raise revenues nor allocate resources with local discretion, but they can influence the city's budgetary process for doing so; and although they have not been able to coordinate service delivery within their districts, their ombudsman role enables them to hold agencies more directly accountable for the jobs they do. Moreover, the 1989 charter revisions included a number of good-faith efforts to assist the boards, particularly those from low-income districts, to carry out their responsibilities. The days of unquestioned citywide dominance of public policy are clearly over.

A final caution is in order. The analysis contained in this book has focused on the inherent divisions between citywide and community-based interests and has suggested that these divisions have been a central focus of regime transformation in New York. Indeed, postreform legitimation through the community board system institutionalizes a community's capacity to cope with the political conflicts arising from these divisions. It is important to keep in mind, however, that the concept of community interest is as vague and often as contentious as the concept of citywide interest. Indeed, the central unifying force in the early community-empowerment movement was the common adversary of reform governance. As New York's postreform regime matures and as the community board system develops, there is every reason to believe that intracommunity political conflicts will prove as numerous and at times as harsh as the battles between citywide and community interests.

NOTES

Chapter One

1. For an analysis of polyarchy, see Dahl 1981, chapter 26, and 1991, chapters 7 and 8.

2. The use of the term *internal critics* distinguishes group theorists troubled by aspects of pluralism from stratification theorists who reject the focus on groups in its entirety.

3. An early exposition of the view that American governance was more or less hostage to the fragmented power of private interests can be found in McConnell 1966.

4. The term *mode of production* comprises two concepts: the forces of production (skill of the work force, level of technology, and available resources), and the social relations of production (the nature of class control at a particular period). To stratificationists, the mode of production refers to the socioeconomic basis for governance in a society.

5. The contextual approach is based largely on my reading of the work of Douglas Yates (1977), Martin Shefter (1976, 1977), and Clarence Stone (1980).

6. The socioeconomic context of government in the United States—private ownership and control of productive capacity—has evolved from the early competitive stages of the Industrial Revolution, through the latter periods of corporate consolidation, into the most recent era of the postindustrial service economy. The liberal political context has been characterized by the increasing enfranchisement of formerly excluded groups and the democratization of governance.

7. For insightful analyses of the concept of urban regimes, see Elkin 1985 and 1987; Stone 1989 and 1993; Horan 1991; and Judd and Kantor 1992, 4–8, 66–77, and 272–282.

8. Stephen Elkin (1987) emphasizes the effects of an urban regime's particular "mobilization of bias" on both its formal structure and its informal interactions.

9. Clarence Stone and Heywood Sanders term the type of intraregime tension being discussed here "a scheme of accomodation between popular control and private ownership" (1987, 270).

10. Because the media use the term *fiscal crisis* to describe any multiyear budget pressures, it is devalued in popular usage. Situations of fiscal stress are often difficult for local officials; however, given our definitional requirements, they do not have to be and generally are not fiscal crises.

11. It is important to remember that economic elites also make extensive political demands on city treasuries. For example, financial interests encourage prodevelopment policies, which often put great pressures on city budgets. Their focus on fiscal stability generally involves cutbacks in the programs directed toward attentive nonelite groups while preserving, "in the public interest," their own municipal largess.

12. Waste's analysis emphasizes aspects of several policy models, including those of Bryan Jones (1983) and Randall Ripley and Grace Franklin (1984). However, it is his adaptation of Downs's life-cycle approach that is of primary interest here.

13. For a particularly insightful analysis of this period in New York City history, see Shefter 1976.

Chapter Two

1. There are many sources focusing on New York politics during the Tammany era. For descriptions of politics at the time, see Myers 1917; Lynch 1927; Werner 1928; Riordan 1963; Mushrat 1971; and Caro 1974. For more analytical examinations, see Shaw 1954; Mandelbaum 1965; Callow 1966; Connable and Silberfarb 1967; Henderson 1976; Shefter 1976; Hershkowitz 1977; and Wade 1990. For an insightful analysis of New York City politics before Kelly's consolidation of the Tammany machine, see Bridges 1984.

2. For analyses of machine politics, see Zink 1930; Banfield and Wilson 1963; Royko 1971; Griffith 1974; Callow 1976; Rakove 1976; Allswang 1977; Wald 1980; Hammack 1982; Teaford 1984, chapter 3; Judd 1988, chapter 3; and DiGaetano 1988.

3. There are competing explanations of the machine's relationship with voters. A cultural perspective suggests the "private-regarding ethos" of lower-income immigrant groups promotes identification with machine-style, quid pro quo politics, while the "public-regarding ethos" of middle- and upper-class WASPs promotes a more "unitarist" conception of politics (Wilson and Banfield 1964). Another view sees community-based politics as the consequence of geographical settlement patterns, suggesting that machines mobilized newcomers concentrated in the city's inner ring in opposition to the middle-class politics of the "urban periphery" (see Wade 1990). Broadening the territorial perspective, Hayes contends that geographical decentralization served as the mechanism for the representation of parochial values in opposition to modernization with its cosmopolitan emphasis (Hayes 1964).

4. For discussions of the Tweed Ring, see Werner 1928, chapter 4; Connable and Silberfarb 1967, chapter 5; and Shefter 1976. For a postive analysis of Tweed's accomplishments, see Callow 1976.

5. See the series of exposés in the *New York Times* for July 1871, particularly July 8, 22, and 29.

6. For discussions of Kelly as Tammany leader, see Werner 1928, chapter 5; Connable and Silberfarb 1967, chapter 6; Shefter 1976.

7. For an analysis of Tammany's control of the New York City legislature, see Shaw 1954, chapters 1 and 2.

8. During Croker's tenure as Tammany leader, there were three investigations of the machine's practices. In 1890, the Fassett Committee explored the connections between city government and Tammany Hall. In 1892, the Lexow Committee, financed by the New York Chamber of Commerce, investigated Tammany's involvement with vice. And in 1899, the Republican-controlled state legislature conducted the Mazet investigations into city corruption. For a brief review, see Werner 1928, chapter 6.

9. For discussions of Croker's term as Tammany leader, see Werner 1928, chapter 6, Connable and Silberfarb 1967, chapter 7. For a "friendly examination" of Croker's career, see Stoddard 1931. For a somewhat fawning perspective on Croker, see Lewis 1901.

10. Croker, whose tenure as Tammany leader was interrupted several times by his own resignations, was succeeded initially by his hand-picked successor, Lewis Nixon, as county leader. Nixon resigned several months later and was replaced by a committee of leaders. Charles Murphy soon moved into the political "vacuum" and assumed control. See Connable and Silberfarb 1967, 231–33.

11. For discussions of Murphy's term as Tammany leader, see Werner 1928, chapter 7, and Connable and Silberfarb 1967, chapter 8. For an analysis of Tammany's relationships with immigrant groups during Murphy's reign, see Henderson 1976.

12. For an analysis of the influence of state Republican boss Thomas Platt see Gosnell 1969.

13. In 1910, Murphy succeeded in electing John Alden Dix governor, Al Smith the assembly majority leader, and Robert F. Wagner, Sr., senate majority leader. All three proved to be both progressive politicians and Tammany loyalists.

14. Much of the labor legislation passed by Tammany loyalists followed the protests surrounding the tragic Triangle Shirtwaist Company fire, which killed 143 workers whose exits had been blocked to prevent illegal work breaks. The fire galvanized union and social reform groups in the city and resulted in the creation of a state legislative committee to investigate the tragedy, chaired by Smith and Wagner. As a consequence of the committee hearings, the factory law reforms were passed.

15. Although reformers only succeeded in electing three fusion mayors during these forty years, a number of "Tammany mayors" proved less than reliable from Murphy's perspective. George McClellan, who served from 1904 until 1909, broke with Murphy midway through his term; William Gaynor (1910–13) and John F. Hylan (1918–25), although picked by Murphy, were products of the Brooklyn machine. Such problems with mayors led Sayre and Kaufman to the conclusion that "the mayoralty is more accurately described as Tammany's Achilles' heel" (1960, 689).

16. Only for two years during Mitchels's fusion administration (1914–15) did reformers control both branches of city government.

17. Reformers were also susceptible to co-optation. In the 1903 mayoral campaign, Murphy endorsed the fusion candidates for comptroller and president of the Board of Aldermen, thereby splitting the fusion vote and electing Tammany candidate, George McClellan, mayor.

18. For analyses of urban reform, see Hofstadter 1955; Lowi 1964; Hayes 1964 and 1967; Hawley 1973; Griffith 1974; Schiesl 1977; Dutton and Northrop 1978; and Lyons 1978.

19. For a review of the events leading up to the Bankers Agreement of 1933, see Beyer 1933 and various issues of the *New York Times* in 1933, particularly those of September 29 and 30.

20. For analyses of LaGuardia's years as mayor, see Garrett 1961 and Caro 1974, chapter 23.

21. The Hare system is based on the notion of the single transferable vote. After candidates obtain sufficient votes for election, all their remaining votes are distributed to the voters' alternative choices until all the elective offices are filled.

22. The 1938 charter gave the Board of Estimate sixteen total votes. The citywide officials—the mayor, council president, and comptroller—cast three votes each for a clear majority. The borough presidents divided the remaining seven votes, with the vote apportioned roughly based on population with Brooklyn and Manhattan having two each and the remaining boroughs one vote each. Under the charter revisions, the board's powers were increased at the expense of the council; this further reaffirmed reform's dominance.

23. Frederick Taylor's notion of "scientific management" was the first theory to suggest a systematic organization of industrial management. Although a more "progressive" approach than social Darwinism's survival of the fittest, the Taylorist perspective still considered workers as merely cogs in an industrial machine.

Chapter Three

1. For an example of radical community organizing prior to the 1960s, see Alinsky 1946. For a historical analysis of community politics during different periods in the United States, see Fisher 1984.

2. For an interesting critique of the conventional distinction between political and administrative decentralization, see Iannello 1988, 5–6.

3. Radical political groups such as the Student Nonviolent Coordinating Committee

and Students for a Democratic Society helped establish neo-Alinsky grass-roots, participatory organizations in some urban neighborhoods (Fisher 1984, chap. 4). Such efforts were founded strategically on the notion that outside organizers should only be catalysts for and not leaders in community organizing; such leadership should emerge from within the community and should be broadly reflective of resident needs. Alternative technology groups, which argued for complete community independence from the values and resources of the larger society, reflected in the most radical sense community-based, participatory values (Morris and Hess 1975).

4. For more recent analyses of the inefficiencies involved in metropolitan decentralization, see Dye 1988 and Dolan 1990.

5. In general, community organizing in the United States has focused on the spatial or consumption issues related to neighborhood and avoided the class-based or production concerns related to the work place (Katznelson 1981). However, there are instances of active labor-union support of community organizing (see Fisher 1984; Fitzgerald and Simmons 1991). Fisher and Kling (1989) argue that it is necessary for community organizers in the 1990s to emphasize ideological cleavages to "bridge the community–class dichotomy" (1989, 200).

6. For an excellent overall analysis of the concept of political participation, see Pateman 1970. For a number of articles advocating the idea of "participatory democracy," see Benello and Rousopoulas 1971.

7. For a useful analysis of the current state of progrowth politics in American cities, see Vogel and Swanson 1989.

8. Because of its divergence from more traditional Civil Rights emphases, the community-control movement was not universally applauded in the African-American community. For a critique, see Rustin 1970.

Chapter Four

1. Neither Mayor Impellitteri nor Mayor Wagner were "Tammany mayors" in the traditional sense. Impelletteri was an outspoken critic of Tammany and Wagner was a classic pragmatic reformer.

2. For an analysis of the impact of the 1938 charter revisions, see chapter two.

3. For a number of years after Tammany Hall's fall in 1933, the Democratic party in the city had been under the leadership of Edward Flynn, the county leader from the Bronx, who was an active proponent of national New Deal politics.

4. For a discussion of Tammany Hall under DeSapio's leadership, see Burns 1961; Moynihan 1961; and Moynihan and Wilson 1964.

5. For useful analyses of Wagner and Lindsay's different approaches to the community component of the War on Poverty program, see David 1971; Viteritti 1979; and Savitch 1990.

6. For an interesting case study of HARYOU, see Day 1987.

7. The New York City Planning Commission and the Bedford-Stuyvestant Restoration Corporation differed as to the boundaries of the community. The chapter employs the city's boundaries, which are the more restrictive of the two (see Gifford 1970).

8. For an analysis of the evolution toward professionalism in community organizations, see the analysis in chapter three.

9. For another view of these two decentralization experiments in New York, see Rogers 1990.

10. One analysis of perceptions about the relationship between contract negotiations and community control indicated that rank-and-file teachers saw some professional benefits from decentralization and were less adamantly opposed to community involvement than their representatives on the UFT (Moskow and McLennan 1970).

11. Many of the community school boards' personnel powers are qualified by the condition that the local boards act in ways "not inconsistent with the provisions of this article or any applicable collective negotiation agreement." As John Theobald points out, this phrase, which makes community control subject to UFT collective bargaining protections, "completely negates the assigned powers and duties" (1970, 197).

12. The eight experimental districts in the revised ONG proposal included three middle-class, white neighborhoods, Bay Ridge in Brooklyn, Maspeth-Ridgewood in Queens, and Wakefield-Edenwald in the Bronx; three "transitional neighborhoods," the Rockaways in Queens, Washington Heights in Manhattan, and Crown Heights in Brooklyn; and two lower-income areas, Bushwick in Brooklyn and the South Bronx. For demographic and ONG programatic descriptions of the communities selected, see Heginbotham 1977, 37–44; Brumback 1977; and Rogers 1990, 162.

13. There were eight city agencies included in the revised ONG program: the Police Department; the Administrations for Environmental Protection; Housing and Development; Human Resources; Health Services; Parks, Recreation, and Cultural Affairs; and the Addiction Services Agency (Lindsay 1977, 261).

Chapter Five

1. For in-depth analyses of the roots of urban fiscal crises in the Northeast, see Sternlieb and Hughes 1976; Alcaly and Mermelstein 1977; and Morris 1980. For in-depth analyses of New York City's fiscal problems, see Reischauer, Clark, and Cuciti 1975; Edel 1977; Shefter 1977; Tabb 1978; and Drennan 1982.

2. A number of study commissions issued reports during this period that highlighted the city's structural fiscal problems. Two of the more prominent were the Temporary State Commission to Make a Study of the Governmental Operations of the City of New York and the Temporary Commission on City Finances (TCCF). Although the TCCF report was not made published until 1977, the commission issued periodic reports to the mayor beginning in 1973.

3. The clearest and most analytically satisfying discussion of the structure and political effects of these state and quasi-public agencies is found in Bailey 1984. Another very useful source for a description of the agencies charged with monitoring the city's fiscal situation in the wake of crisis is Brecher and Hartman 1984.

4. Netzer himself has doubts about the long-term effects of attitudinal changes. He includes the discussion of attitude change under the subheading "A Permanent Change in Outlook?" (Netzer 1990).

5. For an analysis of collective bargaining changes and the gradual reduction in the FCB's direct involvement in union negotiations during the period in question, see McCormick 1984.

6. Although personnel cutbacks due to retrenchment had serious negative effects on services, they were one of several factors found to impact service delivery. Agencies with slack resources and/or innovative managers were able to overcome some of the problems produced by resource reductions. (See Horton and McCormick 1980.)

7. From an interview with Donna Shalala, a member of MAC, where she discusses the transit fare increase. (See Newfield and DuBrul 1981, 169.)

8. Altogether, there were seven governmental agencies charged with developing and monitoring New York City's financial plan: the New York City Office of Management and the Budget; the New York City Office of the Comptroller; the New York City Council's Legislative Office of Budget Review; the New York State Municipal Assistance Corporation; the New York State Financial Control Board; the New York State Office of the Special Deputy Comptroller; and the Federal Office of New York City Finance.

9. Local industries primarily serve local demand, whereas export industries are involved with regional, national, or global markets. (See Drennan 1982.)

10. During the period following the fiscal crisis, state categorical aid to the city also increased substantially. For an analysis of state assistance programs, see Grossman 1984.

11. Developmental policies are designed to improve the overall economic competitive position of a community; redistributive policies are designed to support those on the lower end of the socioeconomic scale; and allocational policies involve the delivery of basic local services. For complete definitions, empirical indicators, and an analysis of the differential effects of each type of policy, see Peterson 1981, chapter 2.

12. The public battle is chronicled in a series of articles and editorials in the *New York Times* between April and December of 1991.

13. The creation of the SCRC was also a manifestation of the increasingly bitter feud between Governor Nelson Rockfeller and Mayor John Lindsay.

14. This constraint was obvious in 1991 when the Dinkins administration formulated a "personnel redeployment program," mandating all city agencies, including the community boards, to hire from a pool of laid-off city workers. The program provoked resistance in several community boards.

15. There is evidence that on some boards factions develop around the city councillors, who nominate one-half of the members. In the late 1980s, Joan Lebow reports that Community Board 5 in Manhattan included a "Greitzer faction" composed of City Council Member Carol Greitzer's twenty-two appointees (1988, 12).

Chapter Six

1. For an analysis of the Board of Estimate's historical evolution, see Viteritti 1990.

2. On the Board of Estimate, the Brooklyn borough president, representing over 2 million residents, had the same one vote as the borough president of Staten Island, who represented fewer than four hundred thousand people.

3. Two charter commissions were formed between 1986 and 1989. The work of the first, chaired by Richard Ravitch, was interrupted when the United States Supreme Court unexpectedly decided to hear an appeal of the *Morris* decision. The Ravitch Commission submitted its proposals, without addressing the Board of Estimate issue, to the voters in November 1988, who approved them by a wide margin. The second commission, chaired by Frederick A. O. Schwarz, Jr., was appointed in December 1989 following the Supreme Court's affirmation of the *Morris* decision. The Schwarz Commission submitted its proposals, including abolition of the Board of Estimate, to the voters in November 1989. They passed with a 55 percent majority.

4. For an analysis of suggested changes in the board's voting procedures, see Gelfand and Allbritton 1989.

5. Conversely, some community activists argued that the charter gave too much power to the CPC and would result in a recentralization of land-use authority in the mayor's office. (See *New York Times*, November 10, 1989, B3.)

6. For an analysis of the effect of increasing city council membership, see Muzzio and Tompkins 1989.

7. The 1938 charter codified New York's already professional expense- and capital-budget procedures and placed a great deal of budget authority in the Board of Estimate. The 1963 charter gave more budgetary control to the mayor. (See SCRC 1973a.)

8. An earlier analysis of community board budgetary behavior appeared in Pecorella 1986.

9. The capital budget was selected because it has been broken down geographically for a longer time than the expense budget. Moreover, the boards usually make more capital-

than expense-budget requests (three times more in fiscal year 1982); see NYC CRC 1989, 6. The research does not include distinctions among board proposals. However, discussions with officials at OMB's Office of Community Board Relations' as well as the actual coding of over 2,300 board-initiated proposals (BIPs) gave us confidence that the proposals did not vary greatly either in the amount of funding requested or in the type of project proposed.

10. The operational distinction between parochial and cosmopolitan strategies is a function of the manner selected to submit BIPs. BIPs can be submitted by the board alone, with a community-based cosponsor, or with a city agency cosponsor. While the first and second options indicate a parochial or community-focused strategy, the third evidences a cosmopolitan or interactive approach.

11. In calculating success ratios, we limited the data to the top ten budget priorities per board for each fiscal year.

12. The cosmopolitanism index is the ratio of BIPs cosponsored by city agencies over total proposals.

13. Because percent minority was highly correlated with low median household income (−0.8), we dropped the former variable from the second equation. The low-income communities in the study shared the following characteristics: median household incomes of less than $10,000 per year, 30 percent or more of residents on some form of public assistance, and large minority (African-American or Latino) populations.

14. For example, Community Board 1 in Staten Island completed such an evaluation as part of a study of the effects of secession from New York City on service delivery within the district.

15. Comments made at the April 1987 meeting of the New York State Political Science Association in New York City.

16. In testimony before the 1989 Charter Revision Commission, John Mudd suggested that district managers' difficulties in coordinating services was largely a function of their roles as community representatives rather than as mayoral appointees.

17. Interview with Diane Morales, director of community services for Manhattan, September 2, 1987.

18. Interview with Jane Planken, director of community boards for Queens, September 1, 1987.

19. Interview with Edward Rogowsky, then director of community boards for Brooklyn, November 4, 1986.

Chapter Seven

1. The 1990 census indicated that 23 percent of New Yorkers had college degrees and nearly 20 percent lived at the poverty level. Board members in the sample were better educated and less likely to be poor than the average New Yorker.

2. For an earlier analysis of these responses, see Pecorella 1988.

3. Respondents were asked to select either community decision making or advisory power for the following items: zoning variances, siting group homes, private development proposals, expense-budget allocations, capital-budget allocations, economic-development-budget allocations, sanitation services, housing maintenance and code enforcement, and police services. The first three items involve land use; the next three involve budget issues; and the final three focus on service delivery.

4. The findings depart from Pecorella 1988 for two reasons: (1) The scale used in 1988 had twelve items; the current scale has only nine items. This was done to better balance the weighting of the three subscales. (2) The strong support and opposition categories were less demanding in the original analysis. The changes modify but do not substantively alter the original findings.

5. Fainstein and Martin's sample included community activists who "sometimes have domains of influence which extend over only a neighborhood, a single school, or association" (1978, 449); ours focused exclusively on members of community boards.

6. Because the terms *liberal* and *conservative* enjoy common usage among attentive publics in New York, respondent ideology was a self-described variable.

7. An analysis of variance (ANOVA) program was used to test the hypothesized relationships. ANOVA is employed when the dependent variable is measured intervally and the independent variables are measured nominally. The beta weights provided are adjusted for all independent variables in the equation.

8. Each advisory power response was given a score of 0 and each decision-making reply a score of 1. Then each respondent's score across the items was divided by the total number of responses. Accordingly, each respondent's scale scores ranged from 0 to 1 with those closer to 0 indicating satisfaction with the board system while scores closer to 1 implied more dissatisfaction and a greater community-control perspective. The average scale scores are adjusted for the effects of all independent variables.

9. Beta weights are standardized scores that indicate the relative impact of a specific independent variable while controlling for other independent variables in the equation.

10. The economic controls employed were crude. An annual household income of $20,000 became the dividing line between lower- and middle-class respondents. At least one-half of the lower-income respondents had incomes of less than $10,000 per year.

11. Many of the requests for zoning variances originate with private developers. However, those requests often place the boards in direct interaction with the Board of Standards and Appeals in New York, which hears requests for zoning variances.

12. Unlike land-use issues and budgetary priorities, which require board member involvement, day-to-day service-monitoring responsibilities are handled by the community boards' district managers. Accordingly, this responsibility was omitted from the analysis of sources of advice.

REFERENCES

Chapter One

Anton, Thomas J. 1963. "Power, Pluralism and Local Politics." *Administrative Science Quarterly* (March): 449–51.

Bachrach, Peter, and Baratz, Morton S. 1962. "Two Faces of Power." *American Political Science Review* 56 (December 1962): 947–52.

Beam, David R., and Colella, Cynthia. 1980. "The Federal Role in the Eighties: Bigger, Broader, and Deeper or Smaller, Trimmer, and Cheaper." In *Fiscal Stress and Fiscal Policy*, 49–68. See Levine and Rubin, 1980.

Bentley, Arthur F. 1908. *The Process of Government*. Chicago: University of Chicago Press.

Blair, John P., and Nachmias, David, eds. 1979. *Fiscal Retrenchment and Urban Policy*. Beverly Hills, CA: Sage.

Bluestone, Barry, and Harrison, B. 1980. *Capital and Communities: The Causes and Consequences of Private Disinvestment*. Washington, DC: The Progressive Alliance.

Dahl, Robert. 1958. "A Critique of the Ruling Elite Model." *American Political Science Review* 52 (June 1958): 466–69.

———. 1961. *Who Governs: Democracy and Power in an American City*. New Haven, CT: Yale University Press.

———. 1981. *Democracy in the United States*. 4th ed. Boston: Houghton Mifflin.

———. 1991. *Modern Political Analysis*. 5th ed. Englewood Cliffs, NJ: Prentice-Hall.

Dahl, Robert, and Lindblom, Charles. 1976. *Politics, Economics, and Welfare*. Chicago: University of Chicago Press.

Danziger, Herbert. 1964. "Community Power Structure: Problems and Continuities." *American Sociological Review* (October): 714–16.

Domhoff, G. William. 1978. *Who Really Rules?* Santa Monica, CA: Goodyear.

Downs, Anthony. 1959. *Inside Bureaucracy*. Boston: Little, Brown.

Elkin, Stephen L. 1985. "Twentieth Century Urban Regimes." *Journal of Urban Affairs* 7, no. 2: 11–28.

———. 1987. *City and Regime in the American Republic*. Chicago: University of Chicago.

Feagin, J. R. 1988. *Free Enterprise City: Houston in Political and Economic Perspective*. New Brunswick, NJ: Rutgers University.

Friedland, Roger; Piven, Francis Fox; and Alford, Robert R. 1984. "Political Conflict, Urban Structure, and the Fiscal Crisis." In *Marxism and the Metropolis*, 2d ed., 273–97. See Tabb and Sawers, 1984.

Gordon, David. 1984. "Capitalist Development and the History of American Cities." In *Marxism and the Metropolis*, 2d ed., 21–53. See Tabb and Sawers, 1984.

Haider, Donald. 1979. "Sayre and Kaufman Revisited: New York City Government Since 1965." *Urban Affairs Quarterly* 15, no. 2 (December): 123–45.

Harvey, David. 1973. *Social Justice and the City*. Baltimore, MD: Johns Hopkins Press.

Hill, Richard C. 1984. "Fiscal Crisis, Austerity Politics, and Alternative Urban Policies." In *Marxism and the Metropolis*, 2d ed., 298–322. See Tabb and Sawers, 1984.

Horan, Cynthia. 1991. "Beyond Governing Coalitions: Analyzing Urban Regimes in the 1990s." *Journal of Urban Affairs* 13, no. 2: 119–36.

Hunter, Floyd. 1953. *Community Power Structure*. Chapel Hill: University of North Carolina.

Jones, Bryan. 1983. *Governing Urban America: A Policy Focus*. Boston: Little, Brown.

Judd, Dennis, and Kantor, Paul. 1992. *Enduring Tensions in Urban Politics*. New York: Macmillan.

Katznelson, Ira; Gille, Kathleen; and Weir, Margaret. 1982. "Race and Schooling: Reflections on the Social Bases of Urban Movements." In *Urban Policy Under Capitalism*, edited by Norman Fainstein and Susan Fainstein, 215–36. Beverly Hills, CA: Sage.

Levine, Charles, and Rubin, Irene, eds. 1980. *Fiscal Stress and Fiscal Policy*. Beverly Hills, CA: Sage.

Levine, Charles; Rubin, Irene; and Wolohojian, George. 1981. *The Politics of Retrenchment*. Beverly Hills, CA: Sage.

Long, Norton. 1958. "The Local Community as an Ecology of Games." *American Political Science Review* 64 (November): 251–61.

Lowi, Theodore. 1967. "Machine Politics: Old and New." *Public Interest* 9 (Fall): 83–92.

————. 1979a. *The End of Liberalism: The Second Republic of the United States*. 2d ed. New York: Norton.

————. 1979b. "The State of the Cities in the Second Republic." In *Fiscal Retrenchment and Urban Policy*, 43–54. See Blair and Nachmias, 1979.

Lynd, Robert, and Lynd, Helen Merrell. 1929. *Middletown*. New York: Harcourt, Brace and World.

McConnell, Grant. 1966. *Private Power and American Democracy*. New York: Vintage Books.

Manley, John. 1983. "Neopluralism: A Class Analysis of Pluralism I and Pluralism II." *American Political Science Review* 77 (June): 368–89.

Markusen, Ann. 1984. "Class and Urban Social Expenditure: A Marxist Theory of Metropolitan Government." In *Marxism and the Metropolis*, 2d ed., 82–100. See Tabb and Sawers, 1984.

Masotti, Louis H. 1979. "The Possibilities for Urban Revitalization: Constraints and Opportunities in an Era of Retrenchment." In *Fiscal Retrenchment and Urban Policy*, 55–68. See Blair and Nachmias, 1979.

Myers, Gustavus. 1917. *The History of Tammany Hall*. New York: Boni and Liveright.

Newfield, Jack, and DuBrul, Paul. 1981. *The Permanent Government*. New York: Pilgrim.

O'Connor, James. 1973. *The Fiscal Crisis of the State*. New York: St. Martin's.

Peters, B. Guy. 1980. "Fiscal Strains on the Welfare State: Causes and Consequences." In *Fiscal Stress and Fiscal Policy*, 23–48. See Levine and Rubin, 1980.

Peterson, Paul. 1981. *City Limits*. Chicago: University of Chicago Press.

Polsby, Nelson. 1963. *Community Power and Political Theory*. New Haven, CT: Yale University Press.

Ricci, David. 1971. *Community Power and Democratic Theory: The Logic of Political Analysis*. New York: Random House.

Ripley, Randall, and Franklin, Grace. 1984. *Congress, the Bureaucracy and Public Policy*. 3d ed. Homewood, IL: Dorsey.

Sayre, Wallace, and Kaufman, Herbert. 1960. *Governing New York City*. New York: Russell Sage Foundation.

Schattschneider, E.E. 1960. *The Semi-Sovereign People*. New York: Holt, Rinehart and Winston.

Schick, Allen. 1980. "Budgetary Adaptations to Resource Scarcity." In *Fiscal Stress and Fiscal Policy*, 113–34. See Levine and Rubin, 1980.

Shefter, Martin. 1976. "The Emergence of the Political Machine: An Alternative View." In *Theoretical Perspectives on Urban Politics*, edited by Willis Hawley and Michael Lipsky, 18–32. Englewood Cliffs, NJ: Prentice-Hall.

———. 1977. "New York City's Fiscal Crisis: The Politics of Inflation and Retrenchment." *Public Interest* 48 (Summer): 98–127.

———. 1985. *Political Crisis/Fiscal Crisis*. New York: Basic.

Stone, Clarence. 1980. "Systemic Power in Community Decision Making: A Restatement of Stratification Theory." *American Political Science Review* 74 (December): 978–90.

———. 1987. "Summing Up: Urban Regimes, Development Policy, and Political Arrangements." In *The Politics of Urban Development*, edited by Clarence Stone and Heywood Sanders, 269–90. Lawrence: University of Kansas Press.

———. 1989. *Regime Politics: Governing Atlanta, 1946–1988*. Lawrence: University of Kansas Press.

———. 1993. "Urban Regimes and the Capacity to Govern: A Political Economy Approach." *Journal of Urban Affairs* 15, no. 1: 1–28.

Tabb, William K. 1984. "The New York City Fiscal Crisis." In *Marxism and the Metropolis*, 2d ed., 323–45. See Tabb and Sawers, 1984.

Tabb, William K., and Sawers, Larry, eds. 1984. *Marxism and the Metropolis*. 2d ed. New York: Oxford University Press.

Truman, David B. 1951. *The Governmental Process*. New York: Knopf.

Waste, Robert J. 1989. *The Ecology of City Policymaking*. New York: Oxford University Press.

Wirt, Frederick. 1974. *Power in the City*. Berkeley: University of California Press.

Wolfinger, Raymond. 1962. "A Plea for a Decent Burial." *American Sociological Review* (December): 841–47.

Wolman, Harold. 1980. "Local Government Strategies to Cope with Fiscal Pressure." In *Fiscal Stress and Fiscal Policy*, 231–48. See Levine and Rubin, 1980.

Yates, Douglas. 1977. *The Ungovernable City: The Politics of Urban Problems and Policy Making*. Cambridge: MIT Press.

Chapter Two

Adrian, Charles R., and Press, Charles. 1977. *Governing Urban America*. 5th ed. New York: McGraw-Hill.

Alford, Robert R., and Lee, Eugene C. 1968. "Voting Turnout in American Cities." *American Political Science Review* 62 (September): 796–813.

Allswang, John M. 1977. *Bosses, Machines, and Urban Voters*. Port Washington, NY: Kennikat.

Beyer, William C. 1933. "Financial Dictators Replace Political Boss." *Municipal Review* (April): 162–71.

Bridges, Amy. 1984. *A City in the Republic: Antebellum New York and the Origin of Machine Politics*. Cambridge and London: Cambridge University Press.

Bryce, James. 1888. *The American Commonwealth*. London: Macmillan.

Callow, Alexander B., Jr., 1966. *The Tweed Ring*. New York: Oxford University Press.

———. 1976. *The City Boss in America*. New York: Oxford University Press.

Caro, Robert A. 1974. *The Power Broker*. New York: Vintage Books.

Connable, Alfred, and Silberfarb, Edward. 1967. *Tigers of Tammany*. New York: Holt, Rinehart and Winston.

Cook, Fred J., and Gleason, Gene. 1959. "The Shame of New York." *The Nation,* October 31.

DiGaetano, Alan. 1988. "The Rise and Development of Urban Political Machines: An Alternative to Merton's Functional Analysis." *Urban Affairs Quarterly* 24 (December): 242–67.

Durand, Edward. 1898. *The Finances of New York City.* New York: Macmillan.

Dutton, William H., and Northrop, Alana. 1978. "Municipal Reform and the Changing Pattern of Party Politics." *American Politics Quarterly* 6 (October): 429–52.

Garrett, Charles. 1961. *The LaGuardia Years.* Camden, NJ: Rutgers University Press.

Gosnell, Harold F. 1969. *Boss Platt and His New York Machine.* New York: Russell and Russell.

Griffith, Ernest. 1974. *A History of American City Government: The Conspicuous Failure, 1870–1900.* New York: Praeger.

Hammack, David C. 1982. *Power and Society: Greater New York at the Turn of the Century.* New York: Russell Sage.

Hawley, Willis D. 1973. *Nonpartisan Elections and the Case for Party Politics.* New York: Wiley.

Hayes, Samuel P. 1964. "The Politics of Reform in the Progressive Era." *Pacific Northwest Quarterly* 55 (October): 157–89.

———. 1967. "Political Parties and the Community-Society Continuum." In *The American Party System,* edited by William Nisbet Chambers and Walter Dean Burnham, 152–81. New York: Oxford University Press.

Henderson, Thomas M. 1976. *Tammany Hall and the New Immigrants: The Progressive Years.* New York: Arno.

Hershkowitz, Leo. 1977. *Tweed's New York.* Garden City, NY: Anchor.

Hofstadter, Richard. 1955. *The Age of Reform: From Bryan to FDR.* New York: Vintage Books.

Judd, Dennis R. 1988. *The Politics of American Cities: Private Power and Public Policy.* 3d ed. Glenview, IL, Boston, and London: Scott, Foresman and Company.

Lewis, Alfred H. 1901. *Richard Croker.* New York: Life.

Lewis, Eugene. 1973. *The Urban Political System.* Hinsdale, IL: Dryden.

Lowi, Theodore. 1964. *At the Pleasure of the Mayor.* New York: Macmillan.

———. 1967. "Machine Politics: Old and New." *Public Interest* 9 (Fall): 83–92.

Lynch, Dennis T. 1927. *"Boss" Tweed.* New York: Boni and Liveright.

Lyons, William. 1978. "Reform and Response in American Cities." *Social Science Quarterly* 59 (June): 118–32.

Mandelbaum, Seymour. 1965. *Boss Tweed's New York.* New York: Wiley.

Merton, Robert K. 1967. *Social Theory and Social Structure.* New York: Free Press.

Mushrat, Jerome. 1971. *Tammany: The Evolution of a Political Machine 1789–1865.* Syracuse, NY: Syracuse University Press.

Myers, Gustavus. 1917. *The History of Tammany Hall.* New York: Boni and Liveright.

Rakove, Milton. 1976. *Don't Make No Waves, Don't Back No Losers.* Bloomington: Indiana University Press.

Riordan, William L. 1963. *Plunkitt of Tammany Hall.* New York: Dutton.

Royko, Michael. 1971. *Boss: Richard J. Daley of Chicago.* New York: Dutton.

Sayre, Wallace, and Kaufman, Herbert. 1960. *Governing New York City.* New York: Russell Sage Foundation.

Schiesl, Martin J. 1977. *The Politics of Municipal Reform: Municipal Administration and Reform in America, 1880–1920.* Berkeley: University of California Press.

Shaw, Frederick. 1954. *The History of the New York City Legislature.* New York: Columbia University Press.

Shefter, Martin. 1976. "The Emergence of the Political Machine: An Alternative View." In *Theoretical Perspectives on Urban Politics*, edited by Willis D. Hawley and Michael Lipsky, 18–32. Englewood Cliffs, NJ: Prentice-Hall.

———. 1977. "New York City's Fiscal Crisis: The Politics of Inflation and Retrenchment." *Public Interest* 48 (Summer): 98–127.

Stoddard, Lothrop. 1931. *Master of Manhattan: The Life of Richard Croker*. New York: Longman, Green.

Teaford, Jon C. 1984. *The Unheralded Triumph: City Government in America, 1870–1900*. Baltimore and London: Johns Hopkins University Press.

Tobier, Emanuel. 1984. "Population." In *Setting Municipal Priorities: American Cities and the New York Experience*, edited by Charles Brecher and Raymond D. Horton, 19–42. New York and London: New York University Press.

Wade, Richard C. 1990. "The Withering Away of the Party Systems." In *Urban Politics New York Style,* edited by Jewel Bellush and Dick Netzer, 271–95. Armonk, NY: M.E. Sharpe.

Wald, Kenneth D. 1980. "The Electoral Base of Political Machines: A Deviant Case Analysis." *Urban Affairs Quarterly* 16 (September): 3–30.

Werner, M.R. 1928. *Tammany Hall*. New York: Doubleday, Doran.

Wilson, James Q. 1962. "Politics and Reform in American Cities," In *American Government Annual, 1962–63*. New York: Holt, Rinehart and Winston.

Wilson, James Q., and Banfield, Edward. 1964. "Public Regardingness as a Value Premise in Voting Behavior." *American Political Science Review* 58 (December): 876–87.

Wilson, Woodrow. 1887. "The Study of Administration." *Political Science Quarterly* 2 (June): 197–222.

Wolfinger, Raymond. 1974. *The Politics of Progress*. Englewood Cliffs, NJ: Prentice-Hall.

Zink, Harold. 1930. *City Bosses in the United States*. Durham, NC: Duke University Press.

Chapter Three

Alexander, E. 1976. "Goal Setting and Growth in an Uncertain World: A Case Study of a Local Community Organization." *Public Administration Review* (March/April): 182–91.

Alinsky, Saul. 1946. *Reveille for Radicals*. New York: Vintage Books.

Altshuler, Alan. 1970. *Community Control: The Black Demand for Participation*. New York: Pegasus.

Anderson, Martin. 1964. *The Federal Bulldozer*. Cambridge: MIT Press.

Arnstein, Sherry R. 1969. "A Ladder of Citizen Participation." *Journal of the American Institute of Planners* 35 (July): 212–21.

Barton, Allen H., et al. 1977. *Decentralizing City Government*. Lexington, MA: D.C. Heath.

Benello, G., and Rousopoulas, David. 1971. *The Case for Participatory Democracy*. New York: Grossman.

Benjamin, Gerald, and Mauro, Frank J. 1989. "The Reemergence of Municipal Reform." In *Restructuring the New York City Government: The Reemergence of Municipal Reform*, edited by Frank Mauro and Gerald Benjamin, 1–15. New York: Annual Proceedings of the Academy of Political Science.

Berndt, H. 1977. *New Rulers in the Ghetto*. Westport, CT: Greenwood Press.

Bish, Robert L., and Nourse, Hugh O. 1980. *Urban Economics and Policy Analysis*. New York: McGraw-Hill.

Boyte, Harry C. 1980. *The Backyard Revolution: Understanding the New Citizen Movement*. Philadelphia: Temple University Press.

Cahn, Edgar S., and Cahn, Jean C. 1968. "Citizen Participation." In *Citizen Participation in Urban Development,* edited by Hans B. Spiegel, 218–22. Washington, DC: Center for Community Affairs.

Carmichael, Stokely, and Hamilton, Charles V. 1967. *Black Power.* New York: Vintage Books.

Caro, Robert. 1974. *The Power Broker.* New York: Vintage Books.

Clark, Kenneth. 1965. *Dark Ghetto.* New York: Harper and Row.

Cole, Robert. 1974. *Citizen Participation and the Urban Policy Process.* Lexington, MA: D.C. Heath.

Cooper, Terry. 1980. "Bureaucracy and Community Organizations: The Metamorphosis of a Relationship." *Administration and Society* (February): 411–44.

Danielson, Michael, and Doig, Jameson. 1982. *New York: The Patterns of Urban Regional Development.* Berkeley: University of California Press.

Davies, J. Clarence. 1966. *Neighborhood Groups and Urban Renewal.* New York: Columbia University Press.

Davis, James. 1973. "Citizen Participation in a Bureaucratic Society: Some Questions and Skeptical Notes." In *Neighborhood Control in the 1970s,* 59–72. See Frederickson, 1973.

Dolan, Drew. 1990. "Local Government Fragmentation: Does It Drive Up the Costs of Government?" *Urban Affairs Quarterly* 26 (September): 28–48.

Donovan, John C. 1967. *The Politics of Poverty.* New York: Pegasus.

Dye, Thomas, R. 1988. *Politics in States and Communities.* Englewood Cliffs, NJ: Prentice-Hall.

Fainstein, Norman, and Fainstein Susan. 1976. "The Future of Community Control." *American Political Science Review* 70 (September): 905–23.

———, eds. 1982. *Urban Policy Under Capitalism.* Beverly Hills, CA: Sage.

Fainstein, Norman, and Martin, Mark. 1978. "Support for Community Control Among Local Urban Elites." *Urban Affairs Quarterly* 13 (June): 443–65.

Fantini, Mario, and Gittell Marilyn. 1973. *Decentralization: Achieving Reform.* New York: Praeger.

Fisher, Robert. 1984. *Let the People Decide.* Boston: Twayne.

Fisher, Robert, and Kling, J. 1989. "Community Mobilization Prospects for the Future." *Urban Affairs Quarterly* 25 (June): 200–211.

Fitzgerald, Joan, and Simmons, Louise. 1991. "From Consumption to Production: Labor Participation in Grassroots Movements in Pittsburgh and Hartford." *Urban Affairs Quarterly* 26 (June) 512–31.

Frederickson, George. 1973. *Neighborhood Control in the 1970s.* New York and London: Chandler Publishing.

Gittell, Marilyn. 1980. *Limits to Citizen Participation: The Decline of Community Organizations.* Beverly Hills, CA: Sage.

Goodman, Robert. 1971. *After the Planners.* New York: Simon and Schuster.

Haeberle, Steven H. 1989. *Planting the Grassroots: Structuring Citizen Participation.* New York: Praeger.

Hallman, Howard. 1974. *Neighborhood Government in a Metropolitan Setting.* Beverly Hills, CA: Sage.

———. 1977. *The Organization and Operation of Neighborhood Councils.* New York: Praeger.

———. 1984. *Neighborhoods: Their Place in Urban Life.* Beverly Hills, CA: Sage.

Hamilton, Charles V. 1969. "Conflict, Race and System Transformation." *Journal of International Affairs* 23: 106–18.

Hampden-Turner, Charles. 1974. *From Poverty to Dignity.* New York: Anchor Books.

Harrington, Michael. 1963. *The Other America*. New York: Macmillan.

Hartman, Chester. 1974. *Yerba Buena: Land Grab and Community Resistance in San Francisco*. Berkeley: University of California, Berkeley.

Hawley Amos H., and Zimmer, Basil G. 1970. *The Metropolitan Community: Its People and Government*. Beverly Hills, CA: Sage.

Hetherington, J.A.C. 1972. "Community Participation: A Critical View." In *Community Economic Development: Problems and Potentials for Minority Groups*, edited by J. Weistart. Dobbs Ferry, NY: Oceana.

Hutcheson, John D., Jr., and Prather, James E. 1988. "Community Mobilization and Participation in the Zoning Process." *Urban Affairs Quarterly* 23 (March): 346–68.

Iannello, Kathleen P. 1988. "Making Sense of Decentralized Implementation." Paper delivered at the annual meeting of the American Political Science Association, Washington, DC, September 1–4.

Judd, Dennis R. 1988. *The Politics of American Cities: Private Power and Public Policy*. 3d ed. Glenview, IL, Boston, and London: Scott, Foresman.

Katznelson, Ira. 1972. "Antagonistic Ambiguity: Notes on Reformism and Decentralization." *Politics and Society* (Spring): 323–36.

———. 1981. *City Trenches: Urban Politics and the Patterning of Class in the United States*. New York: Pantheon.

Katznelson, Ira; Gille, Kathleen; and Weir, Margaret. 1982. "Race and Schooling: Reflections on the Social Bases of Urban Movements." In *Urban Policy Under Capitalism*, 215–36. See Fainstein and Fainsten, 1982.

Kelly, Rita Mae. 1977. *Community Control of Economic Development*. New York: Praeger.

Kleniewski, Nancy. 1984. "From Industrial to Corporate City: The Role of Urban Renewal. In *Marxism and the Metropolis*, 2d ed., 205–22. See Tabb and Sawers, 1984.

Kochen, Manfred, and Deutsch, Karl W. 1969. "Toward a Rational Theory of Decentralization: Some Implications of a Mathematical Approach." *American Political Science Review* 63 (September): 734–94.

Korten, David. 1980. "Community Organization and Rural Development: A Learning Process Approach." *Public Administration Review* (September/October): 480–511.

Kotler, Milton. 1969. *Neighborhood Government*. Indianapolis, IN: Bobbs-Merrill.

Kraus, Jeffrey. 1984. "Neighborhood Organizations and Resource Dependency: The Establishment in the Neighborhood." *Journal of Urban Affairs* 6 (Spring): 116–29.

Lineberry, Robert L. 1970. "Reforming Metropolitan Governance: Requium or Reality." *Georgetown Law Journal* 58 (March/May): 675–718.

Lipsitz, Lewis. 1973. "A Better System of Prisons? Thoughts on Decentralization and Participation in America." In *Neighborhood Control in the 1970s*, 39–58. See Frederickson, 1973.

Lipsky, Michael. 1980. *Street-Level Bureaucracy*. New York: Russell Sage.

———. 1984. "Bureaucratic Disentitlement in Social Welfare Programs." *Social Service Review* (March): 3–27.

Marcuse, Peter. 1982. "Determinants of State Housing Policies: West Germany and the United States." In *Urban Policy Under Capitalism*, 83–115. See Fainstein and Fainstein, 1982.

Marshall, K.E. 1969. "Goals of the Black Community." In *Governing the City*, edited by Robert Connery and Demetrios Caraley, 197–210. New York: Praeger.

Michels, Robert. 1947. *Political Parties*. Reprinted. Glencoe, IL: Free Press.

Mollenkopf, John H. 1984. "The Postwar Politics of Urban Development." In *Marxism and the Metropolis*, 2d ed., 117–152. See Tabb and Sawers, 1984.

Molotch, Harvey. 1976. "The City as Growth Machine." *American Journal of Sociology* 82 (February): 309–30.

Moore, Charles H., and Johnston, Ray E. 1971. "School Decentralization, Community Control, and the Politics of Public Education." *Urban Affairs Quarterly* 7 (June): 421–46.

Morris, David, and Hess, Karl. 1975. *Neighborhood Power.* Boston: Beacon Press.

Moynihan, Daniel Patrick. 1969. *Maximum Feasible Misunderstanding.* New York: Free Press.

Mudd, John. 1984. *Neighborhood Services.* New Haven, CT: Yale University Press.

O'Brien, David. 1975. *Neighborhood Organizations and Interest-Group Processes.* Princeton, NJ: Princeton University Press.

Parenti, Michael. 1970. "Power and Pluralism: A View from the Bottom." *Journal of Politics* 32 (August): 501–30.

Pateman, Carole. 1970. *Participation and Democratic Theory.* Cambridge: Cambridge University Press.

Pecorella, Robert F. 1984. "Coping with Crises: The Politics of Urban Retrenchment." *Polity* 17 (Winter): 298–316.

———. 1985. "Resident Participation as Agenda Setting: A Study of Neighborhood-Based Development Corporations." *Journal of Urban Affairs* 7 (Fall): 13–28.

Perlman, Janice. 1976. "Grassrooting the System." *Social Policy* (September/October): 4–20.

Peterson, Paul. 1970. "Forms of Representation: Participation of the Poor in the Community Action Program." *American Political Science Review* 64 (June): 469–80.

Pettigrew, Thomas F. 1971. *Racially Separate or Together?* New York: McGraw-Hill.

Piven, Francis Fox, and Cloward, Richard. 1971. *Regulating the Poor.* New York: Vintage Books.

———. 1982. *The New Class War.* New York: Pantheon.

Report of the Advisory Commission on Civil Disorders. 1968. New York: Bantam Books.

Robson, William. 1964. *The Governors and the Governed.* Baton Rouge: Louisiana State University Press.

Rogers, David, and Chung, I. 1983. *110 Livingston Street Revisited.* New York: New York University Press.

Ross, Bernard H., and Stedman, Murray S. 1985. *Urban Politics.* 3d ed. Itasca, IL: F.E. Peacock.

Rustin, Bayard. 1970. "The Failure of Black Separatism." *Harper's,* January 25–34.

Salisbury, Robert H. 1964. "Urban Politics: The New Convergence of Power." *Journal of Politics* 26, no. 4 (November): 775–97.

Sawers, Larry. 1984. "The Political Economy of Urban Transportation: An Interpretive Essay." In *Marxism and the Metropolis,* 2d ed., 223–54. See Tabb and Sawers, 1984.

Schmandt, Henry J., and Wendel, George. 1988. "A Content Analysis of Urban Affairs Quarterly." *Urban Affairs Quarterly* 23 (September): 3–32.

Scott, W. Richard. 1969. "Professional Employees in a Bureaucratic Structure: Social Work." In *The Semi-Professions and Their Organization,* edited by Amitai Etzioni, 119–122. New York: Free Press.

Stone, Clarence; Whelan, Robert; and Murin, William. 1986. *Urban Policy and Politics in a Bureaucractic Age.* 2d ed. Englewood Cliffs, NJ: Prentice-Hall.

Strange, J.H. 1972. "Citizen Participation in Community Action and Model Cities Programs." *Public Administration Review* 32 (October): 655–70.

Sundquist, James. 1972. "The Problems of Coordination in a Changing Federalism." In *The New Urban Politics,* edited by Douglas Fox, 196–209. Pacific Palisades, CA: Goodyear.

Tabb, William. 1984. "A Pro-People Urban Policy." In *Marxism and the Metropolis*, 2d ed., 367–82. See Tabb and Sawers, 1984.

Tabb, William, and Sawers, Larry. 1984. *Marxism and the Metropolis*. 2d ed. New York: Oxford University Press.

U.S. House of Representatives. 1964. *Economic Opportunity Act of 1964*. Hearings, Subcommittee on the Poverty Program of the Committee on Education and Labor, 88th Congress, 2d session. Washington, DC: Government Printing Office.

U.S. Statutes at Large, 63, 18–29. 1949. Washington, DC: Government Printing Office.

Ventriss, Curtis, and Pecorella, Robert F. 1984. "Community Participation and Modernization: A Reexamination of Political Choices." *Public Administration Review* (May/June): 224–31.

Viteritti, Joseph, and Pecorella, Robert F. 1987. *Community Government*. New York: Urban Research Center.

Vogel, Ronald K., and Swanson, Bert E. 1989. "The Growth Machine Versus the Anti-Growth Machine." *Urban Affairs Quarterly* 25 (September): 63–85.

Warren, Donald. 1975. *Black Neighborhoods*. Lansing: University of Michigan Press.

Warren, Donald, and Warren, Rachel. 1977. *The Neighborhood Organizer's Handbook*. South Bend, IN: University of Notre Dame Press.

Washnis, George J. 1974. *Community Development Strategies*. New York: Praeger.

Weber, Max. 1968. *Economy and Society,* edited by Guenther Roth and Claus Wittich. Berkeley: University of California Press.

White, Orion, Jr. 1970. "The Problems of Urban Administration and Environmental Turbulence." In *Neighborhood Control in the 1970s*, 103–16. See Frederickson, 1970.

Wood, Robert C. 1959. *Suburbia*. New York: Houghton Mifflin.

———. 1961. *1400 Governments: The Political Economy of the New York Metropolitan Region*. Cambridge: Harvard University Press.

Yates, Douglas. 1973. *Neighborhood Democracy: The Politics and Impacts of Decentralization*. Lexington, MA: D.C. Heath.

Yin, Robert K., and Yates, Douglas. 1975. *Street-Level Government: Assessing Decentralization and Urban Services*. Lexington, MA: Lexington Books.

Zimmerman, Joseph F. 1972. *The Federated City: Community Control in Large Cities*. New York: St. Martin's.

Chapter Four

Barton, Allen H. 1977. "The Problem of Urban Decentralization and the Research Design of the New York City Neighborhood Government Study." In *Decentralizing City Government*, 1–26. See Barton et al., 1977.

Barton, Allen H., et al. 1977. *Decentralizing City Government*. Lexington, MA: Lexington Books.

Bellush, Jewel. 1990. "Clusters of Power: Interest Groups." In *Urban Politics New York Style*, 296–338. See Bellush and Netzer, 1990.

Bellush, Jewel, and Netzer, Dick, eds. 1990. *Urban Politics New York Style*. Armonk, NY: M.E. Sharpe.

Blaustein, Arthur I. 1970. "What Is Community Economic Development?" *Urban Affairs Quarterly* 6 (September): 52–70.

Brager, George A., and Purcell, Francis P. 1967. *Community Action Against Poverty*. New Haven, CT: College and University Press.

Brumback, Ronald. 1977. "Service Integration at the District Level: Seven Examples." In *Decentralizing City Government*, 51–69. See Barton et al., 1977.

Bundy, McGeorge. 1967. *Reconnection for Learning: A Community School System for New York City Schools*. New York: Ford Foundation.

Burns, James MacGregor. 1961. "DeSapio at the Village Barricades." *New York Times Magazine,* August 27, 28 ff.

Cloward, Richard, and Piven, Frances. 1972. *The Politics of Turmoil.* New York: Vintage Books.

Connable, Alfred, and Silberfarb, Edward. 1967. *Tigers of Tammany.* New York: Holt, Rinehart and Winston.

Costikyan, Edward N. 1966. *Behind Closed Doors.* New York: Harcourt, Brace and World.

Costikyan, Edward N., and Lehman, M. 1972. *Restructuring the Government of New York City.* New York: Praeger.

Cronin, Joseph. 1973. *The Control of Urban Schools.* New York: Free Press.

David, Stephen M. 1971. "Welfare: The Community Action Program Controversy." In *Race and Politics in New York City,* edited by Jewel Bellush and Stephen M. David, 30–40. New York: Praeger.

Day, Mary W. 1987. "Harlem Youth Opportunities Unlimited." In *Advocacy in America: Case Studies of Social Change,"* edited by Gladys Walton Hall, Grace C. Clark, and Michael A. Creedon, 11–26. New York: University Press of America.

Eichenthal, David R. 1990. "Changing Styles and Strategies of the Mayor." In *Urban Politics New York Style,* 63–85. See Bellush and Netzer, 1990.

Fantini, Mario D. 1970. "Community Control and Quality Education in Urban School Systems." In *Community Control of Schools,* 40–75. See Levin, 1970.

Fantini, Mario, and Gittell, Marilyn. 1973. *Decentralization: Achieving Reform.* New York: Praeger.

Farr, J.R.; Liebman, L.; and Wood, J.S. 1972. *Decentralizing City Government.* New York: Praeger.

Faux, Geoffrey. 1971. *New Hope for the Inner City.* New York: Twentieth Century Fund.

Fisher, Robert. 1984. *Let the People Decide.* Boston: Twayne.

———. 1985. "Neighborhood Organizing and Urban Revitalization: An Historical Perspective." *Journal of Urban Affairs* 7 (Winter 1985): 47–54.

Fitch, Lyle C., and Walsh, Annmarie Hauck, eds. 1970. *Agenda for a City.* Beverly Hills, CA: Sage.

Ford Foundation. 1973. *Community Development Corporations.* New York: Ford Foundation.

Gerth, H.H., and Mills, C. Wright. 1946. *Max Weber: Essays in Sociology.* New York: Oxford University Press.

Gibbs, Lauren K. 1982. "Local Initiatives: The Current Fashion." *New York Affairs* 7, no. 2: 3–26.

Gifford, Kilvert Dun. 1970. "Neighborhood Development Corporations: The Bedford Stuyvesant Experiment." In *Agenda for a City,* 421–50. See Fitch and Walsh, 1970.

Gittell, Marilyn. 1967. *Participants and Participation.* New York: Praeger.

Goodman, Robert. 1971. *After the Planners.* New York: Simon and Schuster.

Gotterher, Barry. 1975. *The Mayor's Man.* New York: Doubleday.

Haider, Donald. 1979. "Sayre and Kaufman Revisited: New York City Government Since 1965." *Urban Affairs Quarterly* 2 (December): 123–45.

Hampden-Turner, Charles. 1974. *From Poverty to Dignity.* New York: Anchor Books.

Havelick, Franklin J., and Kwartler, Michael. 1982. "Sunnyside Gardens: Whose Land Is It Anyway?" *New York Affairs* 7, no. 2: 65–80.

Heginbotham, Stanley J. 1977. "The Evolution of the District Manager Experiment." In *Decentralizing City Government,* 27–50. See Barton et al., 1977.

Heginbotham, Stanley J., and Andrews, Kenneth H. 1973. *Between Community and City Bureaucracy: Problems and Prospects in Expanding to a City-Wide Program.* New

York: Columbia University, Bureau of Applied Research.

Henderson, Keith M. 1989. "Our Other Governments: The Public Authorities." In *New York State Today,* edited by Peter W. Colby and John K. White, 197–204. Albany: SUNY Albany Press.

Jacobs, Barry. 1982. "Jamaica Center: The Long Road Back." *New York Affairs* 7, no. 2: 50–58.

Jacobs, Jane. 1961. *The Death and Life of Great American Cities.* New York: Vintage Books.

James, George. 1970. "Health for the City." In *Agenda for a City.* See Fitch and Walsh 1970, 421–50.

Levin, Henry M., ed. 1970. *Community Control of Schools.* Washington, DC: The Brookings Institution.

Lewis, Eugene. 1977. *American Politics in a Bureaucratic Age.* Cambridge, MA: Winthrop.

Lindsay, John V. 1970. *A Plan for Neighborhood Government.* New York: Office of the Mayor.

———. 1977. "Program for the Decentralized Administration of Municipal Services in New York City Communities." In *Decentralizing City Government,* 261–72. See Barton et al., 1977.

Local Laws for the City of New York for the Year 1969, No. 39.

Lowi, Theodore. 1964. *At the Pleasure of the Mayor.* New York: Macmillan.

———. 1968. "Gosnell's Chicago Revisited via Lindsay's New York." In *Machine Politics: Chicago Model,* 2d ed., edited by Harold F. Gosnell, v–viii. Chicago: The University of Chicago Press.

Lyke, Robert F. 1970. "Representation and Urban School Boards." In *Community Control of Schools,* 138–68. See Levin, 1970.

McCoy, Rhody A. 1969. "The Year of the Dragon." In *Confrontation at Ocean-Hill–Brownsville: The New York School Strikes of 1968,* edited by M.R. Berube and Marilyn Gittell. New York: Praeger.

Maynard, Robert C. 1970. "Black Nationalism and Community Schools." In *Community Control of Schools,* 100–111. See Levin, 1970.

Moore, Charles H., and Johnston, Ray E. 1971. "School Decentralization, Community Control, and the Politics of Public Education." *Urban Affairs Quarterly* 7 (June): 421–46.

Morris, Charles. 1980. *The Cost of Good Intentions.* New York: McGraw-Hill.

Moskow, Michael H., and McLennan, Kenneth. 1970. "Teacher Negotiations and School Decentralization." In *Community Control of Schools,* 191–218. See Levin, 1970.

Moynihan, Daniel P. 1961. " 'Bosses' and 'Reformers': A Profile of the New York Democrats." *Commentary* (June): 470.

———. 1970. *Maximum Feasible Misunderstanding.* New York: Free Press.

Moynihan, Daniel P., and Wilson, James Q. 1964. "Patronage in New York States, 1955–1959." *American Political Science Review* 58 (June): 286–301.

Mudd, John. 1984. *Neighborhood Services.* New Haven, CT: Yale University Press.

Nordlinger, E.A. 1972. *Decentralizing the City: A Study of Boston's Little City Halls.* Cambridge: MIT Press.

Olstein, Andrea. 1982. "Park Slope: The Warren Street Balancing Act." *New York Affairs* 7, no. 2: 59–64.

Pecorella, Robert F. 1985. "Resident Participation as Agenda Setting: A Study of Neighborhood-Based Development Corporations." *Journal of Urban Affairs* 7 (Fall): 13–28.

Perlman, Janice. 1982. "New York from the Bottom Up." *New York Affairs* 7, no. 2: 27–34.

Pfautz, Harold W. 1970. "The Black Community, the Community School, and the Socialization Process: Some Caveats." In *Community Control of Schools,* 13–39. See Levin, 1970.

Piven, Frances, and Cloward, Richard. 1971. *Regulating the Poor.* New York: Vintage Books.

Piven, Frances. 1972. "Whom Does the Advocate Planner Serve?" In *The Politics of Turmoil,* 43–53. See Cloward and Piven, 1972.

———. 1972. "Rent Strike: Disrupting the Slum System." In *The Politics of Turmoil,* 151–160. See Cloward and Piven, 1972.

Rogers, David. 1968. *110 Livingston Street.* New York: Random House.

———. 1977. *An Inventory of Educational Improvement Efforts in the New York City Schools.* New York: Teachers College Press.

———. 1990. "Community Control and Decentralization. In *Urban Politics New York Style,* 143–87. See Bellush and Netzer, 1990.

Rogers, David, and Chung, Norman H. 1983. *110 Livingston Street Revisited.* New York: New York University Press.

Rourke, Francis E. 1976. *Bureaucracy, Politics, and Public Policy.* Boston: Little, Brown.

Savitch, H.V. 1990. "The Federal Impact on City Politics." In *Urban Politics New York Style,* 245–67. See Bellush and Netzer, 1990.

Sayre, Wallace, and Kaufman, Herbert. 1960. *Governing New York City.* New York: Russell Sage Foundation.

Seeley, David. 1981. *Education Through Partnership.* Cambridge, MA: Ballinger.

Shefter, Martin. 1977. "New York City's Fiscal Crisis: The Politics of Inflation and Retrenchment." *Public Interest* 48 (Summer): 98–127.

Simon, Herbert A. 1946. "The Proverbs of Administration." *Public Administration Review* 6 (Winter): 53–67.

State Charter Review Commission for New York City. 1974. *School Decentralization.* New York: SCRC.

Surkin, Marvin. 1971. "The Myth of Community Control: Rhetorical and Political Aspects of the Ocean Hill–Brownsville Controversy." In *Race, Change, and Urban Society,* edited by Peter Orleans and William Russell Ellis, Jr., 405–22. Beverly Hills, CA: Sage.

Theobold, John. 1970. "Education." In *Agenda for a City,* 165–205. See Fitch and Walsh, 1970.

Viteritti, Joseph P. 1979. *Bureaucracy and Social Justice.* Port Washington, NY: Kennikat.

———. 1983. *Across the River: Politics and Education in the City.* New York: Holmes and Meier.

Viteritti, Joseph P., and Pecorella, Robert F. 1987. *Community Government.* New York: NYU Urban Research Center.

Wade, Richard C. 1990. "The Withering Away of the Party System." In *Urban Politics New York Style,* 271–95. See Bellush and Netzer, 1990.

Walsh, Annmarie Hauck. "Public Authorities and the Shape of Decision Making." In *Urban Politics New York Style,* 188–219. See Bellush and Netzer, 1990.

Yates, Douglas. 1973. *Neighborhood Democracy: The Politics and Impacts of Decentralization.* Lexington, MA: D.C. Heath.

———. 1977. *The Ungovernable City: The Politics of Urban Problems and Policy Making.* Cambridge: MIT Press.

Chapter Five

Adler, Madeleine, and Bellush, Jewel. 1980. "A Look at the District Managers." *New York Affairs* 6, no 1: 49–53.

Alcaly, Roger E., and Bodian, Helen. 1977. "New York's Fiscal Crisis and the Economy." In *The Fiscal Crisis of American Cities,* 30–49. See Alcaly and Mermelstein, 1977.

Alcaly, Roger E., and Mermelstein, David. 1977. *The Fiscal Crisis of American Cities*. New York: Vintage Books.

Bailey, Robert W. 1984. *The Crisis Regime*. Albany, NY: State University of New York.

Bellush, Jewel. 1990. "Clusters of Power: Interest Groups." In *Urban Politics New York Style*, 296–338. See Bellush and Netzer, 1990.

Bellush, Jewel, and Netzer, Dick. 1990. *Urban Politics New York Style*. Armonk, NY: M.E. Sharpe.

Benjamin, Gerald. 1990. "The State/City Relationship." In *Urban Politics New York Style,* 223–44. See Bellush and Netzer, 1990.

Bickford, Jewell. 1980. "On the Road to Coterminality." *New York Affairs* 6, no. 1: 36–44.

Brecher, Charles, and Hartman, James M. 1984. "Financial Planning." In *Setting Municipal Priorities: American Cities and the New York Experience*, 198–240. See Brecher and Horton, 1984.

Brecher, Charles, and Horton, Raymond D. eds. 1984. *Setting Municipal Priorities: American Cities and the New York Experience*. New York: New York University.

———. 1985. "Retrenchment and Recovery: American Cities and the New York Experience." *Public Administration Review* 45 (March/April): 269–75.

David, Stephen, and Kantor, Paul. 1979. "Political Theory and Transformations in Urban Budgeting Arenas: The Case of New York City." In *Urban Policy Making,* edited by Dale Rogers Marshall, 196–215. Beverly Hills, CA: Sage.

Drennan, Matthew. 1982. "Local Economy and Local Revenues." In *Setting Municipal Priorities 1983*, edited by Charles Brecher and Raymond Horton, 15–45. New York: New York University Press.

Edel, Matthew. 1977. "The New York City Fiscal Crisis as Economic History." In *The Fiscal Crisis of American Cities*, 228–45. See Alcaly and Mermelstein, 1977.

Eichenthal, David R. 1990. "Changing Styles and Strategies of the Mayor." In *Urban Politics New York Style*, 63–85. See Bellush and Netzer, 1990.

Fowler, Glenn. 1980. "Community Board Wrap-Up." *New York Affairs* 6, no. 1: 7–9.

Green, Cynthia B., and Moore, Paul D. 1988. "Fiscal Relationship." In *The Two New Yorks,* edited by Gerald Benjamin and Charles Brecher, 211–42. New York: Russell Sage.

Greenblatt, Robert, and Rogowsky, Edward. 1980. "Case Study: The Brooklyn Boards." *New York Affairs* 6, no. 1: 19–25.

Grossman, David A. 1984. "State Aid." In *Setting Municipal Priorities: American Cities and the New York Experience,* 115–37. See Brecher and Horton, 1984.

Hartman, J.M. 1979. "Expenditures and Services." In *Setting Municipal Priorities,* edited by Charles Brecher and Raymond Horton, 50–78. Montclair, NJ: Allanheld, Osmun.

Horton, Raymond D., and McCormick, Mary. 1980. "Services." In *Setting Municipal Priorities, 1981,* edited by Charles Brecher and Raymond Horton, 85–112. Montclair, NJ: Osmun.

Kantor, Paul, and David, Stephen. 1983. "The Political Economy of Change in Urban Budgetary Politics: A Framework for Analysis and a Case Study." *British Journal of Political Science* 13: 254–74. Reprinted in *Enduring Tensions in Urban Politics*, edited by Dennis Judd and Paul Kantor, 564–82. New York: Macmillan.

Lebenstein, David. 1980. "A Report Card." *New York Affairs* 6, no. 1: 10–18.

Lebow, Joan. 1988. "Manhattan's Feisty Community Boards." *Crain's New York Business.* March 7, 11–12.

Levine, Charles H.; Rubin, Irene S.; and Wolohojian, George G. 1981. *The Politics of Retrenchment*. Beverly Hills, CA: Sage.

McCormick, Mary. 1984. "Labor Relations." In *Setting Municipal Priorities: American Cities and the New York Experience*, 302–30. See Brecher and Horton, 1984.

McKinney's. 1972. *Session Laws of New York 1972*. St. Paul, MN: West Publishing.
————. 1975. *Session Laws of New York 1975*. St. Paul, MN: West Publishing.
Morris, Charles. 1980. *The Cost of Good Intentions*. New York: McGraw-Hill.
Netzer, Dick. 1990. "The Economy and the Governing of the City." In *Urban Politics New York Style*, 27–59. See Bellush and Netzer, 1990
Newfield, Jack, and DuBrul, Paul. 1981. *The Permanent Government*. New York: Pilgrim.
New York City Charter and Administrative Code. 1963 and updates. Volume 1. New York: Williams Press.
————. 1976 and updates. Volume 1. New York: Williams Press.
Peterson, Paul E. 1981. *City Limits*. Chicago: University of Chicago Press.
Pitkin, Hanna. 1967. *The Concept of Representation*. Berkeley: University of California Press.
Reischauer, Robert D.; Clark, Peter K.; and Cuciti, Peggy L. 1975. *New York City's Fiscal Problem*. Washington, DC: Congressional Budget Office.
Reeves, Richard. 1977. "How Democracy Died in New York." In *Cities in Change*, 2d ed., edited by John Walton and Donald E. Carns, 534–37. Boston: Allyn and Bacon.
Rich, Richard. 1982. *Participation and Representation in New York City's Community Board System*. Blacksburg: Center for Responsive Government, Virginia Polytechnic Institute and State University.
Savitch, H.V. 1990. "The Federal Impact on City Policies." In *Urban Politics New York Style*, 245–69. See Bellush and Netzer, 1990.
Shefter, Martin. 1977. "New York City's Fiscal Crisis: The Politics of Inflation and Retrenchment." *Public Interest* 48 (Summer): 94–120.
State Charter Revision Commission for New York City. 1973. *Community Boards*. New York: SCRC.
Sternlieb, George, and Hughes, James W. 1976. *Post-Industrial America: Metropolitan Decline and Inter-Regional Job Shifts*. New Brunswick, NJ: Center for Urban Policy Research.
Tabb, William. 1977. "Blaming the Victim." In *The Fiscal Crisis of American Cities*, 315–26. See Alcaly and Mermelstein, 1977.
————. 1978. "The New York City Fiscal Crisis." In *Marxism and the Metropolis*, edited by William Tabb and Larry Sawers, 241–265. New York: Oxford University Press.
Twentieth Century Fund. 1980. *New York World City*. Cambridge, MA.: Oelgeschlager, Gunn & Hain.
Viteritti, Joseph P. 1979. *Bureaucracy and Social Justice*. Port Washington, NY: Kennikat.
————. 1989. "The Tradition of Municipal Reform: Charter Revision in Historical Context." In *Restructuring the New York City Government: The Reemergence of Municipal Reform*, edited by Frank J. Mauro and Gerald Benjamin, 16–30. New York: The Academy of Political Science.
Viteritti, Joseph P., and Pecorella, Robert F. 1987. *Community Government*. New York: The Urban Research Center.
Vitullo-Martin, Julia. 1979. "Municipal Assistance Centaur: Half-Private, Half-Public." *Fiscal Observer* 2: 4–7.
Wolf, Robert. 1980. " 'Intergroup' Dilemmas." *New York Affairs* 6, no. 1: 54–55.

Chapter Six

Adler, Madeleine, and Bellush, Jewel. 1980. "A Look at the District Managers." *New York Affairs* 6, no. 1: 49–53.
Axelrod, Regina. 1980. "Decentralized Service Delivery: Role of the District Manager." *National Civic Review* 69: 321–32.

Bahl, Roy, and Duncombe, William. 1991. *Economic Growth and Fiscal Planning: New York in the 1990s*. New Brunswick, NJ: Center for Urban Policy Research, Rutgers University.

Bailey, Robert W. 1984. *The Crisis Regime*. Albany, NY: SUNY Albany Press.

———. 1989. "Strategic Planning and Large City Governance." In *Restructuring the New York City Government*, 167–79. See Mauro and Benjamin, 1989.

Bickford, Jewell. 1980. "On the Road to Coterminality." *New York Affairs* 6, no. 1: 36–44.

Bolotin, Frederic, and Cingranelli, David. 1983. "Equity and Urban Policy: The Underclass Hypothesis Revisited." *Journal Of Politics* 45: 209–19.

Cingranelli, David. 1983. "The Effects of Neighborhood Context on the Evaluation of Police Services." *Journal of Urban Affairs* 5, no. 4: 255–61.

Community Assistance Unit. 1982. *Complaint Handling by New York City Community Boards*. New York: CAU.

Deutsch, Sylvia. 1988. "Community Boards and Land Use." *Charter Review* 1, no. 3 (Spring): 10.

Elkin, Steven. 1987. *City and Regime in the American Republic*. Chicago: University of Chicago.

Fainstein, Norman, and Fainstein, Susan. 1986. "The Politics of Planning New York as a World City." Paper prepared for the Fulbright Colloquium, Center for Community and Educational Policy Studies, University of Liverpool, September.

Fainstein, Norman, and Martin, Mark. 1978. "Support for Community Control Among Local Urban Elites." *Urban Affairs Quarterly* 13 (June): 443–65.

Fowler, Glenn. 1980. "Community Board Wrap-Up." *New York Affairs* 6, no. 1: 7–9.

Gelfand, M. David, and Albritton, Terry E. 1989. In *Restructuring the New York City Government*, 69–82. See Mauro and Benjamin, 1989.

Grossman, David A. 1982. "Debt and Capital Management." In *Setting Municipal Priorities, 1983*, edited by Charles Brecher and Raymond Horton, 120–51. New York: NYU Press.

Hawkins v. Town of Shaw. 1971. 437 *Federal Reporter 2d*. 1286.

Interface Development Project. 1979. *Community Boards: Technical Assistance Needs and Special Projects*. New York: Interface.

———. 1980. *The Community Board Improvement Project*. New York: Interface.

———. 1981. *Monitoring Community Residences: A Guidebook for Community Boards*. New York: Interface.

Jones, Bryan. 1978. "Distributional Considerations in Models of Government Service Delivery." In *The Politics of Urban Services*, edited by Robert Lineberry, 29–40. Beverly Hills, CA: Sage.

Katz, Daniel, and Kahn, Robert L. 1978. *The Social Psychology of Organizations*. 2d ed. New York: Wiley.

Lebenstein, David. 1980. "A Report Card." *New York Affairs* 6, no. 1: 10–18.

Lebow, Joan. 1988. "Manhattan's Feisty Community Boards." *Crain's New York Business*. March 7, 11–12.

Lineberry, Robert. 1977. *Equality and Urban Policy: The Distribution of Municipal Public Services*. Beverly Hills, CA: Sage.

Lineberry, Robert, and Sharkansky, Ira. 1978. *Urban Politics and Public Policy*. 3d ed. New York: Harper and Row.

Marcuse, Peter. 1987. "Neighborhood Policy and the Distribution of Power: New York City's Community Boards." Paper delivered at the annual meeting of the New York State Political Science Association, New York City.

Mauro, Frank, and Benjamin, Gerald. 1989. *Restructuring the New York City Government: The Reemergence of Municipal Reform*. Montpelier, VT: Capital City.

Mladenka, Kenneth. 1980. "The Urban Bureaucracy and the Chicago Political Machine." *American Political Science Review* 74 (December): 991–98.

Morris v. *Board of Estimate*. 647 F. Supp. 1463 (1986); 831 F.2d 384 (1987); and 489 U.S. 103 (1989).

Mudd, John. 1984. *Neighborhood Services*. New Haven, CT: Yale University Press.

Murphy, Serre, and Wechter, Ira. 1980. "The Boards and the Budget Process." *New York Affairs* 6, no. 1: 45–49.

Muzzio, Douglas, and Tompkins, Tim. 1989. "On the Size of the City Council: Finding the Mean." In *Restructuring the New York City Government*, 83–96. See Mauro and Benjamin, 1989.

New York City Charter and Administrative Code. 1976 and updates. Volume 1. New York: Williams Press.

New York City Charter Revision Commission. 1988. "Land Use and the City Charter." *Charter Review* 1, no. 3 (Spring): 3–5.

———. 1989. "The Budget and the City Charter." *Charter Review* 2, no. 4 (Spring): 3–8.

———. 1990. *Final Report*. New York: Charter Revision Commision.

New York City Office of Management and the Budget. 1979. *Manual for Participation in the Budget Process*. New York: OMB.

———. 1984. *Manual for Participation in the Budget Process*. New York: OMB.

Office of the Mayor. 1987. Memo to community board chairs, June 1.

Pecorella, Robert F. 1986. "Community Input and the City Budget: Geographically Based Budgeting in New York City." *Journal of Urban Affairs* 8, no. 1: 57–70.

Peterson, Paul E. 1981. *City Limits*. Chicago: University of Chicago.

Pfeffer, Jeffrey, and Salancik, Gerald R. 1978. *The External Control of Organizations: A Resource Dependency Perspective*. New York: Harper and Row.

Rich, Richard. 1982. *Participation and Representation in New York City's Community Board System*. Blacksburg: Center for Responsive Government, Virginia Polytechnic Institute and State University.

Schick, Allen. 1974. *Central Budget Issues Under the New York City Charter*. New York: State Charter Review Commission.

Silverman, Ronald H. 1989. "Toward Charter Change for Better Land Governance." In *Restructuring the New York City Government*, 187–202. See Mauro and Benjamin, 1989.

Simon, Herbert. 1946. "The Proverbs of Administration." *Public Administration Review* 6 (Winter): 53–67.

Spinola, Steven. 1988. "Community Boards and Land Use." *Charter Review* 1, no. 3 (Spring): 9.

State Charter Revision Commission for New York City. 1973a. *Charter Reforms of New York City's Planning Function*. New York: SCRC.

———. 1973b. *Community Boards*. New York: SCRC.

———. 1973c. *Financial Reporting for Decentralizing Localities in New York*. New York: SCRC.

———. 1977. *Final Report*. New York: SCRC.

Thompson, James. 1967. *Organizations in Action*. New York: McGraw-Hill.

Viteritti, Joseph. 1990. "The New Charter: Will It Make a Difference?" In *Urban Politics New York Style*, edited by Jewel Bellush and Dick Netzer, 413–28. Armonk, NY: M.E. Sharpe.

———. 1991. *Community Government, The City Council, and the Reform Agenda: The Case of Full Coterminality*. New York: Robert F. Wagner Graduate School of Public Service.

Wirth, Louis. 1938. "Urbanism as a Way of Life." *American Journal of Sociology* 44 (July): 17–28.

Wiseman, Carter. 1981. "Power to the People." *New York* 5 (October): 62–63.

Chapter Seven

Alinsky, Saul D. 1969. *Reveille for Radicals*. New York: Vintage Books.

Bailey, Thomas, and Waldinger, Roger. 1991. "The Changing Ethnic/Racial Division of Labor." In *Dual City: Restructuring New York*, 43–78. See Mollenkopf and Castells, 1991.

Bellush, Jewel. 1990. "Clusters of Power: Interest Groups." In *Urban Politics New York Style*, 269–338. See Bellush and Netzer, 1990.

Bellush, Jewel, and Netzer, Dick. 1990. *Urban Politics New York Style*. Armonk, NY: M.E. Sharpe.

Brown, Karin, and Coulter, Philip B. 1983. "Subjective and Objective Measures of Police Service Delivery." *Public Administration Review* 43, no. 1 (January/February): 50–58.

Cingranelli, David. 1983. "The Effect of Neighborhood Context on the Evaluation of Police Services." *Journal of Urban Affairs* 5, no. 4: 255–61.

Fainstein, Norman, and Fainstein, Susan. 1976. "The Future of Community Control." *American Political Science Review* 70 (September): 905–23.

Fainstein, Norman, and Martin, Mark. 1978. "Support for Community Control Among Local Urban Elites." *Urban Affairs Quarterly* 13 (June): 442–68.

Fisher, Robert. 1984. *Let the People Decide*. Boston: Twayne.

Gittlee, Marilyn. 1980. *Limits to Citizen Participation: The Decline of Community Organizations*. Beverly Hills: Sage.

Hamilton, Charles V. 1990. "Needed, More Foxes: The Black Experience." In *Urban Politics New York Style*, 359–84. See Bellush and Netzer, 1990.

Levy, Frank. 1987. *Dollars and Sense: The Changing American Income Distribution*. New York: Russell Sage.

Mollenkopf, John Hull. 1991. "Political Inequality." In *Dual City: Restructuring New York*, 333–58. See Mollenkopf and Castells, 1991.

Mollenkopf, John H., and Castells, Manuel, eds. 1991. *Dual City: Restructuring New York*. New York: Russell Sage.

Mudd, John. 1984. *Neighborhood Services*. New Haven, CT: Yale University Press.

Nelson, William T. 1992. "Black Mayoral Leadership: A Twenty-Year Perspective." In *Enduring Tensions in Urban Politics*, edited by Dennis Judd and Paul Kantor, 450–57. New York: Macmillan.

Pecorella, Robert F. 1986. "Community Input and the City Budget: Geographically Based Budgeting in New York City." *Journal of Urban Affairs* 8, no. 1: 57–70.

———. 1988. "Community Empowerment Revisited: Two Decades of Integrative Reform." *State and Local Government Review* 20, no. 2 (Spring): 72–79.

Ross, Bernard, and Stedman, Martin. 1985. *Urban Politics*. 3d ed. Itasca, IL: F.E. Peacock.

Wilson, William J. 1978. *The Declining Significance of Race: Blacks and Changing American Institutions*. Chicago: University of Chicago Press.

INDEX

ABOUT THE AUTHOR

Dr. Robert F. Pecorella is an associate professor in the Department of Government and Politics at St. John's University in New York. He is also professor-in-residence with the New York State Assembly Intern Program. He was a consultant on community politics to the New York City Charter Revision Commission. His work has appeared in a number of journals including *Polity*, *Public Administration Review*, and the *Journal of Urban Affairs*. He is a coauthor of *Politics and Structure: The Essentials of American National Government*.